T0155891

Lecture Notes of the Institute for Computer Sciences, Social Informatics and Telecommunications Engineering 395

More information about this series at http://www.springer.com/series/8197

Mahdi H. Miraz · Garfield Southall ·
Maaruf Ali · Andrew Ware ·
Safeeullah Soomro (Eds.)

Emerging Technologies in Computing

4th EAI/IAER International Conference, iCETiC 2021
Virtual Event, August 18–19, 2021
Proceedings

 Springer

Editors
Mahdi H. Miraz
Xiamen University Malaysia
Sepang, Malaysia

Garfield Southall
University of Chester
Chester, UK

Maaruf Ali
Epoka University
Tiranë, Albania

Andrew Ware
University of South Wales
Pontypridd, Mid Glamorgan, UK

Safeeullah Soomro
University of Fairfax
Fairfax, VA, USA

ISSN 1867-8211   ISSN 1867-822X (electronic)
Lecture Notes of the Institute for Computer Sciences, Social Informatics
and Telecommunications Engineering
ISBN 978-3-030-90015-1   ISBN 978-3-030-90016-8 (eBook)
https://doi.org/10.1007/978-3-030-90016-8

This Springer imprint is published by the registered company Springer Nature Switzerland AG
The registered company address is: Gewerbestrasse 11, 6330 Cham, Switzerland

Preface

It is our great pleasure to introduce the Proceedings of the Fourth International Conference on Emerging Technologies in Computing (iCETiC 2021), held during August 18–19, 2021. As in previous years, the conference was supposed to be held at London Metropolitan University, London, UK. However, due to travel restrictions resulting from the spread of COVID-19, iCETiC 2021 was instead held online, as a live interactive virtual conference, to ensure the safety, comfort and quality of experience of the attendees. All matters related to the quality, publication and indexing remained unchanged.

The theme of iCETiC 2021 was 'Emerging Technologies' as outlined by the Gartner Hype Cycle for Emerging Technologies, 2020. This conference drew together international researchers and developers from both academia and industry – especially in the domains of computing, networking and communications engineering.

iCETiC 2021 was organised by the International Association for Educators and Researchers (IAER) and technically co-sponsored by the Chester and North Wales Branch of the British Computer Society (BCS). As a knowledge partner, the European Alliance for Innovation (EAI) also played a significant role, both in organising the conference and publishing the proceedings.

The technical programme of iCETiC 2021 consisted of 13 full papers in oral presentation sessions in the main conference tracks. The primary conference tracks were as follows:

- Track 1 – Information and Network Security;
- Track 2 - Cloud, IoT and Distributed Computing;
- Track 3 - AI, Expert Systems and Big Data Analytics.

Apart from the high-quality technical paper presentations, the technical programme featured four keynote speeches. The keynote speakers were Andrew Ware, from the University of South Wales, UK, Jonathan C. Roberts from Bangor University, UK, Abdullah Uz Tansel from the City University of New York (CUNY), USA and Bekim Fetaji, from Mother Teresa University (MTU), North Macedonia.

It was a great pleasure to work with such an excellent organising committee team, who put in significant effort in organising and supporting the conference. The work of the Technical programme Committee is also much appreciated: they completed the peer-review process of technical papers culminating in a high-quality professional programme.

Yet again, iCETiC 2021 provided an excellent forum for researchers, developers and practitioners to discuss recent advancements in computing, networking and communications engineering. We will continue to strive to ensure that future iCETiC conferences are as successful and stimulating.

Thank you.

Mahdi H. Miraz
Garfield Southall
Maaruf Ali
Andrew Ware
Safeeullah Soomro

Organisation

Steering Committee Co-chairs

Garfield Southall   University of Chester, UK
Maaruf Ali   Epoka University, Albania
Safeeullah Soomro   University of Fairfax, USA
Mahdi H. Miraz   Xiamen University Malaysia, Malaysia and Wrexham
     Glyndwr University, UK

Organising Committee

General Co-Chair

Safeeullah Soomro   University of Fairfax, USA

Advisory Board

Andrew Jones   University of Hertfordshire, UK
Andrew Ware   University of South Wales, UK
Yousuf M. Islam   Daffodil International University, Bangladesh

Technical Programme Committee Co-chair

Mahdi H. Miraz   Xiamen University Malaysia, Malaysia and Wrexham
     Glyndwr University, UK

Web, Publicity and Social Media Chair

Shayma K. Miraz   International Association of Educators and Researchers
     (IAER), UK

Publications Chair

Mahdi H. Miraz   Xiamen University Malaysia, Malaysia and Wrexham
     Glyndwr University, UK

Local Chair

Anowarul Karim   International Association of Educators and Researchers
     (IAER), UK

Track Chairs

Cloud, IoT and Distributed Computing Track Chair

Will Serrano   University College London, UK

Software Engineering Track Chair

M. Abdullah-Al-Wadud   King Saud University, Saudi Arabia

Communications Engineering and Vehicular Technology Track Chair

Mohab A. Mangoud   University of Bahrain, Bahrain

AI, Expert Systems and Big Data Analytics Track Chair

Christian Esposito   Università degli Studi di Salerno, Italy

Web Information Systems and Applications Track Chair

Marie Nour Haikel-Elsabeh   Léonard de Vinci Pôle Universitaire, France

Security Track Chair

Bhawani Shankar   Mehran University of Engineering and Technology,
  Chowdhry   Pakistan

Database System and Application Track Chair

Abdullah Tansel   The City University of New York (CUNY), USA

Economics and Business Engineering Track Chair

Olga Angelopoulou   University of Hertfordshire, UK

mLearning and eLearning Track Chair

Sergey Lupin   National Research University for Electronic
                               Technology (MIET), Russia

General Track Chair

Andrew Jones   University of Hertfordshire, UK

Technical Programme Committee

Renaud Lambiotte	University of Oxford, UK
Ljiljana Trajkovic	Simon Fraser University, Canada
Been-Chian Chien	National University of Tainan, Taiwan
Victor Preciado	University of Pennsylvania, USA
Lin Liu	Tsinghua University, China
Guanghui Wen	Southeast University, China
Nowshad Amin	Solar Energy Research Institute (SERI), Malaysia
AbdelRahman H. Hussein	Al-Ahliyya Amman University, Jordan
Rabie Ramadan	University of Ha'il, Saudi Arabia
Vincenza Carchiolo	Universita di Catania, Italy
Imran Mahmud	Daffodil International University, Bangladesh
G. Sahoo	Birla Institute of Technology, Mesra, India

Brenda Scholtz	Nelson Mandela University, South Africa
Fabiana Zama	University of Bologna, Italy
Jia Uddin	BRAC University, Bangladesh
Fazal Noor	Islamic University of Madinah, Saudi Arabia
Bernhard Peischl	Technische Universität Graz, Austria
Christian Esposito	University of Salerno, Italy
Zainab Alansari	University of Malaya, Malaysia
Arcangelo Castiglione	University of Salerno, Italy
Mohammed Riyaz Belgaum	Universiti Kuala Lumpur, Malaysia
Trupil Limbasiya	NIIT University, India
Zahida Parveen	University of Hail, Saudi Arabia
Balakrishnan K.	Karpaga Vinayaga College of Engineering and Technology, India
Asadullah Shaikh	Najran University, Saudi Arabia
Ibrahim Kucukkoc	Balikesir University, Turkey
Cristóvão Dias	Universidade de Lisboa, Portugal
Samina Rajper	Shah Abdul Latif University, Pakistan
Wasan Shakir Awad	Ahlia University, Bahrain
Prabhat K. Mahanti	University of New Brunswick, Canada
Massimo Ficco	Università degli Studi della Campania Luigi Vanvitelli, Italy
Syed Faiz Ahmed	Universiti Kuala Lumpur, Malaysia
Mohammad Siraj	King Saud University, Saudi Arabia
Anthony Chukwuemeka Ijeh	American University in the Emirates, UAE
José Javier Ramasco	Insitute for Cross-Disciplinary Physics and Complex Systems (IFISC), Spain
Zi-Ke Zhang	Hangzhou Normal University, China
Francisco Rodrigues	University of São Paulo, Brazil
Ahmed N. Al Masri	American University in the Emirates, UAE
Ahmed Bin Touq	United Arab Emirates University, UAE
Daniel Onah	University College London, UK
Oussama Hamid	University of Kurdistan Hewlêr, Iraq
Souvik Pal	Elitte College of Engineering, India
Ali Hessami	Vega Systems Ltd, UK
Ezendu Ariwa	University of Bedfordshire, UK
Mohab A. Mangoud	University of Bahrain, Bahrain
Umair Ahmed	Gulf University Bahrain, Bahrain
Aamir Zeb Shaikh	NED University of Engineering and Technology, Pakistan
Farhat Naureen Memon	University of Sindh, Pakistan
Fida Hussain Chandio	University of Sindh, Pakistan
Riaz Ahmed Shaikh	Shah Abdul Latif University, Pakistan
Muniba Memon	Najran University, Saudi Arabia
Mansoor Hyder Depar	Sindh Agriculture University (SAU), Pakistan
Hamid Tahaei	University of Malaya, Malaysia

Zohreh Dehghani Champiri	University of Malaya, Malaysia
Md Tanvir Arafat Khan	Hanwha Q Cells America Limited, USA
Abhishek Shukla	Dr A. P. J. Abdul Kalam Technical University, India
Shkelqim Hajrulla	Epoka University Albania
Rezaul Azim	University of Chittagong, Bangladesh
Toufique Ahmed Soomro	Quaid-e-Awam University of Engineering and Science Technology, Pakistan
Purushottam Jadhav	Brahma Valley College of Engineering and Research Institute, India
Jinfeng Li	Imperial College London and University of Southampton, UK
Abdul Baqi Khan	Jubail Industrial College and Jubail University College, Saudi Arabia
Swati Namdev	Career College, Bhopal, India
Muhammad Aamir	Sir Syed University of Engineering and Technology, Pakistan
Muhammad Saddam Khokhar	Jiangsu University, China
Man Fung Lo	The Education University of Hong Kong, Hong Kong SAR
Amando Jr. Pimentel	Higher College of Technology, Muscat, Oman
Ezendu Ariwa	University of Wales Trinity Saint David, UK

Contents

Information and Network Security

Hardware Assisted Protocol for Attacks Prevention in Ad Hoc Networks

Vincent Omollo Nyangaresi$^{(\boxtimes)}$

Tom Mboya University College, Homabay, Kenya
vnyangaresi@tmuc.ac.ke

Abstract. The packet exchanges over open communication channels expose ad hoc networks data to numerous security and privacy attacks. To address this issue, many schemes have been developed based on public key infrastructure, tamper proof devices, bilinear pairings or trusted authorities. However, these techniques still have a number of security and privacy challenges or are inefficient in terms of communication, computation or storage overheads. In this paper, an attack prevention protocol is proposed based on elliptic curve cryptography and a combination of private keys and signatures. The results of simulations that were executed showed that the proposed protocol had the lowest computation costs, communication overheads, energy consumption and latencies in terms of signature signing and verification. In addition, this protocol offered non-repudiation, communication session unlinkability, mutual authentication, integrity, location privacy and anonymity. Moreover, it was resilient against message replays and impersonation attacks.

Keywords: Ad hoc networks · Authentication · Efficiency · Privacy · Security · TPD

1 Introduction

One of the most promising components of intelligent transportation system is the vehicular ad-hoc network (VANET) that can improve transport conditions through collaborative driving. However, message exchanges in VANETs is through dedicated short range communication (DSRC) over open wireless channels [1]. This exposes the transmitted packets to both security and privacy attacks such as eavesdropping, impersonation and modifications [2]. The leakage of vehicle's real identity can potentially expose driver's trajectory and locations. As such, it is critical for the messages to be authenticated by all the communicating entities in order to uphold integrity and confidentiality. In addition, authors in [3] explain that communication challenges such as efficiency, privacy and security need to be addressed in these ad hoc networks. Authors in [4] identify security and privacy as crucial issues in VANETs while message interception, tampering and tracking have been noted in [5] as some of the most dangerous attacks in this environment. Since these attacks compromise vehicle safety and privacy of its occupants, it is

M. H. Miraz et al. (Eds.): iCETiC 2021, LNICST 395, pp. 3–20, 2021.
https://doi.org/10.1007/978-3-030-90016-8_1

important that they are addressed. As explained in [6], private and secure communication in VANETs enhance safety and comfort of the drivers. Authors in [7] stress on the significance of message authentication between roadside units (RSUs) and vehicles, while in [8] authors explain that challenges such as privacy and reliability necessitate the enhancement of confidentiality and security of the exchanged data. Owing to the requirements for secure communication in VANETs, authors in [9] identify implementation of integrity, non-repudiation, confidentiality and authentication as being key in these networks. On the other hand, the importance of message authentication, integrity and reliability among vehicles has been highlighted in [10].

During deployments, privacy, security and efficiency have been discussed in [11] as being important for secure data exchanges. This requires that RSUs and vehicles verify the authenticity of all received messages before processing. In addition, captured messages over open channels may facilitate identification of real indentify of vehicles and their subsequent route tracking. To address this, enhanced unlinkability, privacy and anonymous communication need to be implemented in VANETs. On the other hand, the reliance on tamper proof devices (TPDs) and space complexity of authenticating techniques has been presented in [12] as significant challenges. One approach towards privacy protection in VANETs is anonymous authentication [4]. For attacks prevention, symmetric cryptography based approaches are more efficient compared to their asymmetric cryptography based techniques. However, as explained in [12], issues such as key management and non-repudiation still remain unresolved in symmetric cryptography.

1.1 Problem Statement

Security, privacy and efficiency during ad hoc communication are key issues and numerous schemes have been developed to address these issues. The conventional techniques either utilize bilinear pairing (BP), public key infrastructure (PKI), ideal tamper proof devices (TPD), trusted authority (TA), certificates or group signatures. However, BP operations and group signatures require high communication and computation overheads while TA may be a single point of failure during massive authentication process. On the other hand, the conventional authentication techniques based on TPD assume that this hardware device is highly resilient against security and privacy attacks. In addition, PKI based techniques result in problems regarding certificate storage and management. Consequently, conventional ad hoc authentication protocols either do not offer resilience against most of the ad hoc attacks or are inefficient in terms of communication, computation and energy overheads.

1.2 Our Contributions

The main contributions of this paper include the following:

I. Anonymous authentication protocol employing pseudonyms is developed to offer communication entity location and identity privacy in VANETs.
II. Realistic TPD devoid of system key pre-installation is deployed to address side-channel attacks in conventional hardware-based authentication schemes.

III. Intermediary ECC-based ephemerals are utilized to prevent key escrow problems in PKI based schemes.
IV. Individual vehicle signature and group signatures are implemented to provide non-repudiation and confidentiality.
V. We show that techniques in I–IV above rendered the proposed protocol resilient against conventional ad hoc attacks such as impersonation and message replays.

1.3 Organization of the Paper

The rest of this paper is organized as follows: Sect. 2 discusses related work while Sect. 3 details the system model. On the other hand, Sect. 4 presents the simulation and evaluation results while Sect. 5 concludes the paper and gives future directions.

2 Related Work

Over the recent past, numerous schemes have been developed to facilitate secure communication in vehicular networks. For instance, authors in [13] have presented a bilinear based anonymous authentication technique. However, this scheme has high computational costs and never incorporates session unlinkability in its design. Similarly, authors in [14–19] have developed bilinear based authentication schemes, but which have high computational costs. The elliptic curve (EC) pseudonym based technique in [20] has good computational efficiency but requires incorporation of trusted authority (TA) during authentication process. This effectively increases both communication latencies and costs, in addition to TA presenting a single point of failure [21]. Similarly, a hash function based scheme for privacy protection has been presented in [22], but which requires involvement of TA during the verification procedures. In addition, authors in [23] and [24] have deployed TA for the generation of authentication keys between vehicles and RSUs, and hence have similar challenges as schemes in [20] and [22]. Authors in [25] introduce certificate based authentication, but which requires high computation and space complexity. On the other hand, the schemes presented in [26–30] are prone to attacks and are also inefficient. In addition, the scheme in [26] results in high communication overheads. An identity based authentication approach is presented in [2] based on elliptic curve cryptography (ECC). However, this technique requires an ideal TPD for the storage of master keys of each vehicle.

Registration lists and hash functions have been incorporated in [31] during authentication while hash functions and XOR based authentication algorithm has been developed in [32]. Although the techniques in [31] and [32] enhance computational efficiency, their reliance on TA may potentially lead to some bottlenecks within the network. The batch authentication approach developed in [33] achieves some anonymity, but fails to offer resilience against collusion attacks. Authors in [34] have presented an aggregate signature based scheme for privacy preservation, but requires a trusted third for message verification. A PKI-based authentication protocol is developed in [35] but has high storage requirements for the generated vehicle certificates. Authors in [36] have presented an anonymous privacy preserving technique for vehicular networks, but has high communication costs. On the other hand, the anonymous authentication scheme in [37] requires maintenance of certificate revocation list (CRL) which increases its storage costs. Group key based schemes have been presented in [10] and [38–40]. However, in most of these group key signature based schemes, group leaders have high communication energy and computational resources consumption. In addition, group signature verification is computationally intensive, and the group leader can potentially become a network bottleneck. Specifically, the protocol in [40] offers only one-way authentication between TA and participating vehicles.

A conditional privacy preservation technique has been developed in [41], but has high storage requirements. On the other hand, the batch authentication scheme in [42] is susceptible to replay attacks and cannot withstand non-repudiation of the generated signature. An anonymous authentication algorithm developed in [43] achieves low computation overheads but fails to consider communication session unlinkability. On the other hand, the scheme in [44] cannot withstand modification and impersonation attacks. Authors in [45] have combined pseudonyms with group signature for authentication. However, this technique has high space complexity for CRL and high computation costs for CRL verification. On the other hand, the symmetric cryptograph hash function and XOR based scheme in [46] achieves high communication and computation overheads, but fails to consider internal attacks. Identity based VANET authentication scheme has been presented in [47] for privacy preservation. However, these protocols are inefficient and do not offer effective certificate revocation techniques. Similarly, identity based techniques in [48, 49] utilize group signatures for authentication and anonymity enhancement. However, the approach in [48] has high space and computation overheads, while the algorithm in [49] is vulnerable to replay and tracing attacks and cannot offer both backward and forward key secrecy. In addition, they inherit high communication and computation overheads of group signatures. Moreover, the techniques in [49] and [47] have ineffective certificate revocation mechanisms and do not offer mutual authentication.

3 System Model

In this section, the design goals, mathematical preliminaries, system architecture and the procedures of the proposed protocol are discussed.

3.1 Design Goals

In light of the security, privacy and efficiency challenges of the current ad hoc authentication and key management protocols, this paper proposes a hardware assisted protocol for attacks prevention in ad hoc networks. The proposed protocol employs both secret keys and group signatures for mutual authentication, while pseudonyms are deployed to uphold anonymity of the communicating entities. The authentication process is devoid of TA so as to alleviate single point of failure problem. In addition, the deployed TPD is based on realistic security assumptions of it being susceptible to physical and side-channel attacks. As such, no system keys are pre-installed in TPD and hence its failure or capture of secrets stored in it cannot compromise the entire network. Some of the goals pursued include unlinkability, authentication, integrity, non-repudiation, location privacy, anonymity, and resilience against message replays and impersonation attacks.

3.2 Mathematical Preliminaries

The proposed protocol deployed elliptic curve cryptography (ECC) which is a widely implemented cryptographic algorithm due to its high efficiency and superb security. It utilizes less bits than Rivest–Shamir–Adleman (RSA) algorithm for encrypting same length message and hence has less communication, computation and storage complexity. In addition, it requires fewer computation parameters and shorter key lengths, rendering it ideal for resource constrained vehicle TPDs. The following definitions hold for ECC systems:

Denoting a set of all EC points over a restricted field F_θ as $\varepsilon(F_\theta)$ where $\theta > 3$, then $\varepsilon : y^2 = (x^3 + \alpha x + \psi) mod\ \theta$. Here, α, $\psi \epsilon F_\theta$ and $4\alpha^3 + 27\psi^2 \neq 0$.

Let ϕ and ω be two points of group $\bar{g}$. Then if ϕ is not equal to ω, for an additive EC group $\bar{g} = \{(x, y) \epsilon \varepsilon(F_\theta) : x, y \epsilon F_\theta\} \cup \{i\}$ where i is a point at infinity, $\bar{g}$ forms a cyclic group under addition operation $\beta = \phi + \omega$ for $\phi, \psi \epsilon \bar{g}$. Here, β is the intersection of ε and the straight line connecting θ and ϑ. If $\phi = \omega$, then $\beta = \phi + \omega$, but if $\phi = -\omega$, then $\phi + \omega = 0$.

Let $\phi \epsilon \bar{g}_\theta$ and $\mu \epsilon Z_\vartheta^*$ for μ, in this case, scalar multiplication of ε is given by $\phi = \phi + \phi + \cdots \phi$.

Suppose that ϕ and ω are two randomly generated points on ε where $\phi \epsilon \bar{g}$ generates group $\bar{g}$ with large prime order ϑ. Then in EC discrete logarithm (ECDL), given $\phi, \omega \epsilon \bar{g}$, then the problem is to find $x \epsilon Z_\vartheta^*$ such that $\omega = x\phi \epsilon \bar{g}$.

Let ϕ be a generator of $\bar{g}$, $\alpha\phi, \psi \phi \epsilon \bar{g}$ where α, $\psi \epsilon Z_\vartheta^*$ are unknown. Then the EC computational Diffie-Hellman (ECCDH) problem is to calculate $\alpha\psi \phi \epsilon \bar{g}$.

Given ϕ, $\alpha\phi$, $\psi\phi$, $\gamma\phi \epsilon \bar{g}_1$ where ϕ is the generator of $\bar{g}_1$ with large prime order ϑ. Then for α, ψ, $\gamma \epsilon Z_\vartheta^*$, it is computationally cumbersome to decide whether or not $\gamma \equiv \alpha\psi$ mod ϑ.

Suppose that algorithm $\mathfrak{B}$ solves ECDL problem in $\bar{g}$ within some polynomial time with success probability $\mathfrak{K}$, then:

$$\mathfrak{K} = \Pr\left[\mathfrak{B}(\phi, x\phi) = x : x \epsilon Z_\theta^*\right] \geq \xi$$

ECDL hypothesis is defined as $\mathfrak{B}$ in any polynomial time and $\mathfrak{K}$ is negligible.

If ECDL or ECCDH on a group $\bar{g}$ cannot be solved with non-negligible probability ξ in time t, then ECDL or ECCDH is said to be a complex problem on EC.

3.3 System Architecture

In the proposed protocol, the system architecture consists of vehicles Vi fully equipped with online board units (OBUs), roadside unit (RSU), the public internet and the cloud server (CS) as shown in Fig. 1. Each OBU device incorporates a tamper proof device (TPD) to buffer the security secrets. The CS and RSU are trusted network entities but the Vi and internet connections are un-trusted. Whenever Vi wants some services from the cloud server, full authentication must be executed among the CS, Vi and RSU so as to prevent security and privacy attacks that may emanate from the internet.

Once mutual authentication is complete, the V_i need to sign each message transmitted to uphold both security and privacy.

Fig. 1. System architecture

3.4 Proposed Protocol

The proposed protocol consisted of five major phases including initialization, pseudo-identities generation, secret key generation, signature generation and verification. Table 1 presents the notations used in this paper and their brief description.

Table 1. Notations and their descriptions

Notation	Description
CS	Cloud server
V_i	i^{th} vehicle
RSU	Roadside unit
GS	Group signature
θ, ϑ	Large prime numbers
ε	Elliptic curve
$\mathcal{Z}$	CS master key
Б	CS public key
ψ	RSU master key
ȝ	RSU public key
$\check{y}$	Message signature
η_i	RSU nonce
ω_i	V_i pseudo-identity
χ_1, χ_2, χ_3	Hash functions
$\eta_i, R_i, \hat{W}_i$	Nonces
τ_i	Timestamp
$\Delta\tau_i$	Legitimate duration of pseudo identity
β_i	Partial private key of V_i
RegReq	V_i registration request
β_iReq	β_i request
$\hbar_i$	V_i real identity
ζ_i	V_i secret parameter
ς_i	V_i public key
ϕ_i	V_i private key
$\oplus$	XOR operation

As shown in Algorithm 1, during the initialization phase, the RSU and CS agree on θ, ϑ after which they generate ε as in step 1 where $\alpha, \psi \in Z_\theta^*$ and $(4\alpha^3 + \psi^2) \bmod \theta \neq 0$. In step 2, the CS chooses $\mathcal{Z} \in Z_\theta^*$ as its private master key and utilizes it to derive its public master key $Б$. Next, the RSU stochastically chooses $\psi \in Z_\theta^*$ as its private master key and uses it to compute security parameter $\mathfrak{z}$. For improved security and privacy, Z and ψ are only known to CS and RSU respectively and are never shared over the communication channels. In step 4, both CS and V i choose hash functions for subsequent authentication before publishing $\{\phi, \theta, \vartheta, \varepsilon, X_1, X_2, X_3, \bar{g}_i, \mathfrak{z}, Б\}$ (step 5). During V_i registration, the registration request RegReq , together with V_i's true identity $\mathcal{H}_i$ are sent to the corresponding RSU (step 6). At the same time, the V_i obtains the published security tokens which are then buffered in its TPD (step 7). To uphold anonymity, each V_i randomly chooses nonce η_i and employs it to derive its pseudo-identity $\mathcal{W}_i$ and other additional security token $\mho_i$ for later authentication, before sending $\{\mathcal{W}_i, 1, \mho_i\}$ to its RSU (step 9). To prevent impersonation and forgery attacks, the RSU re-computes V_i's $\mathcal{H}_i$ as shown in step 10. This identity is then validated in step 11 such that if it is invalid, RegReq is immediately discarded.

Algorithm 1: Authentication and Key Management

Input: $\theta, \vartheta, Z, \psi, X_1, X_2, X_3, \phi, \eta_i, \tau_i, R_i, \hat{W}_i, L_{2,i}, \omega_i, \Delta\tau_i$

Output: $\varepsilon, Б, \mathfrak{z}, \mathcal{W}_{i,1}, \mho_i, \mathcal{H}_i, \mathcal{W}_{i,2}, \beta_i, L_{1,i}, \beta_i, \zeta_i, \varsigma_i, \varphi, L_{2,i}, L_{3,i}, \text{sign}_i, \breve{Y}_i, GS, \breve{Y}_G, \lambda$

Begin:

1) Agree on θ and ϑ generate $\varepsilon: y^2 = (x^3 + ax + \psi) \bmod \theta$
2) Choose $Z \in Z_\theta^*$ & compute $Б=Z\phi$
3) Select $\psi \in Z_\theta^*$ & compute $\mathfrak{z}=\psi\phi$
4) Choose $X_1, X_2, X_3: \{0,1\}^* \rightarrow Z_\theta^*$
5) Publish $\{\phi, \theta, \vartheta, \varepsilon, X_1, X_2, X_3, \bar{g}_i, \mathfrak{z}, Б\}$
6) $V_i \rightarrow$ RSU: $\{\text{RegReq}, \mathcal{H}_i\}$
7) Buffer $\{\phi, \theta, \vartheta, \varepsilon, X_1, X_2, X_3, \bar{g}_i, \mathfrak{z}, Б\}$ in TPD
8) Choose $\eta_i \in Z_\theta^*$ & compute $\mathcal{W}_{i,1}= \eta_i\phi, \mho_i=\eta_i\mathfrak{z}\oplus\mathcal{H}_i$
9) $V_i \rightarrow$ RSU: $\{\mathcal{W}_{i,1}, \mho_i\}$
10) Re-compute $\mathcal{H}_i=\mho_i \oplus\psi\mathcal{W}_{i,1}$
11) **IF** $\mathcal{H}_i$ is invalid **THEN:** Discard RegReq
12) **ELSE:**
13) Calculate $\mathcal{W}_{i,2}=\mathcal{H}_i\oplus X_1(\psi\mathcal{W}_{i,1}, \tau_i)$
14) RSU$\rightarrow$CS: $\{\mathcal{W}_{i,1}, \mathcal{W}_{i,2}, \tau_i\}$
15) $V_i \rightarrow$CS: $\{\beta_i\text{Req}\}$
16) Select $R_i \in Z_\theta^*$ & compute $\beta_i= R_i\phi, L_{1,i} = X_1(\mathcal{W}_i, \beta_i, Б), \beta_i=(R_i+ ZL_{1,i}) \bmod \theta$
17) CS $\rightarrow V_i: \{\beta_i, \beta_i, \mathcal{W}_i\}$
18) **IF** $\beta_i\phi!= \beta_i+L_{1,i} Б$ **THEN:** Discard $\beta_i\text{Req}$
19) **ELSE:** Choose $\hat{W}_i \in Z_\theta^*$ & compute $\zeta_i=\hat{W}_i\phi$
20) Generate $L_{2,i}=X_2(\mathcal{W}_i, \zeta_i), \omega_i=\beta_i+L_{2,i}\zeta_i$
21) Set $\varsigma_i=(\omega_i, \beta_i)$ as public key & $\varphi=(\beta_i, \hat{W}_i)$ as private key
22) Choose $\bar{g}_i \in Z_\theta^*$ & compute $\bar{G}_i=\bar{g}\phi, L_{2,i}=X_2(\mathcal{W}_i, \zeta_i), L_{3,i}=X_3(\mathcal{W}_i, \rho_i, \zeta_i, \bar{G}_i, \tau_i)$, $\text{sign}_i=[\bar{g}_i + L_{3,i}(\beta_i + L_{2,i}\hat{W}_j)] \bmod \theta, \breve{Y}_i=(G_i, \text{sign}_i)$
23) $V_i \rightarrow$ RSU: $\{\mathcal{W}_i, \zeta_i, \rho_i, \tau_i, \breve{Y}_i\}$
24) **IF** $\Delta\tau_i$ and τ_i are invalid **THEN:** Discard sign_i
25) **ELSE:** Re-compute $L_{1,i}, L_{3,i}$
26) **IF** $\text{sign}_i\phi!= \bar{G}_i+ L_{3,i}(\omega_i+L_{1,i}Б)$ **THEN:** Discard sign_i
27) **ELSE:** Trust sign_i
28) Generate $GS = \sum_{i=1}^n \text{sign}_i$ & compute $\breve{Y}_G=(\bar{G}_1, \bar{G}_2, \bar{G}_3, ..., \bar{G}_n, GS)$
29) WSNS$\rightarrow$CS: $\{\breve{Y}_G\}$
30) **IF** $\Delta\tau_i$ and τ_i are invalid **THEN:** Discard $\breve{Y}_G$
31) **ELSE:** Compute $\lambda = \sum \bar{G}_i + \sum L_{3,i}(\omega_i + L_{1,i}Б)$
32) **IF** λ is invalid **THEN:** Deny resource access
33) **ELSE:** Grant resource access
34) **ENDIF;ENDIF;ENDIF;ENDIF;ENDIF**

END

However, if it is valid, RSU computes pseudo-identity $Ⅲ_{i,2}$ (step 13) before forwarding $\{Ⅲ_{i,1}, Ⅲ_{i,2}, \tau_i\}$ to CS (step 14). Here, current timestamp τ_i served to thwart any packet replays. In step 15, the V_i makes a request $\beta_i Req$ for assignment of its partial secret key β_i from the CS. This secret key is deployed in subsequent signing of its messages to protect integrity of transmitted messages. Upon the receipt of $\beta_i Req$, the CS chooses ephemeral R_i which then it utilizes to derive security tokens β_i, $L_{·1,i}$ and β_i for later message signing and authentication (step 16). In step 17, the CS sends beacon $\{\beta_i, \beta_i, Ⅲ_i\}$ to V_i, which then validates it in step 18 such that if it is invalid, the $\beta_i Req$ is discarded. However, if it is valid, the V_i proceeds to randomly select private nonce $\hat{W}_i$ that it then utilizes to derive security token ζ_i (step 19). In step 20, the V_i derives security parameters $L_{·2,1}$ and ω_i employed for computation of its public key ς_i. Next, the V_i sets ς_i and φ as its public key and private keys respectively for payload protection (step 21). In step 22, signature $sign_i$ for authentication and integrity protection of message $\ell_i \in \{0, 1\}^*$ is derived. The process begins by having the V_i randomly choose security token $\bar{g}_i$ before computing $\bar{G}_i$, $L_{·2,i}$, and $L_{·3,i}$. Thereafter, the V_i generates $sign_i$ and $\breve{y}_i$ before sending beacon $\{Ⅲ_i, \zeta_i, \rho_i, \tau_i, \breve{y}_i\}$ to its RSU (step 23) as shown in Fig. 2.

Upon receiving this beacon, the RSU validates the timestamp τ_i as well as the permissible duration of pseudo identity $\Delta\tau_i$ to prevent message replay attacks (step 24). If these two values are invalid, the received signature is discarded, otherwise the RSU proceeds to re-compute security tokens $L_{·1,i}$ and $L_{·3,1}$ (step 25) that are used to validate the received signature $sign_i$ in step 26. Here, if these security tokens are invalid, the received signature is discarded, otherwise the RSU trusts the V_i (step 27). The proposed protocol also supported group signature GS for authenticating a number of V_i's simultaneously. As evidenced in step 28, upon receiving multiple authentication tokens $\{Ⅲ_i, \varsigma_i, \rho_i, \tau_i \breve{y}_i\}$, $i \in \{1, 2, \ldots n\}$ from V_i group with signature pairs $\{\rho_i, \breve{y}_i\}$, it amalgamates these signatures through GS and $\breve{y}_G$. Thereafter, the RSU sends $\breve{y}_G$ to the CS (step 29) where $\Delta\tau_i$ and τ_i are verified such that if they are invalid, $\breve{y}_G$ is discarded (step 30). However, if it is valid, the CS proceeds to compute security token χ (step 31) which is then verified in step 32 such that if it is invalid, resource access is denied. However, if it is valid, the V_i group is granted access to the requested resources.

4   Results and Discussion

The proposed protocol was simulated in Network Simulator 2 (*NS2.35*) owing to its flexible environment that facilitated evaluation of this protocol with other related conventional protocols. For vehicle mobility modeling, VanetMobiSim was deployed.

As shown in Table 2, Ad-hoc On-demand Distance Vector (AODV) was utilized for routing due to its ability of operating in an environment characterized by network challenges such as packet losses, frequent node mobility and link failures. The simulations were executed on 1000 by 20 m^2 coverage area with maximum vehicle and RSU density of 50 and 6 respectively. A channel bandwidth of 5 Mpbs and slot time of 13 ms was adopted with 1 km maximum RSU transmission range. On the other hand, the least inter-vehicle distance was set to 30 m with 300 m maximum transmission range for each vehicle. The Media Access Control (MAC) layer protocol was IEEE 802.11p which is applicable in DSRC, and the maximum traffic lanes were 4. Thereafter, the simulations were run for 150 s as the required data items were collected.

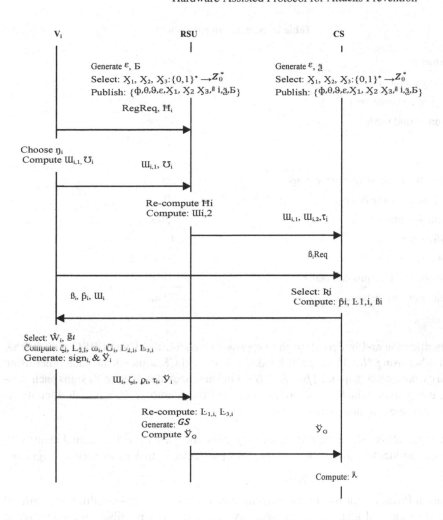

Fig. 2. Message exchanges in the proposed protocol

4.1 Security Evaluation

To assess the security posture of the proposed protocol, Spoofing, Tampering, Repudiation, Information disclosure, Denial of Service, Elevation of Privilege (STRIDE) model was utilized. In this model, the desired security and privacy features include authenticity, integrity, non-repudiability, confidentiality, availability, and authorization for upholding spoofing, tampering, repudiation, information disclosure, denial of service and elevation of privilege respectively.

Unlinkability: to prevent an adversary from associating any two messages of the same V_i, randomly generated security parameter $\bar{g}_i$ was incorporated in signature $sign_i$. This offers strong anonymity to beacon $\{ Ш_i, \zeta_i, \rho_i, \tau_i, \breve{Y}_i \}$ exchanged between the V_i and RSU.

Table 2. Simulation parameters

Parameter	Value
Routing protocol	AODV
Network coverage area	$1000 \times 20 \text{ m}^2$
Channel bandwidth	5 Mpbs
Slot time	13×10^{-6}s
RSU density	6
RSU's maximum transmission range	1000 m
Maximum Vehicle density	50
Simulation time	150 s
Traffic lanes	4
MAC layer protocol	IEEE 802.11p
V_i maximum transmission range	300 m
Least inter - V_i distance	30 m

Authentication and Integrity: in the proposed protocol, the V_i and RSU authenticate each other using $\hbar_i$. On the other hand, the RSU and CS authenticate each other using security parameter $\beta_i\varphi$ and $\{\beta_i + L_{1,i} \, \mathcal{B}\}$. For message integrity, the V_i signs each message using $sign_i$, which is comprised of current timestamp τ_i, V_i's pseudo-identity III, secret parameter ζ and private key φ.

Non-repudiation: since the RSU can easily associate each V_i with its actual identity $\hbar_i$ and pseudo-identity III_i, it is not possible for a particular V_i to deny its message signature $sign_i$.

Location Privacy: during the communication process, pseudo-identities are utilized instead of the real identities of vehicles. As such, it is not possible for an attacker to track V_i's trajectories within the network. It is only the RSU with its master secret key ψ that can validate III_i by executing the following operation: $\hbar_i = \mathcal{O}_i \oplus \psi \mathit{III}_{i,1}$. Consequently, without ψ, an adversary is unable to establish $\hbar_i$ and hence the proposed protocol upholds authorization. Moreover, since ψ is never sent over the communication channel, it is infeasible for an attacker to eavesdrop it. Consequently, the proposed protocol upholds confidentiality.

Anonymity and Privacy: To uphold anonymity of the V_i, only the RSU has the master key ψ necessary for the derivation of real identity of the V_i, $\hbar_i$. As such, other vehicles have no knowledge of the real identities of their neighbours. The utilized pseudo-identities such as $\mathit{III}_{i,1}$ and $\mathit{III}_{i,2}$ coupled with signature $sign_i$ on every message ensures that the exchanged messages are kept secret from the spying eyes of adversaries.

Resilience Against Message Replays and Impersonation Attacks: in the proposed protocol, each message sent by any V_i is signed using $sign_i$ and hence it is infeasible for an attacker to forge this signature for possible impersonation. The usage of timestamps τ_i during the communication process, coupled with the verification of the legitimate duration of pseudo identity $\Delta\tau_i$ thwarts any message replay attacks. As such, an adversary is unable to launch denial of service attacks against legitimate users through impersonating their network access credentials which might knock off these users from the network.

4.2 Performance Evaluation

The cryptographic operations in [50] executed on MIRACL software on a computer system running on Pentium 4 processor were utilized to evaluate the proposed protocol. Here, modular multiplication in Z_θ^*, T_M takes approximately 0.2325 ms, modular exponential operation T_{MX} takes 55.2 ms, modular point addition T_{MA} takes 0.12 ms, EC scalar point multiplication T_S takes 6.38 ms, bilinear paring T_{BP} takes 20.01 ms, while map to point hashing operation T_H takes 6.38 ms.

Computation Costs: in this evaluation, the signing and verification overheads of individual as well as amalgamated signature are computed. Based on Algorithm 1, signature generation in the proposed protocol requires only one T_S of approximately 6.38 ms that is equivalent to $27.44T_M$ operations. On the other hand, signature verification requires three T_S and two point additions. As such, the total computation overheads for signature verification is $((3* 6.38) + (2*0.12))$, yielding 19.38 ms(approximately $83.35T_M$) as shown in Table 3.

Table 3. Computation overheads comparisons

Scheme	Computation overheads			
	Signing		Verification	
	T_M	ms	T_M	ms
[15]	140	32.55	502	116.72
[17]	97	22.55	331	76.96
[19]	110	25.58	384	89.28
[18]	137	31.85	385	89.51
[16]	187	43.48	478	111.14
[14]	113	26.27	388	90.21
Proposed	27.44	6.38	83.35	19.38

The obtained computation overheads are then compared to schemes in [14, 15, 16, 17, 18, 19] as shown in Fig. 3. As shown in Fig. 3, the scheme in [15] had the highest signature verification overheads of 116.72 ms while the proposed protocol had the least signature verification overheads of 19.38 ms.

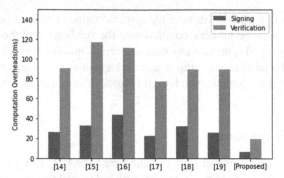

Fig. 3. Computation costs comparisons

On the other hand, the scheme in [16] had the highest signature signing costs of 43.48 ms while the proposed protocol had the least signing costs of 6.38 ms. As such, the proposed protocol was lightweight and hence applicable in resource constrained vehicular OBUs compared with its peers.

Signing and Verification Latencies: to evaluate the proposed protocol against the signature generation and verification latencies, the number of vehicles was varied between 10 and 50 as the values of these latencies were observed. Table 4 presents the results that were obtained.

Table 4. Signature signing and verification latencies

Scheme	Latencies (T_M)									
	Signing					Verification				
	10	20	30	40	50	10	20	30	40	50
[15]	1482	2921	4267	6115	7229	19935	44937	74592	91289	110937
[17]	983	1989	2376	3852	4198	21093	57026	78317	99727	120273
[19]	1128	2392	3949	4372	6061	16038	28723	41218	59022	81291
[18]	1388	2827	4164	6011	7127	18034	30781	43297	61037	82093
[16]	1923	3965	5782	7026	8893	2374	20156	23076	39092	42047
[14]	1022	2298	3845	4278	5967	2103	4315	10097	18092	20136
Proposed	756	984	1023	1793	1931	421	478	512	558	687

As shown in Table 4, there was a general increase in signature signing and verification latencies as the number of vehicles were increased from 10 to 50. This is attributed to the increasing processing at the OBU, RSU and CS as the increment of vehicles implies a surge in the number of transmitted messages. The scheme in [16] had longest signing latencies while the proposed protocol had the shortest signing latencies for all vehicle densities. On the other hand, the scheme in [17] had the longest signature verification latencies while the proposed protocol had the shortest latencies for all vehicle densities.

Transmission Costs: in the proposed protocol, the transmission costs consisted of times-tamp τ_i, pseudo-identities $ıı_i$, $sign_i$ length,β_i, and $\hat{W}_i$. During the authentication process, the V_i sent $ıı_i$, ζ_i, $\check{Y}_i = (\bar{G}_i, sign_i)$, τ_i, in which $ıı_i$, $\zeta_i \in \bar{g}_i$ and $sign_i \in Z_\vartheta^*$. As such, the total transmission cost is 184 bytes as shown in Fig. 4, which is the aggregation of the total length of $4(\bar{g}_i)$, Z_ϑ^* and τ_i.

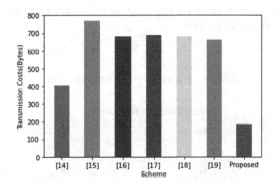

Fig. 4. Transmission costs comparisons

As shown in Fig. 4, the scheme in [15] had the highest transmission costs of 768 bytes followed by the schemes in [14, 16–19] and the proposed protocol with values of 689 bytes, 680 bytes, 680 bytes, 660 bytes, 404 bytes and 184 bytes respectively. Consequently, the proposed protocol had the least bandwidth requirements among its peers. This is due to its bilinear pairing free computations based on lightweight ECC, compared to its peers all of which are based on pairing operations. To investigate how the communication costs were influenced by the increase in signatures, the number of transmitted signatures was increased from 10 to 50 as shown in Fig. 5, below.

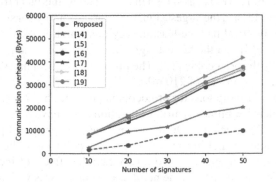

Fig. 5. Communication overheads variations

It is evident from Fig. 5 that as the number of signatures was increased, there was a corresponding increase in communication overheads among all the schemes. As such, the graphs of all schemes assumed nearly the same shape. While the scheme in [15] had the highest communication overheads for all signature densities, the proposed protocol had the least communication overheads for all signature densities. Basically, an increase in the number of signatures imply surging signaling among the network entities during signaling and verification processes, and hence the increase in bandwidth requirements.

Energy Consumption: for this evaluation, energy is obtained from the product of central processing unit maximum power (10.88 watts) and message generation or verification. As such, the energy consumption for the proposed protocol included message signing and verification as shown in Table 5.

Table 5. Signature energy consumption

Scheme	Energy consumption (mJ)	
	Signing	Verification
[15]	367	1247
[17]	220	881
[19]	294	953
[18]	367	953
[16]	440	1173
[14]	293	953
Proposed	69	210

For message signing, the computation involved was: (27.44*0.2325*10.88) while message verification computation was: (83.35*0.2325*10.88). This yielded 69 mJ for signing and 210 mJ for verification. These results were then compared with the values of schemes in [14, 15, 16, 17, 18, 19] as shown in Fig. 6 below. It is clear from Fig. 6 that the protocols in [15] and [18] had the largest signature signing energy consumption of 367 mJ while the proposed protocol had the least energy consumption of 69 mJ. On the other hand, the scheme in [15] had the largest signature verification energy consumption of 1247 mJ followed by the protocol in [16]. The proposed protocol had the least signature verification energy consumption of 210 mJ.

The high energy consumptions for protocols in [14, 15, 16, 17, 18, 19] is due to the computationally intensive bilinear pairing operations that have to be executed during signature signing and verification. On the other hand, the proposed protocol requires lightweight ECC modular multiplications and scalar point multiplication operations, hence its lower energy consumptions. To investigate the effects of increase in number of vehicles on energy consumptions, the number of vehicles was varied between 10 and 50 as shown in Fig. 7.

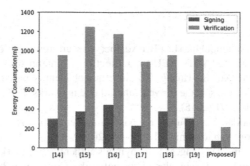

Fig. 6. Signature energy consumption

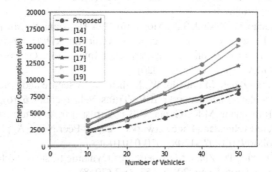

Fig. 7. Energy consumption variations

Based on the results in Fig. 7, there is a general increase in energy consumption as the number of vehicles is slowly incremented from 10 to 50. This is attributed to the surge in the number of transmitted messages when vehicle density is high. Among all these protocols, the one in [19] had the highest energy variations while the proposed protocol had the least energy variations.

5   Conclusion and Future Work

The goal of this paper was to develop an attack prevention protocol for ad hoc networks. To accomplish this, hardware based TPD was deployed, operating under realistic security assumptions. For cryptographic operations, modular multiplication and scalar point multiplication operations over ECC was deployed, coupled with simple XOR operations. The simulations results showed that this protocol had the least computation, communication, energy, and signature signing and verification costs compared with its peers. In addition, signature signing and verification analysis showed the proposed protocol had the lowest latencies. In terms of security, the proposed protocol offered unlinkability, authentication, integrity, non-repudiation, location privacy, anonymity, and was resilient against message replays and impersonation attacks. Future work lies in the formal verification of the security features provided by this protocol.

References

1. Rafsanjani, M.K., Fatemidokht, H.: FBeeAdHoc: a secure routing protocol for BeeAdHoc based on fuzzy logic in MANETs. AEU-Int. J. Electron. Commun. **69**(11), 1613–1621 (2015)
2. He, D., Zeadally, S., Xu, B., Huang, X.: An efficient identity-based conditional privacy-preserving authentication scheme for vehicular ad hoc networks. IEEE Trans. Inf. Forensics Secur. **10**(12), 2681–2691 (2015)
3. Muhammad, M., Safdar, G.A.: Survey on existing authentication issues for cellular-assisted V2X communication. Veh. Commun. **12**, 50–65 (2018)
4. Sun, M., Guo, Y., Zhang, D., Jiang, M.: Anonymous authentication and key agreement scheme combining the group key for vehicular ad hoc networks. Complexity **2021**, 1–13 (2021)
5. Bayat, M., Barmshoory, M., Rahimi, M., Aref, M.R.: A secure authentication scheme for VANETs with batch verification. Wireless Netw. **21**(5), 1733–1743 (2014). https://doi.org/10.1007/s11276-014-0881-0
6. Hamdi, M.M., Audah, L., Rashid, S.A., Mohammed, A.H., Alani, S., Mustafa, A.S.: A review of applications, characteristics and challenges in vehicular ad hoc networks (VANETs). In: 2020 International Congress on Human-Computer Interaction, Optimization and Robotic Applications (HORA), pp. 1–7. IEEE (2020)
7. Asaar, M.R., Salmasizadeh, M., Susilo, W., Majidi, A.: A secure and efficient authentication technique for vehicular ad-hoc networks. IEEE Trans. Veh. Technol. **67**(6), 5409–5423 (2018)
8. Mirsadeghi, F., Rafsanjani, M.K., Gupta, B.B.: A trust infrastructure based authentication method for clustered vehicular ad hoc networks. Peer-to-Peer Netw. Appl. **14**(4), 2537–2553 (2020). https://doi.org/10.1007/s12083-020-01010-4
9. Zhao, H., Sun, D., Yue, H., Zhao, M., Cheng, S.: Dynamic trust model for vehicular cyber-physical systems. IJ Netw. Secur. **20**(1), 157–167 (2018)
10. Cui, J., Tao, X., Zhang, J., Xu, Y., Zhong, H.: HCPA-GKA: a hash function-based conditional privacy-preserving authentication and group-key agreement scheme for VANETs. Veh. Commun. **14**, 15–25 (2018)
11. Nyangaresi, V.O., Rodrigues, A.J., Taha, N.K.: Mutual authentication protocol for secure VANET data exchanges. In: Perakovic, D., Knapcikova, L. (eds.) Future Access Enablers for Ubiquitous and Intelligent Infrastructures, vol. 382, pp. 58–76. Springer, Cham (2021). https://doi.org/10.1007/978-3-030-78459-1_5
12. Liu, Z.C., Xiong, L., Peng, T., Peng, D.Y., Liang, H.B.: A realistic distributed conditional privacy-preserving authentication scheme for vehicular ad hoc networks. IEEE Access **6**, 26307–26317 (2018)
13. Azees, M., Vijayakumar, P., Deboarh, L.J.: EAAP: Efficient anonymous authentication with conditional privacy-preserving scheme for vehicular ad hoc networks. IEEE Trans. Intell. Transp. Syst. **18**(9), 2467–2476 (2017)
14. Xu, Z., He, D., Kumar, N., Choo, K.K.R.: Efficient certificateless aggregate signature scheme for performing secure routing in VANETs. Secur. Commun. Netw. 2020 (2020)
15. Kumar, P., Kumari, S., Sharma, V., Li, X., Sangaiah, A.K., Islam, S.K.H.: Secure CLS and CL-AS schemes designed for VANETs. J. Supercomput. **75**(6), 3076–3098 (2018). https://doi.org/10.1007/s11227-018-2312-y
16. Mei, Q., Xiong, H., Chen, J., Yang, M., Kumari, S., Khan, M.K.: Efficient certificateless aggregate signature with conditional privacy preservation in IoV. IEEE Syst. J. **15**, 245–256 (2020)
17. Li, J., Yuan, H., Zhang, Y.: Cryptanalysis and improvement of certificateless aggregate signature with conditional privacy-preserving for vehicular sensor networks. Networks **317**, 48–66 (2015)

18. Kamil, I.A., Ogundoyin, S.O.: On the security of privacy-preserving authentication scheme with full aggregation in vehicular ad hoc network. Secur. Privacy **3**(3), e104 (2020)
19. Daxing, W., Jikai, T.: Probably secure cetificateless aggregate signature algorithm for vehicular ad hoc Network. J. Electron. Inf. Technol. **40**(1), 11–17 (2018)
20. Alazzawi, M.A., Lu, H., Yassin, A.A., Chen, K.: Efficient conditional anonymity with message integrity and authentication in a vehicular ad-hoc network. IEEE Access **7**, 71424–71435 (2019)
21. Nyangaresi, V.O., Rodrigues, A.J., Abeka, S.O.: Neuro-fuzzy based handover authentication protocol for ultra dense 5G networks. In: 2020 2nd Global Power, Energy and Communication Conference (GPECOM), pp. 339–344. IEEE (2020)
22. Islam, S.H., Obaidat, M.S., Vijayakumar, P., Abdulhay, E., Li, F., Reddy, M.K.C.: A robust and efficient password-based conditional privacy preserving authentication and group-key agreement protocol for VANETs. Future Gener. Comput. Syst. **84**, 216–227 (2018)
23. Wu, L., Fan, J., Xie, Y., Wang, J., Liu, Q.: Efficient location-based conditional privacy-preserving authentication scheme for vehicle ad hoc networks. Int. J. Distrib. Sensor Netw. **13**(3), 1550147717700899 (2017)
24. Cui, J., Zhang, J., Zhong, H., Xu, Y.: SPACF: a secure privacy-preserving authentication scheme for VANET with cuckoo filter. IEEE Trans. Veh. Technol. **66**(11), 10283–10295 (2017)
25. Raya, M., Hubaux, J.P.: Securing vehicular ad hoc networks. J. Comput. Secur. **15**(1), 39–68 (2007)
26. Lu, R., Lin, X., Zhu, H., Ho, P.H., Shen, X.: ECPP: efficient conditional privacy preservation protocol for secure vehicular communications. In: IEEE INFOCOM 2008-The 27th Conference on Computer Communications, pp. 1229–1237. IEEE (2008)
27. Chim, T.W., Yiu, S.M., Hui, L.C., Li, V.O.: SPECS: Secure and privacy enhancing communications schemes for VANETs. Ad Hoc Netw. **9**(2), 189–203 (2011)
28. Shim, K.A.: CPAS: an efficient conditional privacy-preserving authentication scheme for vehicular sensor networks. IEEE Trans. Veh. Technol. **61**(4), 1874–1883 (2012)
29. Liu, J.K., Yuen, T.H., Au, M.H., Susilo, W.: Improvements on an authentication scheme for vehicular sensor networks. Expert Syst. Appl. **41**(5), 2559–2564 (2014)
30. Lim, K., Manivannan, D.: An efficient protocol for authenticated and secure message delivery in vehicular ad hoc networks. Veh. Commun. **4**, 30–37 (2016)
31. Zhong, H., Huang, B., Cui, J., Xu, Y., Liu, L.: Conditional privacy-preserving authentication using registration list in vehicular ad hoc networks. IEEE Access **6**, 2241–2250 (2017)
32. Li, X., Liu, T., Obaidat, M.S., Wu, F., Vijayakumar, P., Kumar, N.: A lightweight privacy-preserving authentication protocol for VANETs. IEEE Syst. J. **14**(3), 3547–3557 (2020)
33. Huang, J.L., Yeh, L.Y., Chien, H.Y.: ABAKA: an anonymous batch authenticated and key agreement scheme for value-added services in vehicular ad hoc networks. IEEE Trans. Veh. Technol. **60**(1), 248–262 (2010)
34. Zhang, L., Wu, Q., Domingo-Ferrer, J., Qin, B., Hu, C.: Distributed aggregate privacy-preserving authentication in VANETs. IEEE Trans. Intell. Transp. Syst. **18**(3), 516–526 (2016)
35. Ying, B., Makrakis, D., Mouftah, H.T.: Dynamic mix-zone for location privacy in vehicular networks. IEEE Commun. Lett. **17**(8), 1524–1527 (2013)
36. Rajput, U., Abbas, F., Oh, H.: A hierarchical privacy preserving pseudonymous authentication protocol for VANET. IEEE Access **4**, 7770–7784 (2016)
37. Wang, S., Yao, N.: LIAP: a local identity-based anonymous message authentication protocol in VANETs. Comput. Commun. **112**, 154–164 (2017)
38. Nyangaresi, V.O., Rodrigues, A.J., Abeka, S.O.: Efficient group authentication protocol for secure 5G enabled vehicular communications. In: 2020 16th International Computer Engineering Conference (ICENCO), pp. 25–30. IEEE, Cairo (2020)

39. Zhang, J., Cui, J., Zhong, H., Chen, Z., Liu, L.: PA-CRT: Chinese remainder theorem based conditional privacy-preserving authentication scheme in vehicular ad-hoc networks. IEEE Trans. Dependable Secure Comput. **18**(2), 722–735 (2019)
40. Azees, M., Vijayakumar, P.: CEKD: computationally efficient key distribution scheme for vehicular ad-hoc networks. Aust. J. Basic Appl. Sci. **10**(2), 171–175 (2016)
41. Lo, N.W., Tsai, J.L.: An efficient conditional privacy-preserving authentication scheme for vehicular sensor networks without pairings. IEEE Trans. Intell. Transp. Syst. **17**(5), 1319–1328 (2015)
42. Zhang, C., Lu, R., Lin, X., Ho, P. H., Shen, X.: An efficient identity-based batch verification scheme for vehicular sensor networks. In: IEEE INFOCOM 2008-The 27th Conference on Computer Communications, pp. 246–250. IEEE (2008)
43. Wei, F., Zeadally, S., Vijayakumar, P., Kumar, N., He, D.: An intelligent terminal based privacy-preserving multi-modal implicit authentication protocol for internet of connected vehicles. IEEE Trans. Intell. Transp. Syst. 1–13 (2020)
44. Li, J., Lu, H., Guizani, M.: ACPN: a novel authentication framework with conditional privacy-preservation and non-repudiation for VANETs. IEEE Trans. Parallel Distrib. Syst. **26**(4), 938–948 (2014)
45. Calandriello, G., Papadimitratos, P., Hubaux, J.P., Lioy, A.: Efficient and robust pseudonymous authentication in VANET. In: Proceedings of the Fourth ACM International Workshop on Vehicular Ad Hoc Networks, pp. 19–28 (2007)
46. Vinoth, R., Deborah, L.J., Vijayakumar, P., Kumar, N.: Secure multi-factor authenticated key agreement scheme for industrial IoT. IEEE Internet Things J. **8**(5), 3801–3811 (2021)
47. Tzeng, S.F., Horng, S.J., Li, T., Wang, X., Huang, P.H., Khan, M.K.: Enhancing security and privacy for identity-based batch verification scheme in VANETs. IEEE Trans. Veh. Technol. **66**(4), 3235–3248 (2017)
48. Lin, X., Sun, X., Ho, P.H., Shen, X.: GSIS: A secure and privacy-preserving protocol for vehicular communications. IEEE Trans. Veh. Technol. **56**(6), 3442–3456 (2007)
49. Shao, J., Lin, X., Lu, R., Zuo, C.: A threshold anonymous authentication protocol for VANETs. IEEE Trans. Veh. Technol. **65**(3), 1711–1720 (2015)
50. Cao, X., Kou, W., Du, X.: A pairing-free identity-based authenticated key agreement protocol with minimal message exchanges. Inf. Sci. **180**(15), 2895–2903 (2010)

Prediction of Android Malicious Software Using Boosting Algorithms

Deepon Deb Nath[1], Nafiz Imtiaz Khan[2(✉)], Jesmin Akhter[3],
and Abu Sayed Md. Mostafizur Rahaman[4]

[1] Department of Information and Communication Technology, Bangladesh
University of Professionals (BUP), Dhaka, Bangladesh
[2] Department of Computer Science and Engineering, Military Institute of Science
and Technology (MIST), Dhaka, Bangladesh
`nafiz@cse.mist.ac.bd`
[3] Institute of Information Technology, Jahangirnagar University, Dhaka, Bangladesh
[4] Department of Computer Science and Engineering, Jahangirnagar
University, Dhaka, Bangladesh

Abstract. Android malware, a group of malicious software variants, including
viruses, ransomware and spyware, designed to cause substantial damage to data
and systems or to access a network without authorization. With an inexorable shift
in technology, Android has supplanted other Mobile platforms by being flexible
and user-friendly to the users. As the number of Android apps continues to grow
every day, the number of malwares aimed at attacking those users is also on the rise.
Thus, it becomes emergent to identify and remove malicious Android applications
before installation to prevent user's loss. Several studies have already been carried
out to anticipate Android malware using machine learning algorithms, while as per
the literature survey conducted by this study, a significant research has not been
found to be focusing especially on the genre of boosting algorithms. Therefore,
the objective of this paper is to classify malicious and benign Android applications
by using Boosting algorithm. To attain the research objective, four widely defined
boosting models viz. AdaBoost, CatBoost, XGBoost, and GradientBoost were
developed whereas, it was found that CatBoost and GradientBoost had the highest
F1 score (93.9%), followed by Adaboost (F1 score 93.5%), and XGBoost (F1
score 93.5%).

Keywords: Android · Malware · Classification · Boosting algorithms · Machine
learning · Static analysis

1 Introduction

Android has proven to be the world's most widely used intelligent terminal operating
system because of its numerous benefits: open-source, extensibility, and convenience.
According to [1] in May 2021, Android has a 72.72% market share worldwide among
mobile operating systems. Therefore, much mobile malware is likely to continue to
be developed and distributed to execute various cybercrimes on mobile phones. As of

M. H. Miraz et al. (Eds.): iCETiC 2021, LNICST 395, pp. 21–36, 2021.
https://doi.org/10.1007/978-3-030-90016-8_2

March 2020 in [2], 482,579 new Android malware samples amounted per month. These malicious apps are mostly distributed through third-party markets, but even Google Android Market cannot assure the applications that it registers into it are virus-free. Malicious apps pose a much more dangerous security risk to users. Spyware, Phishing, Bots, RootExploits, Banking-Trojans, Premium Dialers, SMS Fraud, and other threats are among them. While Android apps are handy for users, private information and vital data (such as information about medical records, bank account, credit card information, and passwords, etc.) are continually under threat as well.

To assure the safety of the Android system, various malware detection techniques have been recommended. Malware detection methods are mainly classified into three types: static detection method, dynamic detection method, and hybrid detection method [3, 4]. The first detection methods take out syntactic features that can be observed when an application is run in a controlled environment, whereas the second methods take out semantic features that can also be observed when an application is run in a controlled environment. This can reveal risks that static analysis cannot, but the time, cost, and computational resources of dynamic detection are comparatively high. Finally, The third method "hybrid detection" refers to a method that combines the first and second methods to accomplish a balance of detection efficiency and efficacy.

As of today, the signature-based detection technique is the most widely utilized. In this method, Experts manually define the signatures of malware and afterwords the malware is identified by looking for signatures in apps. Malware authors can make use of obfuscation technology to change malware's signature, granting malware to simply evade recognition by detection engines which are one of the disadvantages of the signature-based technique. To address this problem, an intelligent malware recognition technique is proposed. Machine learning algorithms are used by the intelligent malware detection technique to identify malware whether the technique is dynamic, static, or hybrid. Hidden patterns in malware can be learned by machine learning algorithms. These patterns have a high degree of generalization and can differentiate between benign and malicious applications. Unlike traditional approaches of malware detection, such as signature-based technique, machine learning (ML) based detection can identify previously undetected types of malware [5] and can deliver improved detection efficiency and efficacy [6].

The primary goals of this research are to examine various boosting algorithms for predicting android malware and to identify the relative feature importance of each features for developing ML models. The structure of the paper is as follows. The literature review on Android malware detection is described in Sect. 2. Section 3 discusses the overall research methodology, while the experimental results, analysis and evaluations are descried in Sect. 4. Finally, the discussion, conclusion and the future plan are narrated in Sect. 5.

2   Literature Review

Machine learning algorithms can be used to learn the most essential patterns from malware samples which can distinguish between dangerous and benign applications. Various ML algorithms such as Support Vector Machines (SVM), Naive Bayes method, Decision Trees, and Random Forest (RF) have been employed in this field to detect unknown harmful executables. These studies demonstrate the effectiveness of machine learning methods in detecting unknown malware.

To illustrate the features of malware which is commonly stated as a feature vector is one of the key tasks of an ML-based malware recognition system. If the feature vector's dimension is very huge, feature selection techniques can be used to lower it's dimension. For extracting behavioral features, malware samples are usually run in a virtual environment or sandbox. Mohaisen et al. [7] studied the behavior of malware illustrations in a simulated environment. Following that, they selected program behaviors such as network activities, file operations, memory operations, and registry key changes to depict malware. Besides, They used K-Nearest-Neighbor (KNN), Linear Regression (LR), the Perceptron, and SVM to categorize malware. Moreover, they extracted 65 features from malware to represent it. Pirscoveanu et al. [8] extracted 151 API calls which were used to characterize malware by running malware samples in the Cuckoo sandbox and classified them using the random forest classifier.

Malicious applications were detected with unauthorized permission attacks by Ankita [9] using 103 malware and 97 benign applications datasets, respectively on Nexus 5 with API level 19. Simple logic, J.48, RF 100, Naive Bayes, RF 10, IBK algorithms, and Sequential minimal optimization were used in the experimental approach. Here, The permission request was extracted by the XML parser, which generated binary malware features that were saved in the Attribute Relation File Format (ARFF). When the random forest algorithm was used, the detection rate was 96.6%. The researchers in [10] proposed a model for monitoring application events, integrating access, modifying permission levels into a critical function (RF) and sensitive APIs to protect users from the high levels of destruction caused by Android malicious applications. A database of 2130 samples is being used to specifically test the effectiveness of the proposed technique. According to experimental results, the proposed method accomplishes a high precision of 88.26%, 88.40% sensitivity, and 88.16% accuracy.

The dynamic detection technique [11] was tested on 4034 malware datasets and 10024 benign datasets. The random forest classifier detected malware on those applications with 96% accuracy while using the ServiceMonitor method. Here features attributes are extracted by the classifier module and this module is trained by using k-fold validation and the Markov chain. Malware retrieved information, like phone IMEI was found with an accuracy of 67%. In interchange for a better service rating, 17% of the detected malicious applications have attached their payload to the device.

Some malware remains dormant on the device after it has been downloaded and installed until an action is taken. Others, on the other hand, execute their payload during download, installation, and runtime [12]. Despite the fact that default permissions are continually encountered during install and download sessions, the access authorization routinely granted by Android users creates a huge space in the device attack vector. Malicious code attaches itself to benign applications during these exercises. At these stages, critical monitoring is essential for improved mobile platform security.

Based on deep learning, a static detection method [13] for packed or encrypted malware has been proposed. From the Android APK file, Bytecode files can be extracted and then converted into a two-dimensional bytecode matrix, and finally used to train and categorize malware using the deep learning algorithm, convolution neural network

(CNN). CNN learned features of bytecode files spontaneously that can be used to categorize malicious applications. The suggested detection method avoids the steps of investigating malware features and crafting malware feature illustrations.

To improve the accuracy and efficacy of comprehensive Android malware detection, the authors in [14] suggested a hybrid model based on convolutional neural networks (CNN) and deep autoencoders (DAE). Here neural networks demonstrate a strong ability to detect malware with 99.80% accuracy. While compared to the CNN-S model, the DAC-CNN model also reduces training time by 83%. To identify zero-day botnet attacks, the deep learning-based model for detecting botnets in real-time has been proposed by Ahmed et al. [15]. In 2019, Ding and Zhu [16] characterize malware as opcode sequences and used a deep belief network (DBN) to extract malware features in an analogous manner. Their experiments demonstrate that the DBN model outperforms baseline models such as the k-nearest neighbor algorithm, SVM, and decision trees as classifiers.

The hybrid detection approach incorporates the advantages of both dynamic and static detection methods to provide strong detection outcomes While analyzing malicious applications. Because the strengths of both methods are combined, it appears that this method has a better detection percentage than static and dynamic methods. A Droid-Detector model [17] for android malware recognition was designed and trained utilizing artificial intelligence's deep learning capability [18]. This model produced detection outcomes with a 96.6% accuracy and a 0.0021% distinction among the algorithms applied. Hybrid technology also allows for precise comparison of static and dynamic detection rates. Using a hidden Markov model [19] and the semantic approach of this method, a hidden example sequence was extracted from job code and API calls. The ROC curve's threshold was determined by reproducibility, precision, and specificity. The Android Buster sandbox was used as an analysis tool to define and determine the application's maliciousness and positivity. However, using the API call sequence to detect android malware does not solve the malware obfuscation problem.

To avoid infecting other network devices, the emulation-based detection tech nique necessarily requires the creation of sandboxes and the configuration of virtual machines systematically and securely. This technique is particularly effective when the Dalvik file (.dex) [20] is properly monitored. When malware is executed in the mobile real OS, detection turn out to be very much difficult. Malicious applications can be recognized in the sandbox environment by getting the dex file and transforming it into a human-readable format. This technique effectively captures zero-day malware [21] and malware that escalates privileges [22]. Sometimes, malware understands the environment's virtual nature and attempts to avoid recognition.

In addition to employing dynamic monitoring tools to achieve malware feature interpretation, decompiling tools such as IDAPro and Captone can be used to obtain the behavior features of malware. Cesare et al. [23] used decompilers to extract a program's control flow graph and identified malware variants by associating control flow graph similarity. Chan and Song [24] suggested a feature set for Android malicious application recognition that incorporated API calls and permissions. Wang et al. [25] categorized malware using application and platform specific static features using linear SVM, logistic regression, Random Forest, and Decision Tree. In paper [26], the authors developed sensitive subgraphs to illustrate static features demonstrating invocation patterns. Classifiers such as Decision Tree, Random Forest, PART, and K-Nearest Neighbor (KNN) were trained using the features, with Random Forest outperforming the others. Optimizing the hyper-parameters of a single class support vector machine used to identify an IoT botnet using the Grey Wolf Optimization swarm intelligence algorithm is described in [27].

In the field of android malware recognition, the N-gram technique has also been analyzed and evaluated in combination with stacked generalization. To assess the usefulness of unigram, bigram, and trigram along with stacking, a detailed analysis was performed in [28]. It has been discovered that when combined with stacking, unigram provides more than 97% accuracy, the highest detection rate while compared to others.

3 Research Methodology

The overview of research methodology is shown in Fig. 1, which includes data acquisition, feature selection, data synthesis, data oversampling, models development, and prediction. The stages are briefly discussed in the following subsections.

3.1 Data Acquisition

The dataset used in the experiment is from the University of Gottingen's Drebin project [29]. 215 features were obtained from 15,036 applications in this dataset (9,476 benign and 5,560 malware). Drebin samples are broadly used in the scien tific community. This dataset was also employed to create and assess a multilevel classifier fusion method for identifying Android malware [30].

3.2 Feature Selection

To lower the dimension of the chosen dataset, the Recursive Feature Elimination (RFE) method was applied. RFE works by deleting features in a recursive manner and then creating a model on the remaining attributes. It determines the combinations of attributes that contribute the most to predicting the target attribute by looking at the model accuracy. In this study, RFE was applied with a Logistic Regression algorithm to select the top 20 features, which are shown in Table 1, for predicting the target variable (type of application).

3.3 Data Synthesis

In this phase, the reduced feature set was processed to feed to the ML mod els. First, the dataset's missing values were addressed; the mean values were substituted for missing numerical cells, whereas the most frequent values were substituted for missing category cells. Second, the target feature was encoded as it was labeled as 'M', short of malware, and 'B', short of Benign. Third, a random train-test split of 75–25 was applied to the dataset, where 75% data was considered as train set while 25% data was considered as the test set.

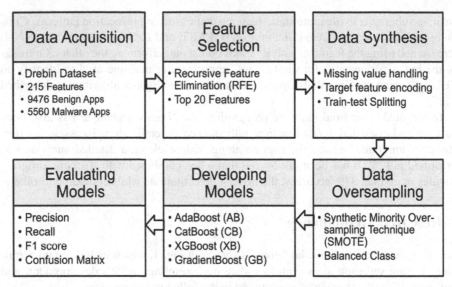

Fig. 1. Overview of research methodology

3.4 Data Oversampling

Drebin dataset had a class imbalance issue [31] as there were 9476 samples labeled as benign while 5560 samples labeled as malignant. It is required to have a similar number of instances for every class so that the ML models do not get biased toward a particular class. To handle the class imbalance problem, the Synthetic Minority Over-sampling Technique (SMOTE) [32] was used as the over-sampling procedure, which removes the imbalances in the classes. This method imitates current minority data instances and makes modest modifications to them, resulting in new minority data instances. Both the malignant and benign classes have exactly 9476 samples after the oversampling technique.

3.5 Developing Models

In this phase, four different ML models were developed by utilizing four algorithms from the domain of boosting algorithms. The algorithms subsume AdaBoost, CatBoost, XGBoost, and GradientBoost. The models were developed by using Python programming language and Sci-kit learn implementation package. The following is a brief overview of the considered algorithms.

1. **AdaBoost** AdaBoost which stands for Adaptive Boosting is a meta-learning ML algorithm, which is used to ameliorate the performance of the model by fitting sequentially to the weak learning models such as Decision Trees [33]. The output of the weak learners is merged into a weighted sum that reflects the final output of the boosted classifier. Because of the strong tugging of weak learners, when examples are misclassified, this classifier is adaptive. It is less prone to overfitting than other learning algorithms, yet being sensitive to noisy input [33].

Table 1. Reduced set of features (n = 20)

SL.	Feature name
1	Send_Sms
2	Ljava.lang.Class.getCanonicalName
3	getCallingUid
4	Use_Credentials
5	Manage_Accounts
6	android.intent.action. send
7	android.telephony.gsm.SmsManager
8	Read_History_Bookmarks
9	android.intent.action.Package_Replaced
10	nfc
11	Bind_RemoteViews
12	TelephonyManager.getDeviceId
13	Modify_Audio_Settings
14	android.intent.action.Timezone_Changed
15	chmod
16	Runtime.load
17	Read_Call_Log
18	SendMultipartTextMessage
19	Write_Calender
20	Write_Gservices

2. **CatBoost** CatBoost is a popular machine learning algorithm that handles categorical features efficiently and takes advantage of dealing with them during training rather than pre-processing time. [34]. It reduces the extensive need for hyper-parameter tuning and has a lower chance of overfitting by applying ordered boosting for getting the best result [35].

3. **XGBoost** XGBoost (eXtreme Gradient Boosting) is a boosting technique that is well known for offering parallel tree boosting that is well utilized for tackling data science issues precisely and efficiently in terms of both speed and performance [36]. This method is also frequently used to predict the polarity of online reviews [37] based on consumer purchase choices, where the essential characteristics are retrieved from the data using ranking scores.

4. **GradientBoost** Gradient boosting is another ML technique for solving classification and regression problems [38]. The basis learners are generally decision trees, and this prediction method is essentially an ensemble form of weak prediction models or base learners. A stage-wise fashioned model, like other boosting methods, is optimized using an arbitrary differentiable loss function.

3.6 Evaluating Models

In this phase, the predictions (malware and benign) are obtained from the ML models and their performance was evaluated. This phase is discussed in detail in Sect. 4 (Result Analysis).

4 Result Analysis

The models were evaluated on both training and test data, whereas the algorithms were trained on training data. Precision, recall, and f1 score are used to assess the models' performance. Because of the oversampling approach, the wellknown performance metric'accuracy' was not employed because it is deceptive in this situation [39]. The performance of the models for both the train as well as test data is shown in Table 2. Also, the performance for the train and the test data is shown in graphical form in Figs. 2 and 3 respectively. For each of the models, the feature importance score for each of the features (n = 20) were obtained. The feature importance score delineates that how useful a particular feature is to develop a particular model [40].

Table 2. Performance measures for the developed models

Model	Train			Test		
	Precision	Recall	F1 score	Precision	Recall	F1 score
AB	0.934	0.933	0.933	0.936	0.935	0.935
CB	0.94	0.94	0.94	0.939	0.939	0.939
XB	0.935	0.935	0.935	0.936	0.935	0.935
GB	0.94	0.94	0.94	0.939	0.939	0.939

Considering the AB model, the train precision, recall and f1-score were 93.4%, 93.3% and 93.3% respectively, while the precision, recall and f1-score for the test dataset were 93.6%, 93.5% and 93.5% respectively (see Table 2). The feature importance and the confusion matrices for the AB model are shown in Figs. 5 and 4 respectively. It can be observed from Fig. 5 that, 'getCallingUid', 'android.telephony.gsm.SmsManager' and 'Send sms' were top three features for developing the AB model. nonetheless, for the test dataset, 2197 samples were correctly classified as Benign, while 2252 samples were correctly classified as malignant (see Fig. 4 (b)).

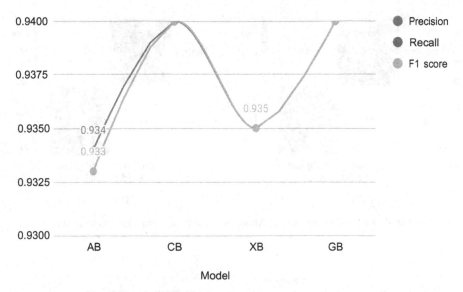

Fig. 2. Performance by developed models on training data

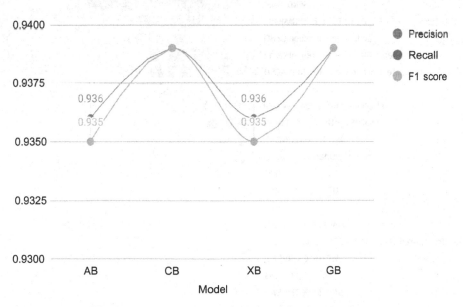

Fig. 3. Performance by developed models on testing data

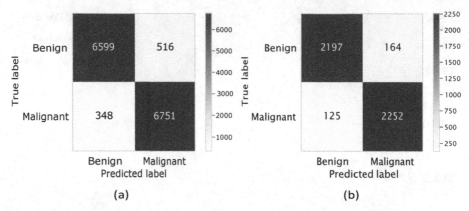

Fig. 4. Confusion matrices of AB classifier for: (a) train data, (b) test data

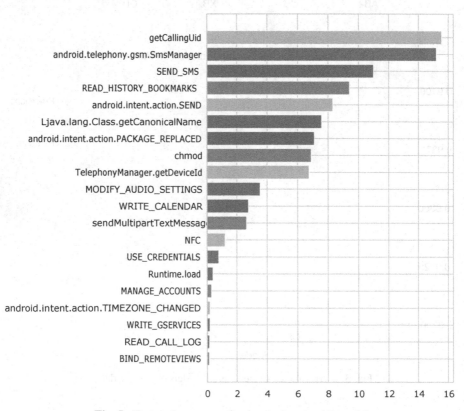

Fig. 5. Feature importance for developing the AB model

For the CB model, precision, recall and f1 score for the train dataset was 94%, while precision, recall and f1 score for the test dataset was 93.9% (see Table 2). The confusion matrices for the CB model are shown in Fig. 6, where for the test dataset, 2197 samples

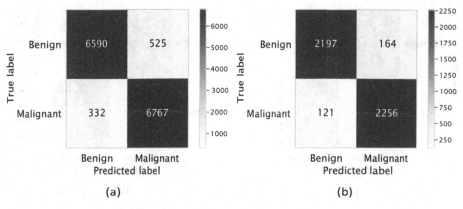

Fig. 6. Confusion matrices of CB classifier for: (a) train data, (b) test data

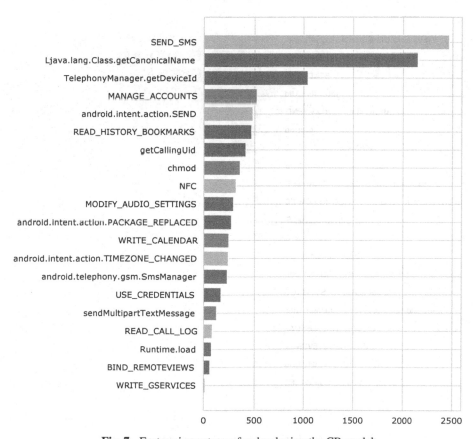

Fig. 7. Feature importance for developing the CB model

were correctly classified as Benign, while 2256 samples were correctly classsfied as Malignant. However, the feature importance for the CB model is shown in Fig. 7. It

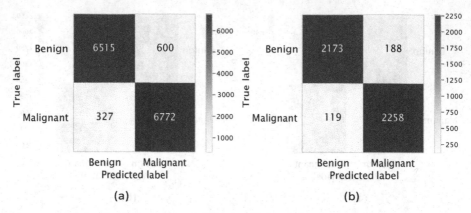

Fig. 8. Confusion matrices of XB classifier for: (a) train data, (b) test data

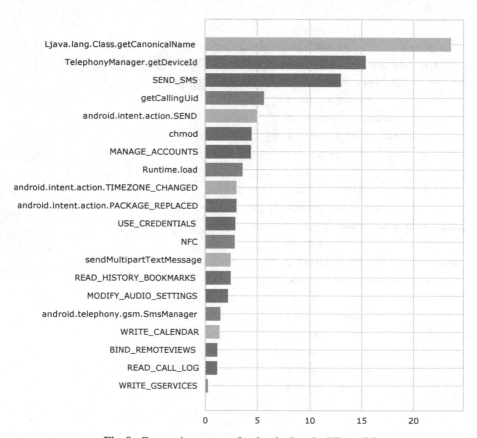

Fig. 9. Feature importance for developing the XB model

can be seen from Fig. 7 that, 'SEND SMS', 'Ljava.lang.class.getCannonicalName' and 'TelephonyManager.getDeviceid' were top three features for developing the CB model.

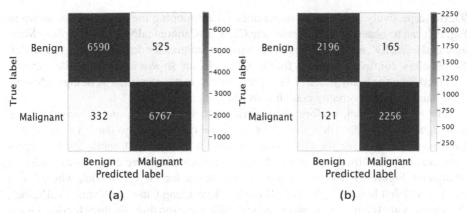

Fig. 10. Confusion matrices of GB classifier for: (a) train data, (b) test data

For the XB model, the precision, recall, and f1 score for the train dataset was 93.5%, while precision, recall and f1 score for the test dataset were 93.6%, 93.5%,

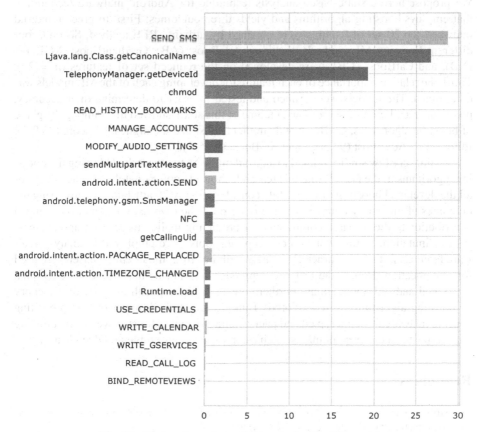

Fig. 11. Feature importance for developing the GB model

93.5% respectively. The feature importance for developing the XB model is shown in Fig. 9. It can be observed that, 'Ljava.lang.Class.getCannonicalName', 'TelephonyManager.getDeviceID', and 'Send sms' were top three features for developing the XB model. Nonetheless, confusion matrices for the XB model are shown in Fig. 8, while it can be observed from the figure that 2173 samples were correctly classified as Benign whereas, 2258 samples were correctly classified as Malignant.

For the GB model, performance metrics (precision, recall, and f1 score) for the train dataset were 94%, while the performance metrics for the test dataset were 93.9%. Confusion matrices for the GB model are shown in figure 10, while 2196 samples were correctly classified as Benign whereas, 2256 samples were correctly classified as Malignant. Figure 11 depicts the feature importance for the GB model, where it can be observed that here also like the XB model, 'Ljava.lang.Class. getCannonicalName', 'Sendsms' and 'TelephonyManager.getDeviceID' were top three features for developing the GB model.

5 Discussion and Conclusions

We propose here a static-based analysis technique for Android malware recognition that employs boosting algorithms and yields three outcomes: First, to predict android malware, top 20 set of features were obtained by utilizing RFE method, Second, four different Boosting ML methods, including AdaBoost (AB), GradientBoost, XGBoost (XB), and CatBoost (CB), were developed on the reduced set of features (n = 20). Third, the relative importance of each feature for developing each of the ML models was determined. The models were trained and tested in order to determine their accuracy, precision, recall, and F1 score. The outcome of this study showed that: among the genre of boosting algorithms, CatBoost and GradientBoost had the highest F1 score (93.9%), followed by AdaBoost (93.5%), and XGBoost (93.5%).

Again, very few studies related to android malware were conducted using the boosting algorithms in the past. While this research showed approximately 93% accuracy for all the developed boosting models while considering only 20 attributes. Considering the outcomes of this study compared to the other published works, this paper has a novel contribution to the research community for predicting malicious android applications. As for limitation, in this work no decompiling tools were employed to analyze malware features, rather the extracted features/attributes from the Drebin dataset were used for classification. Hence, the proposed approach will not be applicable for encrypted or packed android applications. Furthermore, only the algorithms from the category of boosting algorithms were explored. Thus, future studies may work on predicting android malware from encrypted and packed android applications as well as by utilizing algorithms from different domains, such as: traditional, ensemble and deep learning.

References

1. Mobile operating system market share worldwide. https://gs.statcounter.com/os-market-share/mobile/worldwide. Accessed 4 May 2021

2. Development of new android malware worldwide from June 2016 to March 2020. https://www.statista.com/statistics/680705/global-android-malware-volume/. Accessed 4 May 2021
3. Qing, S.H.: Research progress on android security. J. Softw. **27**(1), 45–71 (2016)
4. Lopes, J., Serr~ao, C., Nunes, L., Almeida, A., Oliveira, J.: Overview of machine learning methods for android malware identification. In: 2019 7th International Symposium on Digital Forensics and Security (ISDFS), pp. 1–6. IEEE (2019)
5. Ahvanooey, M.T., Li, Q., Rabbani, M., Rajput, A.R.: A survey on smartphones security: software vulnerabilities, malware, and attacks. *arXiv preprint* arXiv:2001.09406 (2020)
6. Souri, A., Hosseini, R.: A state-of-the-art survey of malware detection approaches using data mining techniques. HCIS **8**(1), 1–22 (2018). https://doi.org/10.1186/s13673-018-0125-x
7. Mohaisen, A., Alrawi, O., Mohaisen, M.: Amal: high-fidelity, behavior- based automated malware analysis and classification. Comput. Secur. **52**, 251–266 (2015)
8. Pirscoveanu, R.S., Hansen, S.S., Larsen, T.M., Stevanovic, M., Pedersen, J.M., Czech, A.: Analysis of malware behavior: type classification using machine learning. In: 2015 International Conference on Cyber Situational Awareness, Data Analytics and Assessment (CyberSA), pp. 1–7. IEEE (2015)
9. Kapratwar, A., Di Troia, F., Stamp, M.: Static and dynamic analysis of android malware. In: ICISSP, pp. 653–662 (2017)
10. Zhu, H.-J., You, Z.-H., Zhu, Z.-X., Shi, W.-L., Chen, X., Cheng, L.: Droiddet: effective and robust detection of android malware using static analysis along with rotation forest model. Neurocomputing **272**, 638–646 (2018)
11. Salehi, M., Amini, M.: Android malware detection using Markov chain model of application behaviors in requesting system services. *arXiv preprint* arXiv:1711.05731 (2017)
12. Mahindru, A., Singh, P.: Dynamic permissions based android malware detection using machine learning techniques. In: Proceedings of the 10th In novations in Software Engineering Conference, pp. 202–210 (2017)
13. Ding, Y., Zhang, X., Hu, J., Xu, W.: Android malware detection method based on bytecode image. J. Ambient Intell. Humaniz. Comput. 1–10 (2020). https://doi.org/10.1007/s12652-020-02196-4
14. Wang, W., Zhao, M., Wang, J.: Effective android malware detection with a hybrid model based on deep autoencoder and convolutional neural network. J. Ambient Intell. Humaniz. Comput. **10**(8), 3035–3043 (2018). https://doi.org/10.1007/s12652-018-0803-6
15. Ahmed, A.A., Jabbar, W.A., Sadiq, A.S., Patel, H.: Deep learning-based classification model for botnet attack detection. J. Ambient Intell. Humaniz. Comput. 1–10 (2020). https://doi.org/10.1007/s12652-020-01848-9
16. Yuxin, D., Siyi, Z.: Malware detection based on deep learning algorithm. Neural Comput. Appl. **31**(2), 461–472 (2017). https://doi.org/10.1007/s00521-017-3077-6
17. Yuan, Z., Yongqiang, L., Xue, Y.: Droiddetector: android malware characterization and detection using deep learning. Tsinghua Sci. Technol. **21**(1), 114–123 (2016)
18. Demetrio, L., Biggio, B., Lagorio, G., Roli, F., Armando, A.: Explaining vulnerabilities of deep learning to adversarial malware binaries. *arXiv preprint* arXiv:1901.03583 (2019)
19. Damodaran, A., Di Troia, F., Visaggio, C.A., Austin, T.H., Stamp, M.: A comparison of static, dynamic, and hybrid analysis for malware detection. J. Comput. Virol. Hacking Tech. **13**(1), 1–12 (2017)
20. Costa, G., Aria, H.: Android malware detection using network behavior analysis and machine learning classifiers (2017)
21. Ashawa, M.A., Morris, S.: Analysis of android malware detection techniques: a systematic review (2019)
22. Lee, H.-T., Kim, D., Park, M., Cho, S.: Protecting data on android platform against privilege escalation attack. Int. J. Comput. Math. **93**(2), 401–414 (2016)

23. Cesare, S., Xiang, Y., Zhou, W.: Control flow-based malware variant-detection. IEEE Trans. Dependable Secure Comput. **11**(4), 307–317 (2013)
24. Chan, P.P.K., Song, W.K.: Static detection of android malware by using permissions and API calls. In: 2014 International Conference on Machine Learning and Cybernetics, vol. 1, pp. 82–87. IEEE (2014)
25. Wang, X., Wang, W., He, Y., Liu, J., Han, Z., Zhang, X.: Characterizing Android apps' behavior for effective detection of malapps at large scale. Future Gener. Comput. Syst. **75**, 30–45 (2017)
26. Fan, M., Liu, J., Wang, W., Li, H., Tian, Z., Liu, T.: Dapasa: detecting android piggybacked apps through sensitive subgraph analysis. IEEE Trans. Inf. Forensics Secur. **12**(8), 1772–1785 (2017)
27. Al Shorman, A., Faris, H., Aljarah, I.: Unsupervised intelligent system based on one class support vector machine and grey wolf optimization for iot botnet detection. J. Ambient Intell. Humaniz. Comput. **11**(7), 2809–2825 (2020). https://doi.org/10.1007/s12652-019-01387-y
28. Islam, T., Rahman, S.S.M.M., Hasan, M.A., Rahaman, A.S.M.M., Jabiullah, M.I.: Evaluation of N-gram based multi-layer approach to detect malware in android. Procedia Comput. Sci. **171**, 1074–1082 (2020)
29. Arp, D., Spreitzenbarth, M., Hubner, M., Gascon, H., Rieck, K., Siemens, C.E.: Drebin: effective and explainable detection of android malware in your pocket. In: NDSS, vol. 14, pp. 23–26 (2014)
30. Yerima, S.Y., Sezer, S.: Droidfusion: a novel multilevel classifier fusion approach for android malware detection. IEEE Trans. Cybern. **49**(2), 453–466 (2018)
31. Kotsiantis, S., Kanellopoulos, D., Pintelas, P., et al.: Handling imbalanced datasets: a review. GESTS Int. Trans. Comput. Sci. and Eng. **30**(1), 25–36 (2006)
32. Chawla, N.V., Bowyer, K.W., Hall, L.O., Kegelmeyer, W.P.: Smote: synthetic minority over-sampling technique. J. Artif. Intel. Res. **16**, 321–357 (2002)
33. Schapire, R.E.: Explaining adaBoost. In: Schölkopf, B., Luo, Z., Vovk, V. (eds.) Empirical Inference, pp. 37–52. Springer, Heidelberg (2013). https://doi.org/10.1007/978-3-642-411 36-6_5
34. Dorogush, A.V., Ershov, V., Gulin, A.: CatBoost: gradient boosting with categorical features support. *arXiv preprint* arXiv:1810.11363 (2018)
35. Prokhorenkova, L., Gusev, G., Vorobev, A., Dorogush, A.V., Gulin, A.: CatBoost: unbiased boosting with categorical features. *arXiv preprint* arXiv:1706.09516 (2017)
36. Chen, T., Guestrin, C.: XGBoost: a scalable tree boosting system. In: Proceedings of the 22nd ACM SIGKDD International Conference on Knowledge Discovery And Data Mining, pp. 785–794 (2016)
37. Nguyen, L.T.K., Chung, H.H., Tuliao, K.V., Lin, T.M.Y.: Using XGBoost and skip-gram model to predict online review popularity. SAGE Open **10**(4), 1–17 (2020). https://doi.org/10.1177/2158244020983316
38. Friedman, J.H.: Stochastic gradient boosting. Comput. Stat. Data Anal. **38**(4), 367–378 (2002)
39. Chawla, N.V.: Data mining for imbalanced datasets: an overview. In: Maimon, O., Rokach, L. (eds.) Data Mining and Knowledge Discovery Handbook, pp. 875–886. Springer, Boston (2009). https://doi.org/10.1007/978-0-387-09823-4_45
40. Zien, A., Kramer, N., Sonnenburg, S., Ratsch, G.: The feature importance ranking measure. In: Buntine, W., Grobelnik, M., Mladenić, D., Shawe-Taylor, J. (eds.) Machine Learning and Knowledge Discovery in Databases, vol. 5782, pp. 694–709. Springer, Heidelberg (2009). https://doi.org/10.1007/978-3-642-04174-7_45

Privacy and Security Factors of Government Websites versus Private Websites in Bangladesh and USA: A Comparative Study

Merina Tanjin[1], Ishorju Agnes Botlero[1], Mourina Tasnim Hridita[1],
Tawsiful Islam Riyadh[1], Md. Mehedi Hassan Onik[1(✉)] iD, and Mahdi H. Miraz[2(✉)] iD

[1] Department of Computer Science, American International University-Bangladesh (AIUB),
Dhaka, Bangladesh
mehedi.onik@aiub.edu, m.miraz@ieee.org
[2] School of Electrical and Computer Engineering, Xiamen University
Malaysia, Sepang, Malaysia

Abstract. Security and privacy are the two most vital aspects of the modern technological evolution, to ensure the required level of trust between the customers and the service providers. Personally identifiable information (PII) is mounting at an exponential rate and so does the associated manifold security risks. In fact, there are many state-of-the-art security and privacy-preserving mechanisms in practice, however, the least developed countries (LDC) are often reluctant to maintain those security standards, in comparison to their counterparts i.e. the developed countries (DC). In addition, government managed websites in LDCs are more exposed to security and privacy vulnerabilities compared with the private sector websites. This study provides a security and privacy assessment model that can thoroughly assess government as well as private websites. To validate the proposed model, this study has selected Bangladesh as a representative of the least developed countries and United States of America (USA) for the developed countries. After a detailed empirical analysis of 20 government and private websites of each of these two countries, this study found that the majority of the public websites in LSD (Bangladesh) were less secure than the private ones, in comparison to those of the DC (USA). Several underlying factors, such as corruption, financial variances, policy issues and lack of skilled workforce in security sector, were the main reasons behind this inequality. This study also outlines some guidelines and recommendations for LDC to eradicate prevailing differences amongst public and private websites' security and privacy standards.

Keywords: Security · Privacy · Government websites · LDC · Private websites · Assessment tool

1 Introduction

As the usage of the Internet is mushrooming, websites and other internet-based applications have become a vital part of our everyday live. According to Firstsiteguide, currently

M. H. Miraz et al. (Eds.): iCETiC 2021, LNICST 395, pp. 37–55, 2021.
https://doi.org/10.1007/978-3-030-90016-8_3

(in 2021) there are more than 1.8 billion websites in the world which was 1.7 billion just one year before (in 2020) [1]. Therefore, it is evident that despite the growing number of mobile applications (apps) and other alternatives, the demand for websites is still significantly on the rise. Business organizations are not only questing for personal data but also images, voice, life style, appearance other multifaceted information. In the era of the 4th industrial revolution [2], various sectors such as healthcare, artificial intelligence (AI), robotics, the Internet of Things (IoT), genetic engineering, quantum computing [3] and more. Therefore, the security and privacy of our digital information, data and applications, have become one of the major concerns in both developed and underdeveloped countries. However, major differences have noticed for two different types of countries, particularly in terms of organizational approaches, government initiatives, infrastructure and services. Developed countries have enough financial, technological and political support, whereas least developed countries have limited resources to fight against cybercrimes.

Bangladesh has become one of the most susceptible countries in cyberspace in the recent years, its current ranking is 25th in the 15/8/2021 Global Cyber security index by International Telecommunication Union [4]. As the number of people using the internet grows in Bangladesh, so does the number of attacks (internet penetration 28.8% in 2021) [5]. In Bangladesh, the level of research conducted on privacy and security is very low, compared to the other domains. Particularly, not enough research comparing the standards, policies and strengths of the local privacy and security measures, with those of the advanced countries, was found. Therefore, cyber-security specialists, researchers and policy makers are not yet well prepared. In addition, the users of websites and mobile apps are not well aware of the privacy and security issues. Due excessive corruptions and lack of accountability in the government sectors, the government websites possess risks and vulnerabilities with regards to privacy and security aspects. On the contrary, private websites, with more traffic and adequate cyber-security team, possess comparatively lower the chance of cyber-attacks.

In this study, selected public and private websites from a least developed country (i.e. Bangladesh) as well as from a developed country (i.e. United States) were evaluated, with regards to their overall privacy and security standards. Some common security aspects, such as authentication process, password recovery process, Captcha, HTTPS, cookies sharing, privacy policies, terms and conditions, etc. were critically analyzed to support our hypothesis. Finally, the research results, including adequate statistical data with comparison and ranking for the websites of both the countries, have been presented.

2 Background Study and Literature Review

Cybersecurity deals with both security and privacy. Security deals with unauthorized access of personal information, that is, the method or tool through which our personal data is protected. On the other hand, privacy protects users' rights to control personal information through laws, regulations and technological architecture. However, both security and privacy intend to protect Personally Identifiable Information (PII) that includes contact details, phone numbers, emails, photos, health data, etc. [3]. In fact, since internet based communication, such as through websites, apps and IoT applications, has rapidly increased in the recent past years, safeguarding users' PII has become a major concern. The main reasons for these intended or unintended privacy and security breaches are poor website and application design, mismanagement of cookies, poor encryption mechanisms, inadequate password protection mechanisms, users' negligence, backdated software, inadequate laws and regulations, lack of law enforcement, etc. [6].

In Bangladesh, government website addresses are formulated as 'XYZ.bd.gov', whereas US government website addresses takes the form of "XYZ.states.gov" [7]. However, private websites may use different domain names with variety of possible extensions such as.net,.com,.bd,.us,.org,.edu, etc. Bangladesh government is rapidly modernizing its public services, though adoption of e-governance to provide various online services to the citizens. These services are mainly provided via different government websites/portals, while some of them are through mobile apps. However, if security measures are not correctly implemented, it can result in great disaster. That is why it is critical to research various aspects of security measures on various websites.

As per the report of the Kaspersky Security Bulletin 2020, Bangladesh was globally ranked 8th where users faced the greatest risk of online infection and the rate was 13.75% [8] The Trend Micro Global Spam Map reveals that about 69.55% Bangladeshi individual users are at computer virus infection risk and about 80% users are already spam attack victims [5]. In fact, there is a recent incident of siphoning $81 million through SWIFT channel from the Federal Reserve Bank of New York account of the central bank of Bangladesh viz. Bangladesh Bank, which was supposedly linked to a customized mul ware attack [5]. Therefore, banks in Bangladesh needs to implement appropriate security measures, particularly with regards to intrusion prevention and detection [5]. In December 2020, three Bangladeshi local private banks reportedly faced major cyberattacks. Considering three such attacks within the short time span of only one month, has raised great concern regarding the strength of their security systems to withstand the escalating threats from scammers [5]. Out of those three banks, the largest victim was Dutch Bangla Bank Limited (DBBL) resulting in a loss of approximately $3 million by the local as well as global cybercriminals [9]. However, the remaining two banks claimed that they could somehow ward off the financial losses [10]. As a matter of fact, numerous Bangladeshi government websites, such as those of the president's as well as the prime minister's offices, were hacked as well [11].

On the contrary, number of cyberattacks in the USA are less than that of Bangladesh. However, cyber-attacks and privacy breaching is also a common phenomenon there. In May 2021, the chief of the U.S. Cyber Command revealed that the number of operations conducted by them surpassed two dozen operations, in order to resist foreign cyber threats anterior to the 2020 U.S. elections. Amongst them, 11 forward hunt operations were conducted in nine different territories [12]. In 2017, a group of hackers, suspected to be Russian origin, breached U.S. State Department's email server and gained illegitimate access to thousands of confidential emails [13]. Another remarkable attack was conducted by some Iranian hackers, targeting to heist the credentials of some lead medical researchers, particularly oncologists, neurologists as well as geneticists, of both the USA and Israel [14].

There is hardly any website which can be considered as completely secure and without the risk of being exploited. Nonetheless, web services have become so intertwined into our daily lives that we have been accustomed to storing and sharing vast amounts of personal information on the internet. In this context, the goal of this research is to provide a strategy for detecting maximal web-application vulnerabilities with minimal expense and effort. It has assessed the vulnerabilities of the chosen Bangladeshi websites against a collection of the most popular and prevalent attack vectors using penetration testing and source code analysis methodologies, which respectively constitute black box as well as white box testing [15] introduced a script that demonstrates how to trade off the application's security requirements. SQL infusion and cross website scripting are two examples of client-side embedded scripts for web interactions. Before they have an impact on the security and classification of the information, such attacks must be identified and evacuated [16]. Computers, projectors, printers, smart watches, smart phones, refrigerators, washing machines and other Internet-connected smart applications are vulnerable to a variety of threats and vulnerabilities. There has been a recent rise in deploying HTTPS protocol, instead of classical HTTPS, for secure communicate and transactions. Meanwhile, the number of browser-trusted certificate authority has increased, while baseline certificate issuing due diligence has decreased [17]. Our study also investigates HTTPS protocol and SSL certificate for ensuring user privacy. The number of services offered by the USA government websites is continuously growing, yet customers are concerned about their personal information being protected. In fact, findings of a study [18] which looked at the privacy policies of 50 USA Senate websites, reveals that only few of them had complete privacy policies in place. The study also identified there is an overall lack of protection of personal data in most of the cases.

3   Proposed Method

Figure 1 illustrates the steps followed this study for investigating the privacy and security aspects of the selected websites. Popular and mostly used ten websites from the government and private sectors of both Bangladesh and USA were selected by this study. Four privacy factors, i.e. (i) password authentication, (ii) privacy policy and law, (iii) third-party data sharing policy and (iv) data access, delete and modification right, were considered.

3.1   Privacy Assessment

A password is one of the authentication mechanisms, which belong to the 'something we know' category. A password is fundamentally a shared secret phrase between the service provider and the user. It is assumed that the password will not be disclosed with any third-party by either the user or the service provider. Thus, it provides the mechanism to authenticate a legitimate user and grant access to the desired services through the website or app. For smooth delivery of services, the security of a password is of paramount importance. Our privacy assessment tool has identified six crucial heuristics for password authentication (PA), i.e. P.1: Password Construction Guidelines, P.A2: Password Recovery, P.A3 CAPTCHA, P.A4: Security Question, P.A5: HTTPS Channel, P. A6: Password Strength Meter. The other factors include: third party data sharing and privacy policy. All the aforementioned factors are investigated by exploring each of the

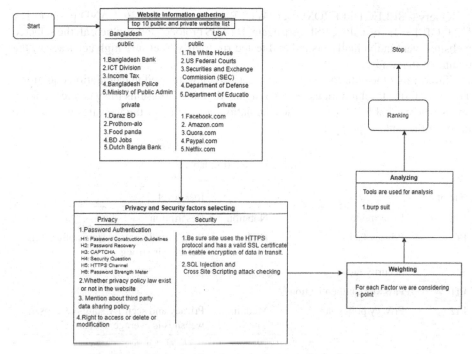

Fig. 1. Architecture of analyzing privacy and security factors

websites considered by this study. Various security measures, such as email verification, user privacy policy and third-party data sharing, have been rigorously investigated.

3.2 Security Assessment

For security purpose, SQL injection and cross-site scripting attack, SSL certificate, cookies collection numbers and HTTPS protocols have been analyzed. Cross-site scripting (XSS) is a client-side code injection technique. In XSS, malicious scripts are injected by the cybercriminals into the web applications, to exploit the system. This is done through inserting scripts via the data input field of any websites, which accepts data without proper validation. These scripts are treated as the source codes of the targeted [15]. Burp Scanner is a tool which can automatically crawl and scan various websites for collecting contents and identifying possible vulnerabilities. Depending on the configuration, the scanner has the capability to discover the contents and functionalities and audit to determine vulnerabilities [19]. SQL injection is considered as the most vulnerable threat because it can exploit the entire database running behind any web application [20]. SQL injection attacks are administered at the application level, regular firewall and or intrusion detection systems (IDS), placed at the network layer, fails to withstand such attacks [21]. If a script is vulnerable, the attacker can put malicious input to alter the SQL statements. To check vulnerability, concatenated 'OR $1 = 1$' in the URL. So, after the input the query becomes like:

Query – SELECT id FROM users WHERE username = 'ABC' AND password = '123' OR 1 = 1. To analyze SSL certificate, HTTPS protocol and cookies, all the selected websites were individually visited and tested rigorously to ensure high accuracy of the results of this study.

Table 1 lists the notation with description which were used in calculation equations. The overall risk level notations are also included. Table 2 presents the websites ranking levels whereas Table 3 represent the calculation equations for the websites which were used for the ranking purpose.

Table 1. Notation table

Factors		Risk level	
Notation	Description	Notation	Description
Pf	Privacy factor	High	Privacy and security status of chosen websites is strong
Sf	Security factor		
Pf1	Password authentication		
Pf2	Privacy policy law	Medium	Privacy and security status of chosen websites is average

Table 2. Overall websites' rankings

	Low	Medium	High
High	Medium	High	Highest
Medium	Low	Medium	High
Low	Lowest	Low	Medium

Table 3. Privacy factors checking of USA and Bangladesh government websites

Equations	Use
For 1st Website, $W_1P_f = (P_{f1} + P_{f2} + P_{f3})$ $W_1S_f = (S_{f1} + S_{f2} + S_{f3})$ Similarly for N^{th} websites, $W_nP_f = (P_{f1n} + P_{f2n} + P_{f3n})$ $WnSf = (S_{f1n} + S_{f2n} + S_{f3n})$	In terms of privacy factor: [Sorting from high to low $(W_1P_fP_{fn}..........W_nP_fP_{fn})$] In terms of security factor: [Sorting from high to low $(W_1S_fS_{fn}..........W_nS_fS_{fn})$]

4 Result and Analysis

In this part of the research, we counted the number of privacy factors fulfilled by each of the investigated websites for both Bangladesh (private government) and the USA (private government). Here, S = secure, NS = not secure, NA = not available, A = available (Table 4 and Table 5). Table 4 presents the overall state of privacy factors in the government websites of Bangladesh and those of the USA. Overall Password authentication states in both cases are almost similar but the privacy policy deemed to be better in the USA websites than those of Bangladesh.

Table 4. Privacy factors checking of USA and Bangladesh government websites

Bangladeshi govt. websites								
	Password authentication guidelines	Password recovery	Captcha	Security question	HTTPS channels	Password strength meter	Privacy third party	Privacy policy law
Passport [22]	S	S	S	NS	S	NS	NA	NA
Income Tax [23]	NS	S	S	S	S	NS	S	A
Bangladesh Police [24]	S	S	S	NS	S	NS	NA	NA
Teletalk [25]	S	S	S	NS	S	NS	NS	A
National University [26]	S	S	NS	NS	S	NS	NA	NA
USA Govt. websites								
US Federal Courts [27]	S	S	NS	NS	S	NS	S	A
Securities and Exchange Commission (SEC) [28]	S	S	NS	NS	S	NS	NS	A
Department of Defense [29]	S	S	NS	NS	S	NS	NS	A
Department of Education [30]	NA	NA	NA	NA	NA	NA	NS	A
The White House [31]	NA	NA	NA	NA	NA	NA	NS	A

4.1 Total Calculation for Privacy (Government Websites)

Weighting: Here, in Table 4 and Table 5, secure/available = 1, not secure/not available = 0. From the previous equation as shown in Table 3, $W_1P_n = (P_{f1}n + P_{f2}n + P_{f3}n)$.

- **For Bangladesh government website:** (Calculating total weight (0/1) of each privacy factors for Bangladesh government websites) *Web1(Passport) = ((1 + 1 + 1 + 0 +*

$1 + 0) + 0 + 0) = 4$, Web2(Income Tax) = $[(0 + 1 + 1 + 1 + 1 + 0) + 1 + 1] = 6$, Web3 (Bangladesh Police) = $[(1 + 1 + 1 + 0 + 1 + 0) + 0 + 0] = 4$, Web4(Teletalk) = $[(1 + 1 + 1 + 0 + 1 + 0) + 0 + 1] = 5$, Web5(National University) = $[(1 + 1 + 0 + 0 + 1 + 0) + 0 + 0] = 3$

$$\text{Total calculation, } W_5P_f = (4 + 6 + 4 + 5 + 3) = 22 \tag{1}$$

- **For the USA government website:** (Calculating total weight (0/1) of each privacy factors for the USA government websites) Web1(US Federal Courts) = $[(1 + 1 + 0 + 0 + 1 + 0) + 1 + 1] = 5$, Web2 (Securities and Exchange commission (SEC)) = $[(1 + 1 + 0 + 0 + 1 + 0) + 0 + 1] = 4$, Web3 (Department of Defense) = $[(1 + 1 + 0 + 0 + 1 + 0) + 0 + 1] = 4$, Web4(Department of Education) = $[(0 + 0 + 0 + 0 + 0 + 0) + 0 + 0] = 0$, Web5(The White House) = $[(0 + 0 + 0 + 0 + 0 + 0) + 0 + 0] = 0$

$$\text{Total calculation, } W_5P_f = (5 + 4 + 4 + 0 + 0) = 13 \tag{2}$$

Here, S = secure, NS = not secure, A = available. Table 5 represents the scenario of privacy factors in private sector websites of both Bangladesh and the USA. The overall result shows similar trends in both the cases.

4.2 Total Calculation for Privacy (Private Websites)

Weighting: Here, secure/available = 1, not secure/not available = 0.

- **For Bangladeshi private websites:** (Calculating total weight (0/1) of each privacy factors for Bangladesh private websites) Web1(Daraz BD) = $[(1 + 1 + 0 + 0 + 1 + 0) + 0 + 1] = 4$, Web2(Prothom Alo) = $[(1 + 1 + 1 + 0 + 1 + 0) + 0 + 1] = 5$, Web3 (Food Panda) = $[(1 + 1 + 0 + 0 + 1 + 0) + 0 + 1] = 4$, Web4(BD Jobs) = $[(1 + 1 + 1 + 0 + 1 + 1) + 0 + 1] = 6$, Web5(DBBL) = $[(1 + 1 + 0 + 0 + 1 + 0) + 0 + 1] = 4$.

$$\text{Total calculation, } W_5P_f = (4 + 5 + 4 + 6 + 4) = 23 \tag{3}$$

- **For the USA Private website:** (Calculating total weight (0/1) of each privacy factors for USA private websites) Web1(Facebook) = $[(1 + 1 + 0 + 0 + 1 + 0) + 0 + 1] = 4$, Web2 (Amazon) = $[(1 + 1 + 0 + 0 + 1 + 0) + 0 + 1] = 4$, Web3 (Quora) = $[(1 + 1 + 1 + 0 + 1 + 0) + 0 + 1] = 5$, Web4(Paypal) = $[(1 + 1 + 1 + 1 + 1 + 0) + 0 + 1] = 6$, Web5(Netflix) = $[(1 + 1 + 1 + 0 + 1 + 0) + 0 + 1] = 5$

$$\text{Total calculation, } W_5P_f = (4 + 4 + 5 + 6 + 5) = 25 \tag{4}$$

Here in Table 6, S = secure, V = valid. Table 6 represents the scenario of security factors with regards to the private sector websites of both Bangladesh and the USA. The overall result demonstrates a similar outcome in both cases.

Similarly, we counted the number of security factors satisfied by each of the investigated websites for both Bangladesh (private & government) and the USA (private & government).

Table 5. Privacy factors checking of USA and Bangladesh private websites

Bangladeshi private websites

	Password authentication guidelines	Password recovery	Captcha	Security question	HTTPS channels	Password strength meter	Privacy third party	Privacy policy law
DarazBD [32]	S	S	S	NS	S	NS	NA	NA
ProthomAlo [33]	NS	S	S	S	S	NS	S	A
Food-Panda [34]	S	S	S	NS	S	NS	NA	NA
BD-Jobs [35]	S	S	S	NS	S	NS	NS	A
Dutch Bangla Bank [36]	S	S	NS	NS	S	NS	NA	NA
USA private websites								
Facebook [37]	S	S	NS	NS	S	NS	S	A
Amazon [38]	S	S	NS	NS	S	NS	NS	A
Quora [39]	S	S	NS	NS	S	NS	NS	A
Paypal [40]	NA	NA	NA	NA	NA	NA	NS	A
Netflix [41]	NA	NA	NA	NA	NA	NA	NS	A

Table 6. Security factors checking of USA and Bangladesh private websites

Bangladeshi private websites

	SSL certificate	Cookies used	HTTPS protocol status	XSS attack	SQL injection
Daraz BD	V	42	Yes/1	S	S
Prothom Alo	V	15	Yes/1	S	S
Food Panda	V	21	Yes/1	S	S
BD Jobs	V	21	Yes/1	S	S
Dutch Bangla bank	V	4	Yes/1	S	S
USA private websites					
Facebook	V	8	Yes/1	S	S
Amazon	V	13	Yes/1	S	S
Quora	V	18	Yes/1	S	S
Paypal	V	102	Yes/1	S	S
Netflix	V	23	Yes/1	S	S

4.3 Total Calculation for Security Factor (Private Websites)

Here, secure/available $= 1$, not secure/not available $= 0$.

From the previous equation, as shown in Table 3, $W_1S_n = (S_{f1n} + S_{f2n} + S_{f3n})$.

- *For Bangladesh private website:*(Calculating total weight (0/1) of each security factors for Bangladesh private websites. Web1(Daraz BD) = [1 + (1 + 1) + (1 + 1)] = 5, Web2(Prothom Alo) = [1 + (1 + 1) + (1 + 1)] = 5, Web3(Food Panda) = [1 + (1 + 1) + (1 + 1)] = 5, Web4(BD Jobs) = [1 + (1 + 1) + (1 + 1)] = 5, Web5(DBBL) = [1 + (1 + 1) + (1 + 1)] = 5*

$$\text{Total equation, } W_5S_f = (5 + 5 + 5 + 5 + 5) = 30 \tag{5}$$

- **For USA private websites:** (Calculating total weight (0/1) of each security factors for the USA private websites). *Web1(Facebook) = [1 + (1 + 1) + (1 + 1)] = 5, Web2 (Amazon) = [1 + (1 + 1) + (1 + 1)] = 5, Web3 (Quora) = [1 + (1 + 1) + (1 + 1)] = 5, Web4(Paypal) = [1 + (1 + 1) + (1 + 1)] = 5, Web5(Netflix) = [1 + (1 + 1) + (1 + 1)] = 5*

$$\text{Total calculation, } W_5S_f = (5 + 5 + 5 + 5 + 5) = 30 \tag{6}$$

Here in Table 7, S = secure, NS = not Secure, V = valid = V, NV = not valid. Table 7 represents the scenario of security factors in the government sector websites of both Bangladesh and the USA. In both cases, a similarity is observed with regards to the implementation of SSL certificate and HTTPS protocols. But in case of security attacks, Bangladeshi websites are comparatively more vulnerable as the USA websites were found to be comparatively more secure.

SSL = secure sockets layer, HTTPS = Hyper Text Transfer Protocol Secure, XSS Cross Site Scripting

4.4 Total Calculation for Security (Government Websites)

- *For Bangladeshi government websites:* (Calculating total weight (0/1) of each security factors for Bangladesh government websites.) *Web1(Passport) = [0 + (1 + 1) + (0 + 0)] = 2, Web2(Income Tax) = [1 + (1 + 1) + (0 + 0)] = 3, Web3 (Bangladesh Police) = [1 + (1 + 1) + (1 + 0)] = 4, Web4(Teletalk) = [1 + (1 + 1) + (1 + 0)] = 4, Web5(National University) = [1 + (1 + 1) + (0 + 0)] = 3*

$$\text{Total calculation, } W_5S_f = (2 + 3 + 4 + 4 + 3) = 16 \tag{7}$$

- *For USA government websites:* (Calculating total weight (0/1) of each security factors for USA government websites.) *Web1(US Federal Courts) = [1 + (1 + 1) + (1 + 1)] = 5, Web2 (Securities and Exchange Commission (SEC)) = [1 + (1 + 1) + (1 + 1)] = 5, Web3 (Department of Defense) = [1 + (1 + 1) + (1 + 1)] = 5, Web4(Department of Education) = [1 + (1 + 1) + (1 + 1)] = 5, Web5(The White House) = [1 + (1 + 1) + (1 + 1)] = 5*

$$\text{Total calculation, } W_5S_f = (5 + 5 + 5 + 5 + 5) = 30 \tag{8}$$

Table 7. Security factors checking of USA and Bangladesh government websites

Bangladeshi govt. websites					
	SSL certificate	Cookies used	HTTPS protocol status	XSS attack	SQL injection
Passport	NV	29	Yes/1	NS	NS
Income Tax	V	4	Yes/1	NS	NS
Bangladesh Police	V	5	Yes/1	S	NS
Teletalk	V	33	Yes/1	S	NS
National University	V	2	Yes/1	NS	NS
USA Govt. websites					
US Federal Courts	V	7	Yes/1	S	S
Securities and Exchange Commission (SEC)	V	18	Yes/1	S	S
Department of Defense	V	17	Yes/1	S	S
Department of Education	V	5	Yes/1	S	S
The White House	V	4	Yes/1	S	S

Figure 2 shows the percentage of cookies used in private websites in both the USA and Bangladesh. In the USA the rate of acceptance of cookies is highest in PayPal comparing to the other websites. In Bangladesh, Daraz BD accepts the highest cookies. The number of other Bangladeshi websites also accept similar number of cookies as Daraz BD, which is comparatively more than those in the USA. note that the first paragraph of a section or subsection is not indented. The first paragraphs that follows a table, figure, equation etc. does not have an indent, either.

Figure 3 shows the percentage of cookies used in public sector websites in both the USA and Bangladesh. In the USA, the rate of acceptance of cookies is highest in the website of the Security and Exchange Commission, followed by that of the Department of Defense, both of which are higher than the other websites. Amongst the Bangladeshi ones, Passport as well as Income Tax websites are ranked the top two in accepting number of cookies. The remaining ones accepts little less cookies, however, the exhibit a similar trend. First Section

Cookies used in private website of USA

Cookies used in private website of bangladesh

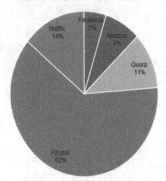
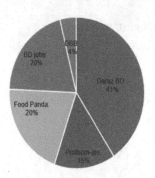

Fig. 2. Cookies of private websites (USA and Bangladesh)

Cookies used in public website of bangladesh

Cookies used in public webaite of USA

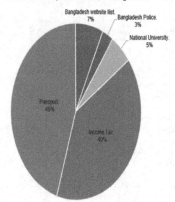
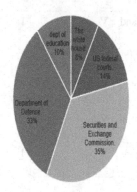

Fig. 3. Cookies of government websites (USA and Bangladesh)

4.5 Total Weight Calculation

Bangladesh government websites:

$$(P_f + S_f) = 22 + 16 = 38 \qquad (1) + (7)$$

Bangladesh private websites:

$$(P_f + S_f) = 23 + 30 = 53 \qquad (3) + (5)$$

USA government websites:

$$(P_f + S_f) = 13 + 30 = 43 \qquad (2) + (8)$$

USA private websites:

$$(P_f + S_f) = 24 + 30 = 54 \qquad (4) + (6)$$

4.6   A Risk Level Analysis

Low = 1–40, Medium = 41–50, High = 50–70 (range level by total factors point). This table (Table 8) shows the final result of the selected websites' privacy and security status by calculating total weight. As it can be seen from the results, the private websites are more secure than the government ones for both Bangladesh and the USA.

Table 8. Overall websites ranking

	Low	Medium	High
Bangladesh government websites	✓		
Bangladesh private websites			✓
USA government websites		✓	
USA private websites			✓

4.7   Website Ranking

Table 9 shows the ranking of the websites according to the privacy factors rating. Table 10 shows the ranking of the websites according to the security factors rating.

Table 9. Privacy-based website rankings (BD and USA)

Bangladesh government website	USA private website
1. Income Tax (6) 2. Teletalk (5), 3. Passport, Bangladesh Police (4) 4. National University (3)	1. US Federal Courts (5) 2. Securities and Exchange Commission (SEC), Department of Defence (4) 3. Department of Education, The White House (0)
Bangladesh private Website	USA private Website
1. BD Jobs (6) 2. Prothom Alo (5), 3. Daraz BD, Food Panda, DBBL (4)	1. Paypal (6) 2. Quora, Netflix (5) 3. Facebook, Amazon (4)

Table 10. Security-based website rankings (BD and USA)

Bangladesh government website	USA government website
1. Bangladesh Police, Teletalk (4) 2. National University (3) 3. Passport (2)	1. US Federal Courts, Securities and Exchange Commission (SEC), Department of Defence, Department of Education, The White House (5)
Bangladesh private website	USA private website
1. Prothom Alo, BD Jobs, Daraz BD,Food Panda, DBBL (5)	1. Paypal, Quora, Netflix, Facebook, Amazon (5)

5 Discussion

In this research, a comparison study of privacy and security factors of the government and private sector websites of both Bangladesh and the USA. From the results of the study, it is evident that the private sector websites outperform the government websites, in terms of maintaining security and privacy aspects, for both of the countries. Analysis of the privacy and security factors reveals the following:

5.1 Privacy Factors

- Financial Issue: From the analysis of our study it is noticeable that the Bangladesh government allocates less funds than the USA, for the purpose of websites' security and privacy aspects. For IT sector's spending of the U.S. federal government, $92.17 billion has been allocated in the 2021 fiscal year budget. The Civilian agencies budgeted $54.36 billion for federal IT spending, while the Department of Defense, a single agency, had the largest funding of $38.8 billion for IT spending as [42]. Considering the financial strength of Bangladeshi, it is neigh impossible to have such a large budget for IT. That being said, the Bangladesh government's budget allocation of $17.2 billion in 2021–2022 fiscal year for the ICT sector is very impressive, which is in fact about 20 percent higher compared to the original budget of the outgoing fiscal year (2019–2020) [43]. Although Bangladesh is gradually expanding its budget allocation for IT sectors, it is still comparatively very low with regards to that of the USA. On the other hand, the local private organization operating in Bangladesh tend to spend comparatively more money for their websites than the government websites, however, the amount is still much less than those of the USA private organizations. For instance, one of the most renowned private e-commerce in Bangladesh, namely Daraz BD, announced to invest 58,948,850.00 $ in 2021 [44] whereas Amazon spent $45.903 billion in the twelve months' time span ending March 31, 2021. This was a 22.97% increase in Amazon's budget compared to the preceding year [45].
- Fewer number of Visitor: In the first 6 months (Feb–July) of 2021, The websites of the government had 90.74k visitors [46] whereas there were 5.29 billion visits to the USA government websites over the past 90 days (April 2021–June 2021) [47]. Therefore, the large difference in the number of visitors between both the countries is clearly distinguishable.

- On the contrary, the total engagement of the Daraz BD website in 6 months is 6.80M [48] while it is 2.72 billion for Amazon [49].
- Maintenance: For the government websites, the maintenance process, such as information updating, security checking, speed optimization, etc. in Bangladesh is much slower than the USA. Figure 4 demonstrates the statistics for daily visitors for the USA government websites. Bangladesh government does not publicly disclose any such information.

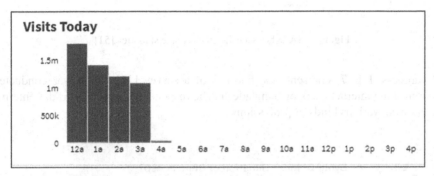

Fig. 4. USA daily website visitor's statistics [47]

5.2 Security Factors

- Vulnerabilities: In 2021 as shown in Fig. 5 till now the most cyber incidents cases were registered in December, 2020.

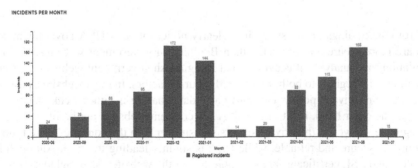

Fig. 5. Bangladesh cyber-attack statistics from 2020–2021 [50]

On the contrary, the cyber security market size of the USA was valued $167.13 billion in 2020 and is predicted to have a 10.9% increase in the compound annual growth rate (CAGR), from 2021 to 2028. In fact, such growth can be attributed to the growing sophistication of the cybercrimes (see Fig. 6).

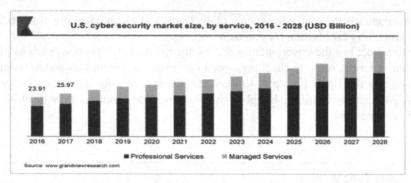

Fig. 6. USA cyber security market size statistics [51]

- Awareness: Fig. 7 represents the findings of a survey [16] which was conducted amongst the internet users of Bangladesh. The respondents were day-to-day internet users from various kinds of professions.

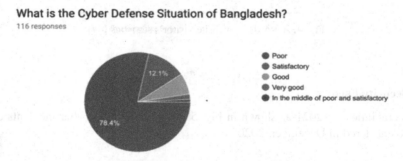

Fig. 7. Bangladesh cyber defense statistics

From the findings of our study, it is clearly noticeable that USA government websites are more secure and protected than Bangladesh government websites. From the calculations and analysis, it is evident that Bangladesh government websites are highly vulnerable with regards to both privacy and security factors. In most websites, password authentication, privacy policy and third-party data sharing is either weak or not available. On the other hand, most of the USA government websites are highly secure and impregnable. However, the private sectors websites in both the countries were found to be similarly secure and reliable, while USA is slightly leading the race. Although http protocols and SSL certificates are available for all the websites of Bangladesh government, most of them are vulnerable for SQL injection and Cross-site Scripting attack. Some of the websites also demand unnecessary cookies. Nevertheless, USA government websites are impenetrable. Security factors for private websites of both countries are as stable as USA government websites.

Finally, based on the outcome of this study, the followings are the recommendations to improve the security and privacy factors for the both countries:

1. Government agencies must be aware of the need to address such flaws and must take the required actions to strengthen the security of these web applications.
2. It is essential to tighten the security of the respective web servers, to prevent the vulnerabilities identified in this research. The foremost tasks in achieving this is to make sure all the plug-ins, libraries, database server software, etc. are always kept up-to-date, particularly by applying the security patches supplied by the vendors.
3. While designing, developing and deploying the websites, the developers must concentrate on the prospective requirements and how to quickly deal with them.

6 Conclusions

The article presented a comparative study of security and privacy aspects of the government and private sector websites of the least developed countries (LDC) vs. the developed countries (DC). While Bangladesh has been chosen as the representative of the LDC, the USA was nominated to represent the DC. Based on the usage and popularity, the websites were selected for inclusion in this study. To ensure representativeness of the sample, a wide variety of government and private sectors websites from both countries were considered, such as government services, news and media, banks, defense, e-commerce, etc. The key goal of the study was to find the most susceptibility and user privacy amongst the selected web services with the least amount of effort, to aid tasks of the future developers and software testers. Most of the selected web applications in this study from Bangladesh, particularly the government ones displayed major security risks and lack user privacy, which need to be resolved with utmost urgency. The USA websites showed comparatively better performance in this regard. In the future, we would like to explore a variety of other web services employing a broader set of vulnerabilities as well as new attack vectors.

References

1. Djuraskovic, O.: How-many-websites. https://firstsiteguide.com/how-many-websites/. Accessed 08 Mar 2021
2. Saad, M., et al.: Exploring the attack surface of blockchain: a comprehensive survey. IEEE Commun. Surv. Tutor. **22**, 1977–2008 (2020). https://doi.org/10.1109/COMST.2020.2975999
3. Onik, M.M.H., Kim, C.-S., Lee, N.-Y., Yang, J.: Privacy-aware blockchain for personal data sharing and tracking. Open Comput. Sci. **9**, 80–91 (2019). https://doi.org/10.1515/comp-2019-0005
4. Global Cybersecurity Index ITU. https://www.itu.int/en/ITU-D/Cybersecurity/Pages/global-cybersecurity-index.aspx. Accessed 05 May 2021
5. Chaudhry, J., Qidwai, U., Miraz, M.H., Ibrahim, A., Valli, C.: Data security among ISO/IEEE 11073 compliant personal healthcare devices through statistical fingerprinting. Presented at the (2017)
6. Onik, M.M.H., Chul-Soo, K.I.M., Jinhong, Y.: Personal data privacy challenges of the fourth industrial revolution. In: 2019 21st International Conference on Advanced Communication Technology (ICACT), pp. 635–638. IEEE (2019). https://doi.org/10.23919/ICACT.2019.870 1932

7. Abu-Shanab, E.A., Baker, A.N.A.: Evaluating Jordan's e-government website: a case study. Electron. Gov. Int. J. **8**, 271–289 (2011)
8. Kaspersky: Kaspersky Security Bulletin 2020 Statistics, 26 (2020)
9. Akinbowale, O.E., Klingelhöfer, H.E., Zerihun, M.F.: Analysis of cyber-crime effects on the banking sector using the balanced score card: a survey of literature. J. Financ. Crime (2020). https://doi.org/10.1108/JFC-03-2020-0037
10. Joveda, N., Khan, M.T., Pathak, A., Chattogram, B.: Cyber laundering: a threat to banking industries in Bangladesh: in quest of effective legal framework and cyber security of financial information. Int. J. Econ. Financ. **11**, 54–65 (2019). https://doi.org/10.5539/ijef.v11n10p54
11. UNB: Several government websites hacked. https://www.thedailystar.net/country/bangla desh-government-websites-hacked-demanding-quota-system-reform-1561267. Accessed 10 Apr 2021
12. Gazis, O.: U.S. launched "more than 2 dozen" cyber operations to protect election. https://www.cbsnews.com/news/election-interference-us-cyber-command-nsa-nakasone/. Accessed 13 May 2021
13. Baezner, M., Robin, P.: Cyber-conflict between the United States of America and Russia
14. Jasper, S.E.: U.S. Cyber threat intelligence sharing frameworks. Int. J. Intell. Count. Intell. **30**, 53–65 (2017). https://doi.org/10.1080/08850607.2016.1230701
15. Moniruzzaman, M., Chowdhury, F., Ferdous, M.S.: Measuring vulnerabilities of Bangladeshi websites. In: 2nd International Conference on Electrical, Computer and Communication Engineering, ECCE 2019 (2019). https://doi.org/10.1109/ECACE.2019.8679426
16. Dikhit, A.S., Karodiya, K.: Result evaluation of field authentication based SQL injection and XSS attack exposure. In: IEEE International Conference on Information, Communication, Instrumentation and Control, ICICIC 2017, 1–6 January 2018 (2018). https://doi.org/10.1109/ICOMICON.2017.8279148
17. Clark, J., Van Oorschot, P.C.: SoK: SSL and HTTPS: revisiting past challenges and evaluating certificate trust model enhancements. In: Proceedings of IEEE Symposium on Security and Privacy, pp. 511–525 (2013). https://doi.org/10.1109/SP.2013.41
18. Kuzma, J.: An examination of privacy policies of US Government Senate websites. Electron. Gov. **7**, 270–280 (2010). https://doi.org/10.1504/EG.2010.033592
19. Kim, J.: Burp suite: automating web vulnerability scanning (2020)
20. Natarajan, S.: Available Online through CODEN : IJPTFI Research Article. 8, 25990–25994 (2017)
21. Salih, A.K., Yousif, M.: Dynamic analysis tool for detecting SQL injection dynamic analysis tool for detecting SQL injection. Int. J. Comput. Sci. Inf. Secur. **14**, 224–232 (2016)
22. Passport. http://www.dip.gov.bd/. Accessed 10 Mar 2021
23. IncomeTax. https://nbr.gov.bd/publications/income-tax/eng. Accessed 10 Mar 2021
24. BangladeshPolice. https://www.police.gov.bd/. Accessed 10 Mar 2021
25. Teletalk. https://www.teletalk.com.bd/bn/. Accessed 10 Mar 2021
26. NU. https://www.nu.ac.bd/. Accessed 02 May 2021
27. US court. https://www.uscourts.gov/. Accessed 10 Mar 2021
28. SEC. https://www.sec.gov/. Accessed 05 Mar 2021
29. Defense. https://www.defense.gov/. Accessed 21 Apr 2021
30. USEducation. https://www.ed.gov/. Accessed 10 May 2021
31. WhiteHouse. https://www.whitehouse.gov/. Accessed 10 Mar 2021
32. Daraz. https://www.daraz.com.bd/. Accessed 16 May 2021
33. Prothom-Alo. https://www.prothomalo.com/. Accessed 10 Mar 2021
34. Food-panda. https://www.foodpanda.com.bd/. Accessed 10 Mar 2021
35. BD jobs. https://www.bdjobs.com/. Accessed 10 Mar 2021
36. DBBL. https://www.dutchbanglabank.com/. Accessed 10 Mar 2021

37. Facebook. https://www.facebook.com/. Accessed 10 Mar 2021
38. Amazon. https://www.amazon.com/. Accessed 10 Mar 2021
39. Quora. https://www.quora.com. Accessed 10 Mar 2021
40. Paypal. https://www.paypal.com/. Accessed 10 Mar 2021
41. Netfllix. https://www.netflix.com. Accessed 10 Mar 2021
42. Mlitz, K.: U.S. federal government IT expenditure 2011–2021. https://www.statista.com/sta tistics/506409/united-states-federal-it-expenditure/. Accessed 08 Apr 2021
43. Kabir, S.A.: Budget for building Digital Bangladesh (2021). https://www.thedailystar.net/bus iness/economy/news/budget-building-digital-bangladesh-2110485
44. Correspondent, S.: Daraz to invest Tk 500 crore in infrastructure development. https://www. newagebd.net/article/107500/daraz-to-invest-tk-500-crore-in-infrastructure-development. Accessed 08 Apr 2021
45. Amazon Research and Development Expenses 2006–2021. https://www.macrotrends.net/sto cks/charts/AMZN/amazon/research-development-expenses. Accessed 03 June 2021
46. Total Visits to bangladesh.gov.bd. https://www.similarweb.com/website/bangladesh.gov.bd/. Accessed 10 Mar 2021
47. analytics.usa.gov. https://analytics.usa.gov/. Accessed 10 Apr 2021
48. Similarweb. https://www.similarweb.com/website/daraz.com.bd/. Accessed 22 Mar 2021
49. Similarweb Amazon. https://www.similarweb.com/website/amazon.com/. Accessed 09 Mar 2021
50. Bangladesh cyber attack. https://www.cirt.gov.bd/incident-reporting/statistics/. Accessed 20 May 2021
51. Cyber Security. https://www.grandviewresearch.com/industry-analysis/cyber-security-market. Accessed 15 Apr 2021

Protecting Web Applications from Web Scraping

Baftjar Tabaku ⓘ and Maaruf Ali$^{(\boxtimes)}$ ⓘ

Epoka University, Rruga Tiranë-Rinas, Km 12, 1032 Vorë, Tiranë, Albania
maaruf@ieee.org

Abstract. Automated software programs called, "bots", are being used extensively to extract, collect and harvest information from the Internet across any website that can be accessed. This unsolicited and intrusive gathering of information, knowns as "web scraping" is then subsequently used in a way that can lead to damaging the integrity, authenticity and reputation of the victim website. The problems of web scraping are identified, along with the methods used to prevent the web scraping are explored and explained. Prevention using rate limit detection, identification of automated traffic and known malicious entities are described including the use of honey-potting. The success of using these techniques is concluded by the positive outcome of the results.

Keywords: Web scraping · Web data extraction · Web harvesting · Web crawling · Information extraction · Google cloud services · Data integration · Interoperability

1 Introduction

1.1 Background

The Internet always is considered a data centre where an outstanding amount of information has become easily accessible to be used through a web-browser. Web-scraping is considered an internet-based data collection technique where a script of code will make continuous automated requests to different webpages and then store the data taken from these webpages for further offline processing.

There is an increasing demand for new and fresh data, however, this cannot be done manually. Manual extraction of data by an end user is almost impossible because of the sheer required volume of information to be collected. This web collection of data has evolved into an automated processes most often using bots, this new concept is known as "Web Scraping".

Without any protection will leave web-applications vulnerable to web-scraping that will compromise the security of the users' data. This will consequently allow third parties to use this data in a way that the original data owners never intended nor permitted. This treatise describes a few techniques to prevent web-scraping. To implement this, Google Cloud Platform was utilised.

M. H. Miraz et al. (Eds.): iCETiC 2021, LNICST 395, pp. 56–70, 2021.
https://doi.org/10.1007/978-3-030-90016-8_4

1.2 Web Scraping

Web scraping is a widely used method of collecting internet data where a code script will be executed repeatedly making requests across different websites and then storing their responses, the data, for offline processing. By leaving websites or web-applications unprotected and vulnerable, it will lead to compromising the security, integrity and reputation of the website. This is because the sensitive and valuable data that has now been extracted without the original owner's permission - can be used by the third parties in ways not originally intended. Figure 1, below, show a typical web scraping scenario.

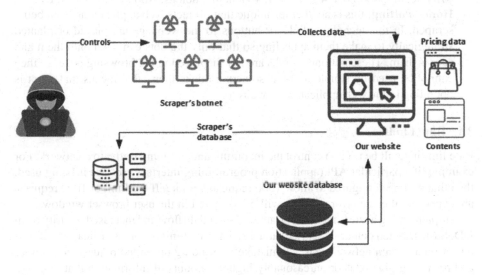

Fig. 1. General website content scraping schema.

2 Preventing Web Scraping

Web scraping is a content extracting process using bots to extract valuable data from one or more websites. It is different from "screen scraping" where only copies of the pixels that are displayed on a screen are made. Web scraping in contrast will only extract the HTML source code and its associated data. After that the scraper can replicate the entire source website source anywhere else, e.g. on a different e-commerce website.

To prevent web-scraping four methods are mentioned here:

1. **Rate limiting:** this limits the rate of requests on a website made from a client to a server that provides the service. For example, if the website service is configured to only 50 requests per second for a client (depending on the service provider capacity), then if this number of requests is exceeded, an error will occur and this client cannot then generate any more requests according to the limit threshold.
2. **Identifying the automated traffic:** this can be identified by detecting non-human behaviour in web traffic information exchange. One of the traffic indicators which

can be utilised is the volume of traffic request, (e.g. making more than 10,000 requests on a given day on a server, even if the rate limit is never exceeded). This will be done automatically on a periodic time per minute or 24-h daily.

3. **Known malicious identifiers:** one of the best practices to protect web applications is to reject different requests from known malicious entities and end users. There are online services and websites that maintain lists of banned or black IPs which can be used to deny their access for the web applications by blocking their IPs. The scraping endpoint user can also be identified by the user-agent. If there is someone trying to scrape the website then its user-agent will contain at least one of these terms like 01h4x.com, 360Spider, 404checker, 404enemy, 80legs, Abonti, Aboundex, etc.

4. **Honey Potting:** this is another technique that protects web applications from being scraped. In this technique, links or buttons to the webpage are placed or planted strategically to make them appealing so that only the bots can latch onto them and access them. These buttons or links are not displayed in the browsing page, so they cannot be used by simple users, if someone clicks them, that means that a bot is operating in the web application or website.

2.1 Rate Limit

Rate limiting will be used to control the incoming and outgoing traffic to a network. For example, if a particular API (application programming interface) service is being used, then that will be configured to allow 1000 requests/minute. If the limit of 1000 requests are exceeded, then an error message will be triggered in the user browser window.

Implementing a rate limit is important for better data flow and increased security from DDoS (distributed denial-of-service) attacks. The rate limit becomes critically useful, if a user on a certain network makes a mistake by sending unlimited requests to a server and retrieving gigabytes or unreasonably higher amounts of information that will also overload the network for everyone. With rate limiting, these attacks would be easily caught and managed by termination (by blocking their requests). Figure 2, below, shows a bar graph display of exceeding the rate limit where the attack condition is detected, managed by blocking and the subsequent reduction of the traffic requests with time.

Types of Rate Limiting

1. *User Rate Limiting.*
   The most popular rate limiting is the user rate limiting where the number of requests that a user will make to an API key or an IP (depends on the user agreed preferences) address. If the user exceeds the request number limit, then any further request for this user will be denied until they reach out to the developer and the API request time limit is reset. Figure 3, below, shows an example where the policy configuration is set to five requests within a ten second window with one retry permitted with a 500 ms delay.

2. *Geographic Rate Limit.*
   To increase the security in certain geographic locations, a regional rate limit can be set with an added temporal or period of operation as well. For example, if in a

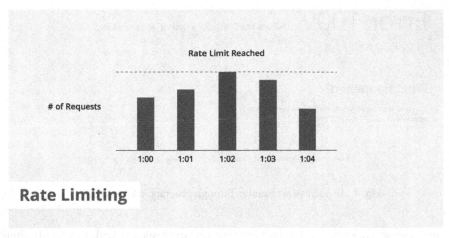

Fig. 2. Rate limit threshold detection and application of rate limiting [1].

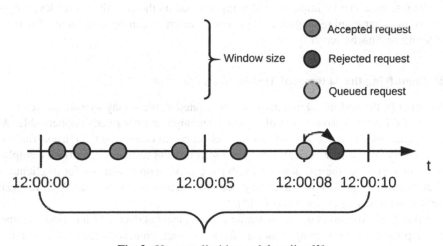

Fig. 3. User rate limiting and throttling [2].

particular region at a certain time the developers expect a low rate of requests, they can set up a lower rate of requests per second limit. This action will prevent potential attacks and risks of suspicious activity for the targeted web-applications. An example of an access denied and the geographic blocking reason message is shown in Fig. 4, below.

3. *Server Rate Limit.*
   Certain servers will handle certain aspects of their applications and their rate limit will be defined based on a server level-basis. This will allow developers finer control to give them the opportunity to increase or decrease the rate limits on a server-by-server basis. As shown in Fig. 5, below, if Server C exceeds its rate limit, then traffic may be diverted or load balanced to Server B. The servers send information about

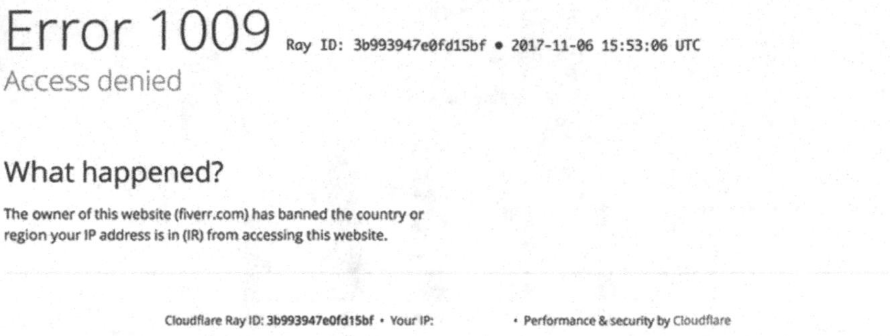

Error 1009 Ray ID: 3b993947e0fd15bf • 2017-11-06 15:53:06 UTC
Access denied

What happened?

The owner of this website (fiverr.com) has banned the country or
region your IP address is in (IR) from accessing this website.

Cloudflare Ray ID: 3b993947e0fd15bf • Your IP: • Performance & security by Cloudflare

Fig. 4. IP address(es) banning through geographic location [3].

the request volumes and the rate-limiting service responds with the rate-limiting decisions.

The rate limit can be implemented using various methods at the server level using various programming languages. For this research, it can be implemented using a Nginx or Apache server.

2.2 Identifying the Automated Traffic

A bot, that is, the end-user generating the automated traffic – may submit queries for a variety of different reasons, most of which are benign and not overly monetisable. As an example, rank bots periodically scrape web pages to determine the current ranking for a <query,URL> pair. A Search Engine Optimization company (SEO) may employ a rank bot to evaluate the efficacy of its web page ranking optimisations for its clients. If a client's current rank is low, a user may need to generate many NEXT PAGE requests to find it in the search engine's results [5].

Figure 6, above, shows the query traffic for a typical bot over a 24-h period. Another way of protecting the web-applications from web-scraping is to identify automated traffic. A group of end-users scraping a webs-application or website would try to prevent extending the rate-limits by slowing down their rate request quota or even making them at random times. Doing this they are still detectable through their access patterns.

The bot end users can be detected by analysing their automated traffic on our applications and identifying entities (end-users, in this case bots) that does not behave as usual normal users when accessing our application.

[6] identified the patterns that indicate typical automated traffic. There are two main patterns in particular that identify the automated traffic which are:

1. The traffic volume, entities or end-users will usually send more than +500 requests to a web-server from a single IP address in a time interval that usual human users can never cannot complete in that same time period.
2. The event periodicity, where the end-users or bots send requests to a server that website or web-application is hosted on every minute on an exact time period from the previous one.

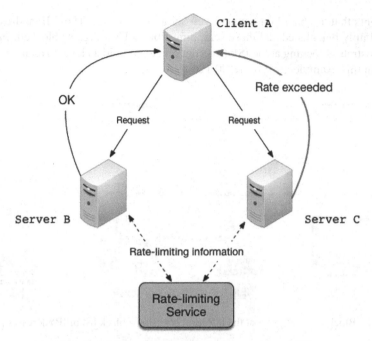

Fig. 5. Global rate-limiting with a central server [4].

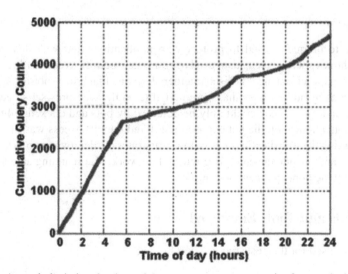

Fig. 6. A graph depicting the time of day versus aggregate queries for a typical bot [5].

2.3 Known Malicious Identifiers

An alternative way of protecting web-applications or websites from web scraping is to block access to the website or web-applications from these malicious entities or end-users (bots). This can be accomplished by checking the blacklisted IP addresses or

User-Agents that are based on popular web-scraping libraries. These IP addresses can then be simply blacklisted and those scrapping library User-Agents blocked. Figure 7, below, illustrates blocking at the ISP (internet service provider) level to an international website, in this example, to 198.51.100.126.

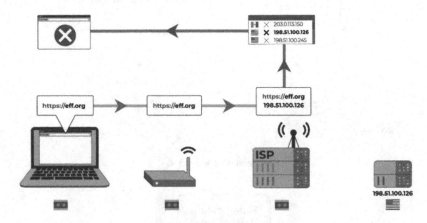

Fig. 7. Blocking of websites at the ISP level by using a black list of IP addresses [7].

2.4 Honey-Potting

This sneaky technique is used to protect web applications and websites from web-scraping. A honeypot is a mechanism used in computer security to detect illegal attempts at using information in an unauthorised manner. The way that honey-potting was used in this project was by adding links that were invisible on the web-browser screen and not clickable by end users. They could only be detected by bots and clicked only by them. By clicking on a honeypot, the bot exposed itself and then its access was blocked from further accessing the website. Figure 8, below, illustrates the deployment of a honeypot at the periphery and outside the enterprise internal network. The scanning attack is caught and logged by the honeypot network entity.

3 Methods and Tools Employed

The hardware used for this research is listed below:

- Device name DESKTOP-F7RINFF
- Processor Intel® Core™ i7-7700HQ CPU @ 2.80 GHz 2.81 GHz
- Installed RAM 16.0 GB (15.9 GB usable)
- Device ID A3604B8D-083F-44CC-AEBD-E10B0FCEF4B6
- Product ID 00331-10000-00001-AA770
- System type 64-bit operating system, ×64-based processor
- Pen and touch No pen or touch input is available for this display.

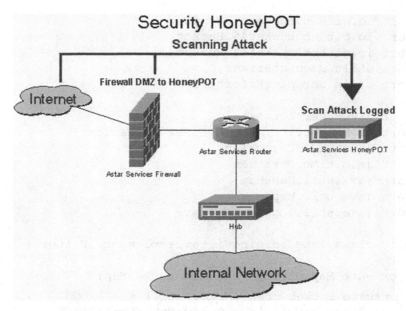

Fig. 8. Deployment of an information system honeypot [8].

- Edition Windows 10 Pro
- Version 20H2
- Installed on 1/23/2021
- OS build 19042.1083
- Experience Windows Feature Experience Pack 120.2212.3530.0

3.1 Experimental Part

There are different methods used to prevent web-applications from web-scraping, limiting the rate of the API was implemented.

API Rate Limiting
Even if there are different methods used to limit the rate of the API, in this experiment, a java servlet filter was used that was setup to limit the request rate using the Bucket4J library. This limited the incoming requests based on a token-bucket algorithm.

The example used here had one endpoint, where the users were taken from the database. Without rate-limiting the users' data at this endpoint would mean that their data could be scrapped and collected. However, by implementing the rate limiting method, it prevented the scraping part.

It was implemented using the Rate Limiting Filter class based on Bucket4J [9]. By using this filter, the rate limit that an IP can send and receive requests would be limited to 50 requests/second. For a better result, the IP addresses are stored to a hash-map where the IP are the keys and the buckets are the values.

The Java code utilised for this project is given next.

```java
import io.github.bucket4j.Bandwidth;
import io.github.bucket4j.Bucket;
import io.github.bucket4j.Bucket4j;
import utils.RequestParser;
import utils.ScrapingEnforcer;

import javax.servlet.*;
import javax.servlet.http.HttpServletRequest;
import java.io.IOException;
import java.time.Duration;
import java.util.HashMap;
import java.util.Map;
import java.util.logging.Filter;

public class RateLimitingFilter implements Filter {

    private Map<String, Bucket> bucketMap;

    private Bucket createNewBucket() {
        Bandwidth limit = Bandwidth.simple(1, Dura-
tion.ofSeconds(1));
        return Bucket4j.builder().ad-
dLimit(limit).build();
    }


    @Override
    public void init(FilterConfig filterConfig) {
        bucketMap = new HashMap<>();
    }

    private Bucket getBucket(String ip) {
        if (!bucketMap.containsKey(ip)) {
            bucketMap.put(ip, createNewBucket());
        }
        return bucketMap.get(ip);
    }

    @Override
    public void doFilter(ServletRequest servletRequest,
ServletResponse servletResponse,
                          FilterChain filterChain) throws
IOException, ServletException {
        HttpServletRequest httpRequest = (HttpS-
ervletRequest) servletRequest;
        String ip = RequestParser.getClientIp(httpRe-
```

```
quest);
        Bucket bucket = getBucket(ip);


        // tryConsume returns false immediately if no to-
kens available with the bucket
        if (bucket.tryConsume(1)) {
            // the limit is not exceeded
            filterChain.doFilter(servletRequest,
servletResponse);
        } else {
            // limit is exceeded
            ScrapingEnforcer.enforce(servletResponse);
        }
    }
}
```

This filter will constantly check and ensure if an IP address has yet exceeded its rate limit. If the rate limit is exceeded, then a 429-error status code that says "Too many requests" will be shown.

The next segment of code shows the client or UserServlet.java [9].

```java
import com.fasterxml.jackson.databind.ObjectMapper;
import models.EventConstants;
import models.User;
import repositories.EventLogRepository;
import repositories.UserRepository;
import utils.RequestParser;
import utils.RequestType;

import javax.servlet.annotation.WebServlet;
import javax.servlet.http.HttpServlet;
import javax.servlet.http.HttpServletRequest;
import javax.servlet.http.HttpServletResponse;
import java.io.IOException;
import java.sql.SQLException;
import java.sql.Timestamp;
import java.util.List;

@WebServlet(name = "servlets.UserServlet")
public class UserServlet extends HttpServlet {

    private final UserRepository userRepository = UserRe-
pository.getRepo();
    private final EventLogRepository eventLogRepository =
EventLogRepository.getRepo();

    private void preProcessResponse(HttpServletResponse
response) {
        response.setContentType("application/json");
        response.setHeader("Access-Control-Allow-Origin",
"*");
    }

    private void handleInvalidRequest(HttpServletResponse
resp) throws IOException {
        resp.setStatus(HttpS-
ervletResponse.SC_BAD_REQUEST);
        resp.getWriter().write("Invalid Request");
    }

    private void logGetUsersByPage(HttpServletRequest re-
quest) {
        try {
            eventLogRepository.insertEventLog(
                    RequestParser.getClientIp(request),
                    EventConstants.GET_USERS_BY_PAGE,
                    RequestParser.getPageNumber(re-
```

```
quest).toString(),
                      new Timestamp(System.currentTimeMil-
lis())
          );
     } catch (SQLException throwables) {
        throwables.printStackTrace();
     }
  }

  private void handleGetUsersByPage(HttpServletRequest
request, HttpServletResponse resp) throws IOException {
     ObjectMapper mapper = new ObjectMapper();
     resp.setStatus(HttpServletResponse.SC_OK);
     List<User> users = userRepository.getTweetsBy-
Page(RequestParser.getPageNumber(request));
     resp.getWriter().write(mapper.writeVal-
ueAsString(users));
     logGetUsersByPage(request);
  }

  @Override
  protected void doGet(HttpServletRequest req, HttpS-
ervletResponse resp) throws IOException {
     preProcessResponse(resp);
     RequestType requestType = RequestParser.parse-
Request(req);
     switch (requestType) {
        case INVALID:
           handleInvalidRequest(resp);
           break;
        case GET_USERS_BY_PAGE:
           handleGetUsersByPage(req, resp);
           break;
        default:
           throw new IllegalStateException("Unex-
pected value: " + requestType);
     }
  }
}
```

It was also necessary to include some URL specifications that were recorded through an xml file [9]:

```xml
<?xml version="1.0" encoding="UTF-8"?>
<web-app xmlns="http://xmlns.jcp.org/xml/ns/javaee"
        xmlns:xsi="http://www.w3.org/2001/XMLSchema-instance"
        xsi:schemaLocation="http://xmlns.jcp.org/xml/ns/javaee
http://xmlns.jcp.org/xml/ns/javaee/web-app_4_0.xsd"
        version="4.0">

<filter>
<filter-name>RateLimitingFilter</filter-name>
<filter-class>servlets.RateLimitingFilter</filter-class>
</filter>

<filter-mapping>
<filter-name>RateLimitingFilter</filter-name>
<url-pattern>/users/*</url-pattern>
    </filter-mapping>

    <filter>
        <filter-name>HighVolumeFilter</filter-name>
        <filter-class>servlets.HighVolumeFilter</filter-class>
    </filter>

    <filter-mapping>
        <filter-name>HighVolumeFilter</filter-name>
        <url-pattern>/users/*</url-pattern>
    </filter-mapping>

    <filter>
        <filter-name>EventPeriodicityFilter</filter-name>
        <filter-class>servlets.EventPeriodicityFilter</filter-class>
    </filter>

    <filter-mapping>
        <filter-name>EventPeriodicityFilter</filter-name>
        <url-pattern>/users/*</url-pattern>
    </filter-mapping>

    <filter>
        <filter-name>MaliciousIdentifierFilter</filter-name>
        <filter-class>servlets.MaliciousIdentifierFilter</filter-class>
```

```
    </filter>

    <filter-mapping>
        <filter-name>MaliciousIdentifierFilter</filter-
name>
        <url-pattern>/users/*</url-pattern>
    </filter-mapping>

    <servlet>
        <servlet-name>UserServlet</servlet-name>
        <servlet-class>servlets.UserServlet</servlet-
class>
    </servlet>

    <servlet-mapping>
        <servlet-name>UserServlet</servlet-name>
        <url-pattern>/users/*</url-pattern>
    </servlet-mapping>

    <servlet>
        <servlet-name>HoneyPotServlet</servlet-name>
        <servlet-class>servlets.HoneyPotServlet</servlet-
class>
    </servlet>

    <servlet-mapping>
        <servlet-name>HoneyPotServlet</servlet-name>
        <url-pattern>/honeypot/*</url-pattern>
    </servlet-mapping>

</web-app>
```

Rate limiting is not the best nor safest way to protect an application from being scraped, because the correct rules must be defined to set the right value for the rate-limit. Since IP addresses are used, a malicious user can define or change its IP proxy several times and then it can still scrape the web-application without limits. This action can also ban or prevent users that share one single IP address from using the web-application. Since there are too many users with the same IP address, then they will all be banned even if they are not doing anything. Due to these issues and reasons, it is important that this technique should be configured properly to give protection.

4 Results and Discussion

There is a plethora of penetration tools: illegal, legal, customised and Metasploit. The Metasploit tool that was used for testing was very comprehensive, effective and power-ful. It offers a lot of options and possibilities to use it both manually or automatically according to the needs of the user.

By doing these experiments manually, it gave more possibilities to control the process flow and finer opportunities and control over exploiting a certain process - even if it meant that more time was required. Every IT system needs continuous work to always be one step ahead from the malicious attackers.

5 Conclusions

Response Rate limiting can be a great method to help fight against infrastructure attacks as well as block other types of suspicious activity like bots or different malicious activity in the attacked web applications or web pages.

There are various methods that can be utilised to implement rate limiting whether it be at the server level or user level. This can be implemented by blocking the access of the various IP addresses that are in the blacklist or by geographical location banning.

If an HTTP error code 429 Too Many Requests error is being experienced for a particular API, the developers should still be reachable to inform them to check their documents to verify what the rate limit is currently configured to be. The developers need to be instructed to modify their usage to fit within those limits according to the app-usage or requests to the website or web-application.

References

1. https://www.keycdn.com/img/support/rate-limiting-md@2x.webp. Accessed 26 July 2021
2. https://docs.mulesoft.com/api-manager/2.x/_images/throttling-rejected-request.png. Accessed 26 July 2021
3. McDonald, A.: Why geoblocking means the web is no longer worldwide, The Conversation, 11 December 2018. https://assets.weforum.org/editor/large_C_uKFkQFhmf1jdl_nGv-PBZrkpdLGrkDvMt6T-xcM40.png. Accessed 26 July2021
4. https://engineering.grab.com/img/beyond-retries-part-1/image1.png. Accessed 26 July 2021
5. King, I., Baeza-Yates, R. (eds.): Weaving Services and People on the World Wide Web, 1st edn. Springer, Heidelberg (2009). https://doi.org/10.1007/978-3-642-00570-1
6. Buehrer, G., Stokes, J.W., Chellapilla, K., Platt, J.C.: Classification of Automated Web Traffic, Microsoft, pp. 1–27 (2009). https://www.microsoft.com/en-us/research/wp-content/uploads/2016/02/ClassAutoSearchTraffic.pdf. Accessed 26 July 2021
7. https://ssd.eff.org/files/2020/04/25/circumvention-networkshutdown.jpeg. Accessed 26 July 2021
8. https://upload.wikimedia.org/wikipedia/commons/7/76/Honeypot_diagram.jpg. Accessed 26 July 2021
9. Bukhtoyarov, V.: bucket4j. https://github.com/vladimir-bukhtoyarov/bucket4j/blob/master/doc-pages/basic-usage.md. Accessed 26 July 2021

Cloud, IoT and Distributed Computing

Integrated CMOS Active Low-Pass Filter for IoT RFID Transceiver

Mahfuzur Rahman[1] ⓘ, Md. Faishal Rahaman[1] ⓘ, Md. Moazzem Hossan Munna[1] ⓘ,
Kelvin Jian Aun Ooi[2] ⓘ, Khairun Nisa' Minhad[2] ⓘ,
Mohammad Arif Sobhan Bhuiyan[2(✉)] ⓘ, and Mahdi H. Miraz[2(✉)] ⓘ

[1] Southern University Bangladesh, Chittagong, Bangladesh
[2] Xiamen University Malaysia, Sepang, Malaysia
arifsobhan.bhuiyan@xmu.edu.my, m.miraz@ieee.org

Abstract. While providing unique identity to the objects, analogous to wireless sensor network (WSN) technologies, radio frequency identification (RFID) technology can be used to automate data collection and thus can significantly limit human involvements as well as errors. Therefore, utilisation and implementation of RFID technology in multifaceted applications has recently been widely observed. In the modern internet of things (IoT) radio frequency identification (RFID) transceivers, the low pass filter (LPF) circuits play an important role to suppress the unwanted high frequency signals and noises. The LPF circuit performance greatly influences the overall performance of the transceivers. However, the passive types of LPFs in modern devices highly suffer from several drawbacks such as low-quality factors, less tuning ability, unwanted harmonic interruptions and the large die size. On the contrary, active types of low pass filters can resolve these limitations to some extent. Therefore, this research presents an active LPF design for 90 nm complementary metal oxide semiconductor (CMOS) technology in Cadence environment. The simulation results reveal that the proposed active low pass filter can achieve 6.5 dB gain with 35.48 MHz bandwidth while having 20.87 dB noise figure. The designed circuit consumes 1.56 mW power from a 1.3 V DC supply, for its smooth operation. The core die size of the proposed LPF is only 85.29 μm^2 and therefore, suitable for compact modern transceiver applications.

Keywords: CMOS · Inductorless · IoT · LNA

1 Introduction

The advancement of technology has opened new horizons for mankind by conceiving and materialising the concept of IoT which is considered as the next step in the internet revolution. The incorporation of the Internet with next generation radio communication technologies as well as embedded wireless sensor networks is notably playing a vital role in the paradigm shift of connecting our everyday devices through the Internet and transforming them into the 'smart' ones - intelligent and context-aware. As we keep on

© ICST Institute for Computer Sciences, Social Informatics and Telecommunications Engineering 2021
Published by Springer Nature Switzerland AG 2021. All Rights Reserved
M. H. Miraz et al. (Eds.): iCETiC 2021, LNICST 395, pp. 73–84, 2021.
https://doi.org/10.1007/978-3-030-90016-8_5

forwarding, IoT is expected to find its place in almost all facets of human life where everything will be connected through a wireless network for exchanging information amongst different nodes in real-time, to facilitate fast and accurate decision making, as shown in Fig. 1. Today's smart world, comprising various smart aspects such as smart health-care, homes, offices, traffics, cities, industries, etc., makes the best use of this technology for a better present and future.

In fact, the twenty-first century is perceived as the IoT-enabled era, leveraged with a network of networks comprising multifaceted smart devices powered by both hardware and software. All IoT devices, ranging from household to industry, should be distinctively identifiable through an embedded system and be connected from everywhere, to provide with better services and greater values [1–3]. Therefore, it has become a dire necessity to ensure a completely seamless, highly secure and exceedingly efficient IoT network facilitating multidimensional information technology (IT) services [1, 4], such as data integration and analysis from diverse sources, comprehensive security, scalability and flexibility, device diversity, management and power efficiency, etc. Apart from these, as the volume of the IoT network is rapidly growing, to uniquely identify each device from billions of devices has becoming a big concern. As a consequence, the current radio frequency identification (RFID) standard, protocol, hardware, and security are required to be modified and/or adapted to satisfy the requirements of IoT devices [5].

Fig. 1. The IoT is everywhere [6].

To simply put, Radio frequency identification (RFID) is a very broad term representing a system which transmits wireless signals, particularly electromagnetic radio waves, containing the unique identity of any object. RFID enables identification from a certain distance and unlike barcode technology, it does not require line of sight. The technology comprises mainly transponders (or tags) and readers, as shown in Fig. 2. The transponder, which is fundamentally an integrated circuit (IC) with an antenna, stores information about its identification along with some additional information which is, generally, transferred to the reader on request. In RFID communication, a reader receives data from the transponders wirelessly using different frequency bands which are decided by the respective nature of the applications. Currently, RFID operating frequencies, ranging from 30 to 300 kHz (commonly known as low frequency (LF)) and 3 MHz to 30 MHz (commonly known as high frequency (HF)), are widely used in industrial applications. 300 MHz to 3 GHz band, referred to as Ultra-high-frequency (UHF), RFID mainly operates at 900 MHz and using smaller antenna it delivers comparatively a higher data rate than HF. Other frequencies, such as 2.45 GHz and 5.8 GHz, which have smaller antennae and are suitable for less populated frequency ranges, are also suggested for RFID operation [7].

Semi-passive of semi-active transponders may optionally be equipped with embedded battery. However, in such cases the battery is primarily utilised in order to administer the chip. Analogous to the functionalities of an active tag, the energy harvested from the electromagnetic field is used for waking up the chip as well as transmitting the data to the reader. The semi-passive or semi-active tags are occasionally called battery-assisted passive tags [8].

A passive tag is batteryless and uses the energy induced by the electromagnetic wave propagated by the antenna of the reader, in order to powering up the chip as well as for transmitting the data to the reader. A passive tag reflects the energy obtained from the reader or receives and momentarily stores the energy in order to process the response [9].

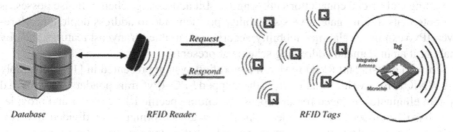

Fig. 2. The RFID communication [10].

The RFID systems use varying frequencies for different purposes that require various types of receivers. As per the findings of a survey conducted by NECTEC, the delay in the deployment of RFID occurred due to four (4) determinants: RFID standard, cost, technology aptness as well as lack of knowledge [11]. For efficient data transmission, the level of security of an RFID network is reduced considering the resource scarcity of the technology. Therefore, user privacy remains as a major concern. The reader, of an RFID eco-system, is the most expensive component. For instance, the cost of a small automated materials handling (AMH) can be US $50,000 [12]. Moreover, a limitation is placed on RFID tag implementation when the reader is used. However, such shortcomings can easily be subdued by deploying wireless network interface card (WNIC). With the use of Wi-Fi networks and an internet protocol version 6 (IPv6) address as tag ID, a novel RFID tagging system has been introduced [13]. The electronic product code (EPC) of a transponder is mapped with the interface ID (64 bit) of an IPv6 address as a unique identifier of an object. However, the implementation of a readerless RFID system should ensure several factors, such as privacy, standards, data management, mobility and scalability [14].

In RFID ecosystems, an identification number is required to track any product or object. This number should be unique to ensure security and proper communication. Therefore, a new global address structure is necessary for RFID systems. In fact, IPv6 addressing scheme, which establishes object-to-object communication, can be utilised to serve this purpose. EPC, extended unique identifier (EUI)-64, uniform resource identifier/locator (URI/URL), medium access control (MAC) addresses, etc. are examples of identification codes. In fact, for energy efficient communications amongst the nodes of WSN/IoT networks, MAC protocol has been the principal target for finding the most optimised and appropriate adaptive approach [15]. Moreover, most identification codes utilise large numbers and thus, require voluminous addressing schemes. IPv6 (128 bits) addressing scheme is becoming an essential future network infrastructure because of its large address space. IPv6 uses a unique local address with an anycast communication scheme, which exhibits service discovery and self-organisation via auto-configuration. Furthermore, making use of IPv6 header information, improved service capabilities were achieved. Moreover, IPv6 addressing scheme facilitates multi-homing. A fusion of IPv6 with wireless systems, such as the IEEE 802.11 protocol (Wi-Fi), will reduce the current problems of dual scarcity in the internet protocol version 4 (IPv4) addressing scheme, i.e. security and quality of service (QoS) from the IP side as well as spectrum and bandwidth limitations from the wireless side. IPv6 is set to gradually supersede IPv4 while providing end-to-end connections utilising 128-bit addressing scheme. It also possesses the potentials to eliminate IPv4's scalability problem due to address depletion. Moreover, IPv6 exhibits scalability, mobility, security and multicast/anycast features, thereby making it an in-demand addressing scheme at present.

Instead of using an RFID reader, the modified system presented in [13] can simply use WNIC to receive information from the mapped EPC–IPv6 transponder. The proposed system eliminates the need for an expensive vendor-specific RFID reader and provides a global ID number to every object. An IPv6 address format is subdivided into two portions. The initial 64 bits represent the subnet, whereas the remaining 64 bits represents the interface/device ID. The subnet or network prefix is used to signify the 'physical' location predefined by the router. An interface/device ID is required in order to uniquely identify or tracking any object. A simple algorithm is used to generate a modified EUI-64 by converting a MAC address. In this algorithm, the seventh bit of the MAC address, which is also known as the global flag, is reversed. Then extra bits are placed in between the third and the fourth bytes of the address. This modified version of the address, i.e. the EUI-64 address, is then utilised as the interface ID, the second part of an IPv6 addressing scheme.

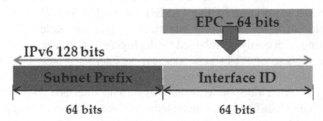

Fig. 3. The IoT RFID mapping with EPC [16].

Similarly, EPC-64 bits can be inserted into the IPv6 addressing scheme to be utilised as an interface ID in a readerless RFID system. Thus, the product information inside

EPC-64 bits will be held by the IPv6 address structure to track any product destination information. Figure 3 shows the modified address structure after the later 64 bits being replaced by the EPC-64 bits. In this manner, all the product information previously held by the EPC will be mapped directly onto the interface ID part of the IPv6 addressing scheme [16]. Thereafter, this modified and mapped address should be stowed in the RFID transponder memory, which can be a non-volatile memory, such as electrically erasable programmable read-only memory (EEPROM). In this way, each of the RFID tags become addressable in any IPv6 networks, providing provisions for physical location identification too.

Figure 4 shows the communication procedure through IEEE 802.11b between an RFID tag with the mapped EPC–IPv6 address structure and a computer with WNIC. The RFID tag will store the entire EPC–IPv6 address by using the mapping mechanism of this address. The RFID tag can be consigned to a range of 1–100 m in the industrial, scientific and medical (ISM) frequency band of 2.4 GHz. When an IPv6 RFID tag enters a Wi-Fi network, the system that contains WNIC will recognize it. First, WNIC will broadcast a message and all the RFID tags in that Wi-Fi network will receive this message. After receiving the message, the RFID transponder will send the acknowledgment packet. WNIC will then obtain the RFID transponder IP address from the acknowledgment packet [17].

Fig. 4. The communication procedure through IEEE 802.11b between an RFID tag with the mapped EPC–IPv6 address structure and a computer with WNIC.

Figure 5 exhibits the fragment of an IoT RFID front-end. In such arrangement, along with other circuits., a low pass filter (LPF) is considered as a very substantial block which suppresses every type of undesirable signals or noises [18]. An LPF design requires a tank circuit to customise the cut-off window. However, on-chip inductors are not advisable to be utilised, due to immoderate loss and comparatively bigger die size [19–22]. As the inductors are an inherent part of amplifier and filter design, CMOS based active inductors are being introduced in order to overcome the shortcomings of the on-chip inductors [23].

The downscaling of integrated circuits (IC) technology allow the designers to design low-power, low-cost but compact wireless communication systems [24–27]. A low pass filter is an inherent block for all the modern transceivers. The LPF performance determines the overall transceiver functionality. Therefore, this research proposes a completely integrated active inductor based low pass filter design in Generic Process Design Kit (GPDK) 90 nm CMOS process for IoT RFID transceiver applications.

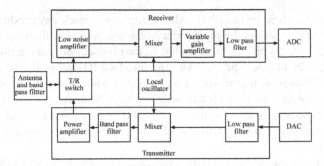

Fig. 5. The front-end block diagram for the design of IoT-RFID [24].

2 Proposed LPF

In conventional low pass filter design, inductors and resistors are generally used. The structure of the low pass filter usually adopts conventional resistive feedback method since it experiences high power consumption as well as parasitic capacitance at high frequencies. The proposed LPF is designed in three successive steps: common gate input buffer, active inductor based tank circuit and common drain output buffer as illustrated in Fig. 6.

Fig. 6. The realisation of the LPF.

The common gate input buffer, as demonstrated in the schematic in Fig. 7, has a good impedance match characteristic. In this structure, the bottom NMOS (M11) functions as a simple MOS resistor whereas the top transistor M8 adjusts the input impedance through its transconductance. The biasing voltages (Vb and V2) keep both the transistors in 'on state' for smooth operation of the LPF.

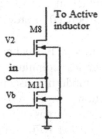

Fig. 7. Common gate input buffer.

The input buffer is followed by the frequency decisive tank circuit which consists of a double feedback active inductor as shown in Fig. 8 [28]. To satisfy the gyrator-capacitor model, in this active inductor, M3 and M4 act as non-inverting transconductors (gM1) whereas M2 act as an inverting transconductor (−gM2). Therefore, -gM2 and gM1 constitute the gyrator. This gyrator builds up the inductor at node 1 because of the parasitic capacitances at node 3. The equivalent RLC circuit is presented in Fig. 8.

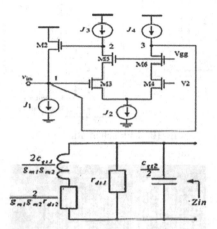

Fig. 8. Double feedback active inductor and its equivalent [27].

The final stage of this LPF is the common drain output buffer which offers a very small impedance, suitable for accomplishing a better output impedance matching. In the output buffer, as shown in the schematic diagram in Fig. 9, the transistor M10 functions as an active resistor. Figure 10 exhibits the final schematic diagram of the proposed LPF. In this LPF, adjusting the aspect ratio of the transistors M2, M3, M4, M8 and M10 results in the adjustment of the LPF gain and NF. However, a compromise has been made to these transistor aspect ratios to reach the best trade-off between the gain and the minimum NF. The W/L ratios of the transistors are presented in Table 1, the biases are set as V1 = 0.60 V, V2 = 0.40 V and Vgg = 0.80 V.

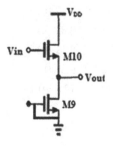

Fig. 9. Common drain output buffer.

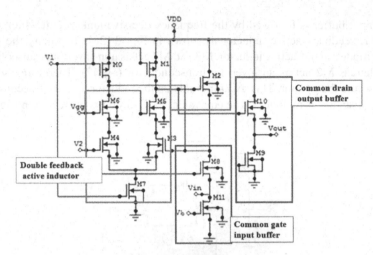

Fig. 10. LPF schematic circuit.

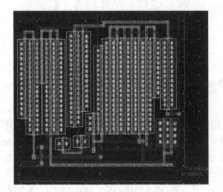

Fig. 11. LPF core layout.

Table 1. Transistors' W/L Aspect Ratio for the LPF.

Transistors	W/L ratio (μm/μm)
M0, M1	1.27/0.13
M2	0.84/0.13
M3, M4	9.11/0.13
M5, M6	0.36/0.13
M7	12.15/0.13
M8	3.66/0.13
M9	25/0.13
M10	4.58/0.13
M11	8/0.13

The LPF's core layout has been designed utilising the EDA tools of cadence ADE (Analog Design Environment), as shown in Fig. 11. The LPF successfully bring about a small core die area of 85.28 μm^2 only.

3   Results

The schematic and layout design of the proposed LPF have been considered utilising GPDK-90 nm CMOS process technology with cadence ADE tool. The simulation uses a 1.3 V DC supply as VDD and the temperature has been set to 300 K. For this LPF performance study various aspects such as gain, noise figure and bandwidth have been considered.

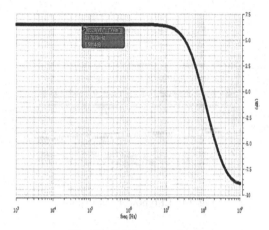

Fig. 12. LPF gain analysis.

Figure 12 shows the AC analysis of the LPF where a moderate peak gain of 6.5 dB is reported. The gain is flat and the cut off frequency is 35.48 MHz. Figure 13 shows the noise analysis of the LPF which shows a 20.78 dB noise figure at 35 MHz offset. The noise figure seems to be quite high which is mainly because of the flicker noise contribution at the low frequencies.

The power consumption of the proposed low pass filter for its operation is only 1.56 mW, as shown in Fig. 14. This reasonably low consumption could have been achieved due to the application of smaller but optimised transistors in the design.

Table 2 summaries the performance of the proposed LPF design, with regards to various parameters. This LPF achieved a moderate gain, a very small core die area and an extremely low power dissipation.

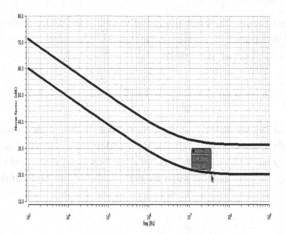

Fig. 13. LPF noise analysis.

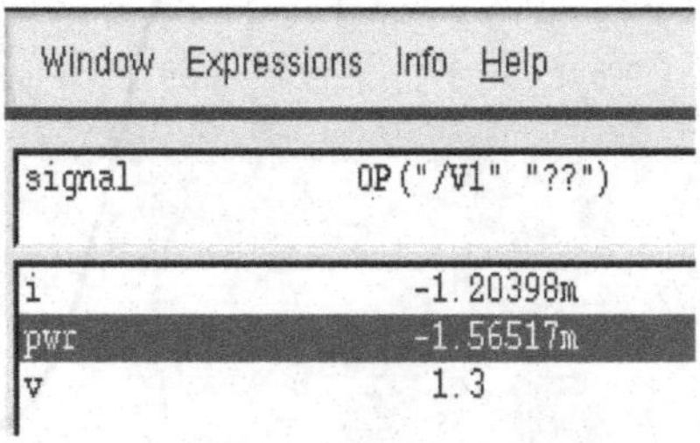

Window Expressions Info Help	
signal	OP("/V1" "??")
i	−1.20398m
pwr	−1.56517m
v	1.3

Fig. 14. LPF power dissipation.

Table 2. Performance summery of the LPF

Parameters	Value
Technology	90 nm CMOS
Gain (dB)	6.5
Supply Voltage (V)	1.3
Bandwidth (MHz)	35.48
NF min (dB)	20.78
Power Consumption (mW)	1.56
Chip Area (μm^2)	85.28

4   Conclusions

IoT RFID is considered as one of the most advantageous devices for the present as well as the future of the smart connected world. In this research, a low power compact LPF has been designed and simulated in GPDK 90-nm CMOS technology for IoT RFID transceiver. It exhibits a high gain of 6.50 dB, a competitive noise figure of 20.56 dB with a wide bandwidth of 35.48 MHz. The LPF operates with a single 1.3 V supply voltage and consumes only 1.56 mW power. In this design, avoiding passive spiral inductors helped to keep the die area very small which is only 85.28 μm^2. Overall, such LPF increases the performance of the IoT RFID transceiver.

Acknowledgements. The authors acknowledge the support of the grant FRGS/1/2020/TK0/XMU/02/5 from the Ministry of Higher Education (MoHE), Malaysia.

References

1. Miraz, M.H., Ali, M., Excell, P.S., Picking, R.: Internet of nano-things, things and everything: future growth trends. Future Internet **10**(8), 68 (2018)
2. Bhuiyan, M.A.S., et al.: CMOS series-shunt single-pole double-throw transmit/receive switch and low noise amplifier design for Internet of Things based radio frequency identification devices. Informacije MIDEM **50**(2), 105–113 (2020)
3. Farooq, H., Rehman, H.U., Javed, A., Shoukat, M., Dudley, S.: A review on smart IoT based farming. Ann. Emerg. Technol. Comput. (AETiC) **4**(3), 17–28 (2020). https://doi.org/10. 33166/AETiC.2020.03.003, http://aetic.theiaer.org/archive/v4/v4n3/p3.html.
4. Badal, M.T.I., Reaz, M.B.I., Bhuiyan, M.A.S., Dhawale, C.A,.; Nano CMOS charge pump for readerless RFID PLL. Informacije MIDEM **49**(2), 53–60 (2019)
5. Bhuiyan, M.B.I., Reaz, M.B.I., Jalil, J., Rahman, L.F., Chang, T.G.: A compact transmit/receive switch for 2.4 GHz reader-less active RFID tag transceiver. J. Central South Univ. **22**(2), 546–551 (2015)
6. https://www.electronicproducts.com/wp-content/uploads/sensors-and-transducers-sensors-vppo-iot-aug2014-lores.gif. Accessed 9 May 2021
7. Badal, M.T.I., Reaz, M.B.I., Jalil, Z., Bhuiyan, M.A.S.: Low power high-efficiency shift register using implicit pulse-triggered flip-flop in 130 nm CMOS process for a cryptographic RFID tag. Electronics **5**(4), 92 (2016)
8. Kantareddy, S.N.R., Mathews, I., Bhattacharyya, R., Peters, I.M., Buonassisi, T., Sarma, S.E.: Long range battery-less PV-powered RFID tag sensors. IEEE Internet Things J. **6**, 6989–6996 (2019)
9. Philipose, M., Smith, J.R., Jiang, B., Mamishev, A., Sumit, R., Sundara-Rajan, K.: Battery-free wireless identification and sensing. IEEE Perv. Comput. **4**, 37–45 (2005). https://doi.org/ 10.1109/MPRV.2005.7
10. https://www.mdpi.com/sensors/sensors-18-03584/article_deploy/html/images/sensors-18-03584-g001-550.jpg. Accessed 9 May 2021
11. SRII: Report on Development plan for RFID in Industry and Service (RFID). NECTEC (2006)
12. Ayre, L.B.: RFID Costs, Benefits, and ROI: Number 5, July 2012. https://www.journals.ala. org/index.php/ltr/article/view/4513. Accessed 12 Nov 2020
13. Dinesh, V., Gupta, R.: IPv6 vs EPC (2004). http://www.worldinternetcenter.com/Pubs/Pub s2004/feb05/IPv6vEPC.pdf. Accessed 12 Nov 2020
14. Bi, H.H., Lin, D.K.J.: RFID-enabled discovery of supply networks. IEEE Trans. Eng. Manag. **56**, 129–141 (2009). https://doi.org/10.1109/TEM.2008.922636
15. Ubrurhe, O.N.H., Excell, P.S.: A review of energy efficiency in wireless body area/sensor networks, with emphasis on MAC protocol. Ann. Emerg. Technol. Comput. (AETiC) **4**(1), 1–7 (2020). https://doi.org/10.33166/AETiC.2020.01.001, http://aetic.theiaer.org/archive/v4/ v4n1/p1.html.

16. Bhuiyan, M.A.S., Minhad, K.N.B., Uddin, M.J., Reaz, M.B.I., Badal, M.T.I., Ullah, H.: CMOS LNA for IoT RFID. In: 2nd IEEE International Conference on Artificial Intelligence in Engineering and Technology (IICAIET 2020), pp. 1–4 (2020)
17. Bhuiyan, M.A.S., Taib, M.T.B.M., Reaz, M.B.I., Hasim, F.H., Ali, S.H.M.: Design of a band-pass filter in 0, 18 μm CMOS for 2, 4 GHz reader-less RFID transponder. Tech. Gaz. **24**(1), 31–34 (2017)
18. Pérez-Bailón, J., Calvo, B., Medrano, N.: A CMOS low pass filter for SoC lock-in-based measurement devices. Sensors **19**(23), 5173 (2019)
19. Zhang, C., Shang, L., Wang, Y., Tang, L.: A CMOS programmable fourth-order Butterworth active-RC low-pass filter. Electronics **9**(2), 204 (2020)
20. Deeb, A., Abugharbieh, K.: A CMOS gm-C low-pass filter for direct conversion receivers with tuning capability. In: 2019 Southeast Con, pp. 1–4 (2019)
21. Bhuiyan, M.A.S., Reaz, M.B.I., Omar, M.B., Badal, M.T.I., Jahan, N.A.: Advances in active inductor based CMOS band-pass filter. Micro Nanosyst. **10**(3), 3–10 (2018)
22. Sreenivasulu, P., Rao, G.H., Rekha, S., Bhat, M.S.: A 0.3 V, 56 dB DR, 100 Hz fourth order low-pass filter for ECG acquisition system. Microelectron. J. **94**, 104652 (2019)
23. Badal, T.I., Reaz, M.B.I., Bhuiyan, M.A.S., Kamal, N.: CMOS transmitters for 2.4-GHz RF Devices: design architectures of the 2.4-GHz CMOS transmitter for RF devices. IEEE Microwave Mag. **20**(1), 38–61 (2019)
24. Folla, J.K., et al.: A low-offset low-power and high-speed dynamic latch comparator with a preamplifier-enhanced stage. IET Circ. Dev. Syst. **15**(1), 65–77 (2021)
25. Bhuiyan, M.A.S., Badal, M.T.I., Reaz, M.B.I., Crespo, M.L., Cicuttin, A.: Design architectures of the CMOS power amplifier for 2.4 GHz ISM band applications: an overview. Electronics **8**(5), 477 (2019)
26. Alam, M.J., Bhuiyan, M.A.S., Badal, M.T.I., Reaz, M.B.I., Kamal, N.: Design of a low-power compact CMOS variable gain amplifier for modern RF receivers. Bull. Electr. Eng. Inform. **9**(1), 87–93 (2020)
27. Folla, J.K., et al.: An 8.72 μW low-noise and wide bandwidth FEE design for high-throughput pixel-strip (PS) sensors. Sensors **21**(5), 1760 (2021)
28. Yodprasit, U., Ngarmnil, J.: Q-enhancing technique for RF CMOS active inductor. In: 2000 IEEE International Symposium on Circuits and Systems (ISCAS 2000), pp. V-589–V-592 (2000)

LoRa IoT WSN for E-Agriculture

Tea Osmëni$^{(\boxtimes)}$ ⓘ and Maaruf Ali ⓘ

Epoka University, Rruga Tiranë-Rinas, Km 12, 1032 Vorë, Tiranë, Albania
`maaruf@ieee.org`

Abstract. This paper presents the research carried out in the application of wireless sensor networks to aid agriculture and cultivation using Albania as an example. Utilisation of artificial intelligence, machine learning to aid agriculture are presented. For a primarily agricultural-based economy with rugged terrain, power availability is the biggest problem along with security. The research presents various technologies that may be applied to aid the farmer. The conclusion of the research finds that Internet-of-Things (IoT) using Long Range (LoRa) Wireless Sensor Networks (WSNs) is the most secure solution for productive and economic farming in semi-developed countries.

Keywords: LoRa · IoT · E-Agriculture · WSN · Wireless Sensor Network

1 Introduction

1.1 Background

Three issues were taken into consideration regarding WSNs (Wireless Sensor Networks) at the onset of this research, these being:

1. The effective radio coverage field (network field) by the sensors. This is related to the sensor receiver sensitivity. The sensitivity of the other types of sensors will also affect the domain of the area or volume being monitored, for example, the IR (infrared) radiation of intruders in the farmer's area.
2. Prolonging the operational life of the network when the number of sensors is greater than operational necessity. This could be required for the simple case to ensure network redundancy and fault tolerance. Some of them could then be scheduled to have their power turned off to save energy.
3. The network needs to be secured against intrusion, spoofing and data theft for protection against hacking.

1.2 Purpose

The purpose of this project was to present several issues regarding wireless connectivity, more specifically related to farming. The research questions to be answered were:

- How could a farmer best make use of the radio network coverage map?
- What issues do we face in using WSNs (Wireless Sensor Networks)?
- Which is the best solution to mitigate against security attacks in agriculture?

M. H. Miraz et al. (Eds.): iCETiC 2021, LNICST 395, pp. 85–93, 2021.
https://doi.org/10.1007/978-3-030-90016-8_6

1.3 Approach

The starting point was a feasibility study where the focus lay on different reference literature study. This would result in a number of hypotheses, which were analysed after the case study. This consisted of implementing the WSN and a skeleton of the coverage map of Tirana, the capital city of Albania, which was performed in Matlab®. After the case study was completed, an evaluation of the issues regarding energy, power consumption and security in agriculture was performed. In the evaluation, the hypotheses were to be confirmed or denied, based on the empirical findings from the case study.

1.4 Literature Review

Based on the literature review, agriculture can be considered a complex dynamic biological production system affected by many parameters: human behaviour, machines used, nature, chemicals, biology, weather and the climate.

Data fusion is necessary to increase the effectiveness of decision making from the myriad of sensors. Maintaining the security of the information flow has become paramount for data integrity, security and privacy with the rise in cybercrime. WSNs and IoTs have now become essential for enabling remote real-time information gathering, analysis and decision making applicable to agriculture using the least amount of labour.

2   IoT (Internet of Things) Domain Model Concepts

This section presents the application of IoT in Albania and other developing countries for a sustainable future.

In general, IoT as the acronym represents, are Internet (connected) of things (objects, devices). These devices come in all sizes and communicate with one another using the Internet, unattended and autonomously.

2.1 IoT Utilisation in Albanian Agriculture

Developed countries continue to extend its network of IoT investing time in research and money to convert the abstract into material reality all with the goal of a sustainable future.

IoT sensors continue to be deployed from the microscopic level to an industrial scale, from underground, overground, in the sea, in humans and animals to space. Applications of IoTs in agriculture is also accelerating, for monitoring and controlling ground water, irrigation, crop growth, harvesting and crop health. All the vast amount of data generated can be saved in the cloud, processed by it and made easily accessible to the farmers and by institutions [1].

How can IoT help in the evolution of a country, currently speaking, the evolving of agriculture in Albania (or any developing country)? Well, in a lot of ways actually, such as:

- Weather monitoring, pest control, nutrient and greenhouse gases emission management [2, 3].
- Information to aid governments and farmers to design business models fusing smart agriculture and optimising the smart food supply chains by making them smarter [1, 4].
- Water supply control and management of irrigation to prevent wastage and thus help prevent flooding or drought - a common problem in Albania [1]. Smart water monitoring using IoTs can help agriculture use 30%–50% less energy and water. Currently many places lack adequate water resources and suffer from poor management leaving many without access to potable water.

2.2 IoT Domain Model Requirements

The six primary requirements for IoT deployment are next explained.

Physical Entity User Interaction, Mediated or Physically via IoT.

I. Application
A agrarian IoT system using WSNs actively monitors its farming environment taking measurements of the temperature, humidity, rainfall, air pressure, light intensity, soil moisture. These are some physical attributes essential for helping to achieve high yield and high cultivation products. These parameters can be displayed on a mobile application on the farmer's phone, tablet or desktop computer. For modelling purposes, the farm is the Physical Entity and the application is the user.

The Physical Entity is an Identifiable Component of the Physical Realm that is for the User's Goal Completion Interest.

II. Environment
Optical sensors may be used for smoke, sand, fog, haze, pollen, precipitation measurements to determine air visibility. The information may used to provide safety information for traffic or air traffic management systems.

III. Living Being
Crop growth monitoring systems allied to WSNs are also being used to determine the rate of growth of plants, fruits, vegetables and crops and the effect of crop spraying of liquid fertilisers. Growth monitors, such as that shown in Fig. 1, below are deployed. These have vegetable/fruit growth sensors. In such a scenario, the fruits are Physical Entities.

Software Components are the Resources that Send Information or Data for Actuation of the Physical Entities.

IV. Resources.
It comes in two contexts: Network Resource and On-Device Resource. We are interested in the Network Resources, as we will see below that we need a wireless connection for the transmission to be done (actually by using WSN). For example, HBase2 is a distributed,

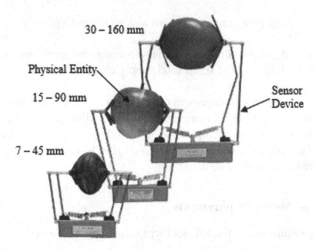

Fig. 1. Physical Entity as part of the physical environment. Adapted from [5].

open-source, column-oriented database offering distributed information management. The Network Resources here are the libraries and components of the HBase software.

A Service Offers a Standardised and Unambiguous Interface with the Functionalities for Interacting with the Related Processes of the Physical Entities.

V. Interacting Services

A resource hungry service that requires high CPU utilisation, memory and storage requirements may be divided as smaller tasks running across multiple machines in a distributed manner, invoking each other for convenient and scalable processing. These subservices in themselves will require smaller resources and less power. A balance and trade-off will need to be established taking into account the increased networking overhead of inter-communication and possible combined increase in the total power of all the host machines.

Devices are Defined as Real-World Technical Artefacts for Bridging the Digital World Internet with the Physical Entities.

VI. Devices

Typical devices needed in our case are both simple sensors that will measure sound, possibly seismic activity, light, thermal, acoustic or lux sensors, but also complex ones like IR or UV cameras. A device can be unitary as well as a conglomerate of devices. The Domain Model for IoT does not define this granularity due to the application dependence of the sensor.

Figure 2, shows that the sensors to be utilised in e-agriculture are at Stage 1 of the four stage IoT Solutions Architecture. Figure 2 also shows the complexity of the end-to-end solution that must be thought out for a seamless fault free solution to the deployment of IoTs in any application and not just in e-agriculture. A clear overview of Fig. 2 is given in [7], which also proposes a final fifth stage with the goal of "initiating a user's control over the structure".

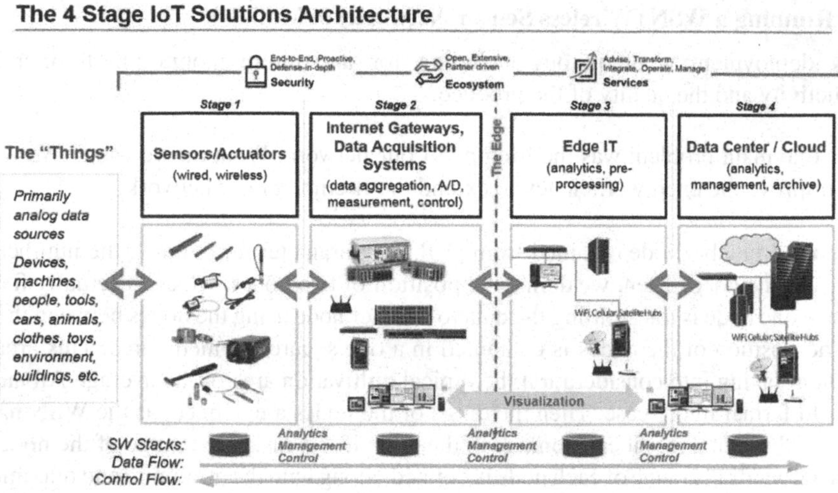

The 4 Stage IoT Solutions Architecture

Fig. 2. The four stage IoT solutions architecture [6].

3 Methodology and Steps

3.1 Coverage Map Regarding Albanian Farms

Ensuring full network coverage via radio in WSNs is a major problem due to the varying and harsh RF propagation environment. Radio coverage planning and monitoring is essential, just like in a mobile cellular network. Three models to deal with this coverage issue are [8]:

- Binary model – each sensor's RF (radio frequency) coverage area is modelled by a circle of a predefined radius.
- Probabilistic model – a stochastic process to describe an event taken place in the coverage of a sensor is either not detected or detected based on a probability distribution measure.
- The third model deals with the coverage problem by considering the trajectory (and velocity) of how the targets are travelling through the sensor's sensing field.

The Matlab® code obtained from [9] takes into consideration the visualisation of the coverage map, communication links and directional antenna. The simulation does include directional and bi-directional antennae, but in this scenario, we only discuss in terms of the directional antenna, because we want the transmission to be done to a specific location. The specific locations here are Tirana with its longitude and latitude, as well as some urban areas not so far from Tirana, in terms of agricultural urban areas. Site Viewer is part of Matlab® which is not free to use. So the main problem, the coverage area and how we can be adapt it in terms of the IoT systems, as an advantage for the agricultural sector of Albania was focussed upon.

3.2 Running a WSN (Wireless Sensor Network) in Matlab®

WSN deployment is ubiquitous including for agriculture monitoring to increase productivity and the quality of the produce.

• So, one main problem was the lifetime of our network. What do we want? We want to improve the energy efficiency to extend the lifetime of our network.

In the Matlab® code obtained from [10], the parameter for defining the number of nodes are included. Then, we define the position of two nodes, which is actually fixed, because one node is transmitting the data to another node using the nodes between them.

The position of the nodes is contained in a one square kilometre area. This area is sufficient taking into consideration the typical cultivation area of the average Albanian freehold farmer in our case. Then the range of the nodes are defined, as the WSN has a range of the signal that it can connect to the node if it is inside the range of the node.

Afterwards the range of each node is defined, along with the minimum and maximum energy, energy consumption per cycle (every time a node forwards a packet or a data).

It is a basic scenario as the range of all the nodes need to be checked to ensure connectivity. In this simulation, 20 nodes were chosen, which is a large number of nodes. Some typical farms were taken into consideration with wireless connectivity for assessment of surveillance and safety.

WSNs still have several shortcomings in terms of poor energy efficiency, routing overhead, limited onboard or embedded computational capability, secure packet delivery and many more. However, efficient power utilisation and access is still a major problem [11, 12]. The number of the sensor nodes are high and they are densely deployed in the farm to offer and ensure network redundancy in case of faulty nodes. The density is the number of the neighbouring nodes that it can interact with. The algorithms should be self-organising and scalable for the large number of entities comprising the IOTs. After executing the code, the results shown in Figs. 3 and 4 were obtained, as shown below.

As the process runs, it is shown which are the dead nodes and the routing nodes that the transmission proceeds. To conserve power, unused and redundant path sensors may be turned off.

3.3 LoRa WSN as the Best Solution

As soon as the code is executed, it starts to send data. As soon as a dead node is obtained, the transmitting node will change its path by itself.

But a problem may be encountered, due to cyberattacks. So security of the farming data generated and dissemination need to be ensured to prevent network disruption and other types of attacks. [13] discusses a security model to ensure against such attacks.

We do know that in order for a wireless communication to be conducted, we need three elements: wireless hosts (laptops, mobile), wireless link (to link the communication from the source to the destination) as well as the base station or access point. So, in such a case, LoRa WSN will behave as the access point.

The server will act as the wireless host and if we look carefully in Fig. 5, the wireless link that will be used is LoRaWAN-59, which in general is used to provide coverage on demand for IoT projects.

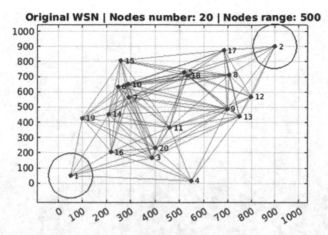

Fig. 3. Scene 2 with 4 hops, 3 dead nodes and routing nodes 1, 3, 9, 2 with 5844 packets sent.

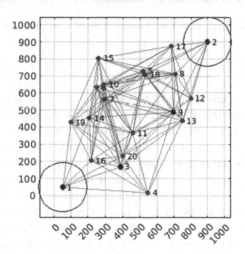

Fig. 4. Scene 3 with 4 hops, 9 dead nodes and routing nodes 1, 3, 9, 2 with 6595 packets sent.

LoRa WSN is the proposed solution by Girard et al. [14], which involves a third trusted party to avoid the problems of cryptographic key sharing.

The end node usually must use secret keys for a lifetime without updating. In the scheme proposed in [14], the end node can update the keys anytime. Chirp spread spectrum methodology modulation of LoRa technology is implemented. Figure 5 below shows the scheme using LoRa WSN.

Fig. 5. The topology of WSN for monitoring of agriculture conditions [11].

4 Conclusions

An explanation of the Domain Model for the IoT concepts was given to see how connections of different devices was done and as well as the requirements needed for an IoT system. The last step is necessary in order to determine the interactivity of the different configurations between the services and the users. This step will help farmers and governments design business models applicable to smart agriculture or e-agriculture.

The three main problems that might occur in future implementations, regarding coverage map, where we have adapted a Matlab® simulation in terms of the longitude and latitude of Tiranë and urban zones around it was described adapting it to our case.

Afterwards, we introduce WSN (Wireless Sensor Network) as a need in agriculture for monitoring, in order to improve farming quality and productivity. We evaluated the WSN issues by illustration with a Matlab® simulation, to justify our explanations to prove our point in terms of nodes, where nodes work as base stations (access points). As the process runs, it is shown which are the dead nodes and the routing nodes that the transmission proceeds. If extra sensors are deployed, these may be turned off to conserve power.

Finally, we have shown that in terms of security, LoRa WSN would be the best choice, after reviewing several publications. We do know that in order for a wireless communication to be conducted, we need three elements: wireless hosts (laptops, mobile), wireless link (to link the communication from source to destination) as well as the base station or access point. So, in such a case LoRa WSN will behave as the access point.

The server will act as the wireless host and specifically the wireless link will be LoRaWAN-59, which in general is used to provide coverage on demand for IoT projects.

References

1. Westbase.io: IoT for farming in developing countries – how can it help, 24 October 2018. https://www.westbase.io/iot-for-farming-in-developing-countries/. Accessed 21 July 2021
2. Lalitha, A., Suresh, B., Purnima, K.S.: Internet of Things: applications to developing country agriculture sector. Int. J. Agric. Sci. **10**(20), 7410–7413 (2018). https://74.220.219.42/files/articles/10_20_21_IJAS.pdf. Accessed 21 July 2021
3. Madushanki, A.A.R., Halgamuge, M.N., Wirasagoda, W.A.H.S., Syed, A.: Adoption of the Internet of Things (IoT) in agriculture and smart farming towards urban greening: a review. Int. J. Adv. Comput. Sci. Appl. **10**(4), 11–28 (2019). https://thesai.org/Downloads/Volume 10No4/Paper_2-Adoption_of_the_Internet_of_Things.pdf. Accessed 21 July 2021
4. Dlodlo, N., Kalezhi, J.: The Internet of Things in agriculture for sustainable rural development. In: 2015 International Conference on Emerging Trends in Networks and Computer Communications (ETNCC), 17–20 May 2015, pp. 13–18 (2015). https://doi.org/10.1109/ETNCC.2015.7184801
5. https://phyto-sensor.com/img/FI-fruits.jpg. Accessed 19 July 2021
6. Fuller, J.R.: The 4 Stages of an IoT Architecture. TechBeacon, 26 May 2018. https://tec hbeacon.com/sites/default/files/4_stage_iot_solutions_architecture_0.jpeg. Accessed 19 July 2021
7. Stokes, P.: 4 Stages of IoT architecture explained in simple words, 5 December 2018. https://medium.datadriveninvestor.com/4-stages-of-iot-architecture-explained-in-sim ple-words-b2ea8b4f777f. Accessed 21 July 2021
8. Wu, S.-L., Tseng, Y.-C.. Wireless Ad Hoc Networking, 1st edn. Auerbach Publications/Taylor & Francis Group, New York (2007). https://doi.org/10.1201/9781420013825
9. https://www.mathworks.com/help/antenna/ref/coverage.html. Accessed 25 July 2021
10. Silva, C.: matlab-wsn-code-with-swarm-optimization-ACO-Ant-colony-optim. GitHub. https://github.com/cesarfgs/matlab-wsn-code-with-swarm-optimization-ACO-Ant-colony-optimization. Accessed 25 July 2021
11. Akyildiz, I.F., Levine, D., Joe, I.: A slotted CDMA protocol with BER scheduling for wireless multimedia networks. IEEE/ACM Trans. Netw. **7**(2), 146–158 (1999). https://doi.org/10. 1109/90.769764
12. Esteves, E.: On the reverse link capacity of cdma2000 high rate packet data systems. In: 2002 IEEE International Conference on Communications. Conference Proceedings. ICC 2002 (Cat. No.02CH37333), vol. 3, pp. 1823–1828 (2002). https://doi.org/10.1109/ICC.2002.997163
13. Prodanović, R., et al.: Wireless sensor network in agriculture: model of cyber security. Sensors (Basel, Switzerland) **20**(23), 6747 (2020). https://doi.org/10.3390/s20236747. https://www.ncbi.nlm.nih.gov/pmc/articles/PMC7728362/. Accessed 21 July 2021
14. Girard, P.: Low Power Wide Area Networks Security, 9 December 2015. https://docbox.etsi.org/Workshop/2015/201512_M2MWORKSHOP/S04_WirelessTechnoforIoTandSecu rityChallenges/GEMALTO_GIRARD.pdf. Accessed 21 July 2021

Integrating the Meteorological Data into a Smart City Service Using Cloud of Things (CoT)

R. Surendran[1]([⊠]), T. Tamilvizhi[2], and S. Lakshmi[3]

[1] Center for Artificial Intelligence & Research (CAIR), Chennai Institute of Technology, Chennai, India
surendranr@citchennai.net
[2] Department of Information Technology, Vel Tech Multi Tech Dr. Rangarajan Dr. Sakunthala Engineering College, Chennai, India
[3] Department of Physics, Chennai Institute of Technology, Chennai, India

Abstract. The Cloud of Things (CoT) offers consistent and adaptable access to the global resources and data. It is being achieved through data integration and resource co-allocation techniques. The data integration is a process of collecting the data from various resources. The users are requesting the meteorological data to propose the smart city service. The proposed smart city service integrates the meteorological data from the meteorological towers. The data centers acts as a broker between the service requestor and the provider. If the requested data unavailable, the nearest tower collects from other towers using co-allocation technique. The resource co-allocation technique involves the analysis of available towers based on the user's request. The meteorological towers hold the weather forecasting data and distribute it across the wide geographical areas. This includes temperature, humidity, precipitation, wind speed and atmospheric pressure. These data are heterogeneous in nature which makes data integration through MapReduce technique and virtual machinery. This research work produces accurate and faultless forecast data for the user through CoT techniques. The proposed work experimental results are proved that the service will be a time and cost effective one for the smart city.

Keywords: Cloud of Things · Resource monitoring technique · Meteorological data · Data integration · MapReduce · Virtual machine

1 Introduction

The Cloud of Things (CoT) is a combination of Cloud Computing and Internet of Things. The resource management technique of CoT consists of resource requisition, resource allocation, resource monitoring, resource matchmaking, resource scheduling and resource brokering. Figure 1 represents the design of allocating the resources to the requestor is based on the system generated prediction and the resource requestor requests the resource through Cloud portal [1]. The resource broker provides an efficient service for the resource requestor and provider service. It resents as system generated prediction. The system generated prediction works with respect to the priority and reservation.

© ICST Institute for Computer Sciences, Social Informatics and Telecommunications Engineering 2021
Published by Springer Nature Switzerland AG 2021. All Rights Reserved
M. H. Miraz et al. (Eds.): iCETiC 2021, LNICST 395, pp. 94–111, 2021.
https://doi.org/10.1007/978-3-030-90016-8_7

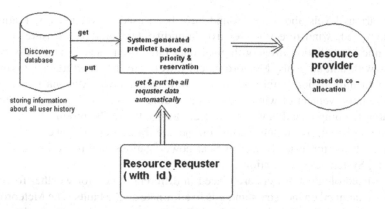

Fig. 1. System generated prediction based resource co-allocation system

In the data integration service, weather data requested peoples are called as resource requestor. The data centers are called as the resource providers. The system generated prediction is act as a resource broker. The data integration process is working based on MapReduce concepts. The scheduling queues are involved to predict the resource allocation for the requestor. It has data storage facilities from the discovery database. It stores current data as well as user history. If the resource goes unavailable/failure to respond to the requestor, the co-allocation plays the vital role here. The response time may be varied for every resources with respect to the distance. The system generated prediction is used to select the matched resources for the requestor from the resource provider. This process is called as resource co-allocation system. This resource co-allocation system matches with meteorological data integration process.

The Climatology and Weather Forecasting is vital on account that it helps to decide the future local weather expectations. Through the location of latitude, one can decide the probability of precipitation and snow accomplishing the surface. We can additionally be in a position to perceive the thermal energy from the solar that is available to a region. The Climatology is the scientific method through which one can find out about climates, which suggests the climate stipulations over a duration of time. The need to gather real-time meteorological data to be used in forecasting is regularly popular and essential to the protection of lifestyles and property. Indeed, one can discover observers or applications of automated instruments tasked with series of meteorological data spread, frequently densely, throughout many nations of the world. A meteorological tower is a facility, on land with instruments and tools for measuring atmospheric prerequisites to grant data for weather forecasts and to find out about the climate. The measurements taken consist of temperature, atmospheric pressure, humidity, wind speed, wind direction, and precipitation amounts. Wind measurements are taken with as few different obstructions as possible, whilst temperature and humidity measurements are stored free from direct solar radiation, or insolation. Manual observations are taken at least once daily, whilst automatic measurements are taken at least as soon as an hour.

A measurement tower or meteorological mast (met tower), is a free standing tower or an eliminated mast. Generally a met tower will have anemometers, wind direction vanes, temperature and pressure sensors, and other measurement devices attached to it at various levels above the ground have been used in weather observation data for wind speed, wind direction, relative humidity, temperature, pressure and background nuclear radiation. Meteorological data have been used in countless types of analyses with unique goals. Meteorological towers are the structures supplying nonstop in situ information within the lower atmospheric layer. Met masts are imperative in the improvement of wind farms, as particular understanding of the wind speed is essential to comprehend how a good deal electricity will be produced, and whether or not the mills will live to tell the tale on the site. Measurement towers are also used in other contexts, for instance near nuclear power stations, and by Automated Surface Observing System (ASOS) stations.

The Meteorological Towers are placed in different region for weather forecasting. These are examined on industry standards to eliminate all the faults. The Meteorological monitoring towers are often the first physical structures evident at proposed green field nuclear sites. New construction at existing nuclear facilities may necessitate the moving of a meteorological monitoring tower due to space considerations. Aging towers may need to be replaced if they have not been properly maintained. Tower siting considerations, power and communication issues must be addressed before construction can begin. Other tower construction management tasks that need to be considered include Federal Aviation Administration (FAA) and Federal Communications Commission (FCC) considerations, site access, local and state permitting and tower engineering based on soil conditions.

The meteorological monitoring tower should be located at an elevation near that of the finished plant grade. Topography and obstructions must be considered for tower placing. In concerning wind sensors, Regulatory guide indicates that the sensors ought to be situated over level to open territory [2]. To provide accurate temperature measurement, the tower should not be located near heat or moisture sources such as large parking lots or water bodies. At a proposed nuclear facility, one would not want to place the tower so close to the proposed plant site that construction activities could impact the meteorological measurements.

Other tower siting considerations would include accessibility, not only for the construction of the tower but for maintaining the tower and the meteorological equipment once the tower is erected and providing data [3]. After siting criteria considered, the exact tower location can be determined. The precise tower location is required for surveying the site and for locating where soil boring. To provide accurate temperature measurement, the tower should not be located near heat or moisture sources such as large parking lots or water bodies [4].

2   Related Works

The existing data integration processes are need to improve with modern technologies like Artificial Intelligence, Machine Learning, Cloud Computing, Internet of Things, Big data. The data integration process starts with data collection. Then collected data are stored and maintained separately in the cloud storage. The resource providers are only considering the resource allocation process. Also have some limitations in the existing system. Such as.

1. Queue handling issue for the large number of request from the user.
2. Time and cost is the challenging task to balanced priority with advanced reservation technique.
3. The database connectivity problem may exist due to insufficient data, while system generated prediction system.

Alfonso Quarat et al. integrate the weather data for smart city in Transport Territory and Tourism (TCUBE) project [5]. Service Oriented Architecture (SOA) and Web service concepts are play important role in this work. The advantage of the work is high accuracy for minimum number of data. The disadvantage of the work is not suitable large amount of data. ArcDualKc model developed for integrating the forecast meteorological data [6]. The benefits of this model is reliable results of spatial weather data determination. Limitation of this model is need to be improve the accuracy for the remote sensing data. Jairam Singh Yada et al. created snow cover pattern methodology for one region [7]. The advantage of the work is efficient meteorological data sets integration. The disadvantage of the work is need to utilize many QoS factors to integrate high level.

Sleiman Farah et al. integrate the meteorological weather data with respect to the climate change [8]. The pros of the work is high energy saving technique and also reduce the annual heating rate. The cons of the work is need to utilize huge number of data sets. The integral regression model was developed to predict the temperature based on meteorology data [9]. The benefits of the work has been predicted weather data dynamically at any time. The Drawback of the work is need to be improve with modern techniques like Quantum Computing, Artificial Intelligent. Machine Leaning, Cloud Computing, Internet of Things. Sasalak Tongkaw designed a mobile application to collects durian resources [10]. The information can be utilized for carrying out a geographic data arrangement of durian asset the executives and the nearby insight of Thai durian grounds-keepers by planning to utilize a similar data set framework. This work was implemented through System Development Life Cycle (SDLC), Waterfall model and Geographic Information System (GIS). The advantages of this work it clarifies a durian varieties study structure in detail. The disadvantage of this work is experimental setup and results not shown properly for the researchers.

Martin JánosMayer aggregates the meteorological datasets and then improve the reliability of photovoltaic design models [11]. This work utilized the following methodologies. Such as Optimization techniques, Data aggregation process and Differential evolution methods. The benefits of this work is high accuracy on simulation and optimization processes. The downside of this work is the aggregation methods not suitable for variety of datasets. Masayuki Maki et al. developed the weather prediction data using cloud computing techniques [12]. The Visualization technique is a vital role in this work to analysis the radar data. This works provides the access of multimedia data efficiently. The limitations of this work is its take more time and cost. Dynamic Memory Manager helps to find the hardware for the Real-Time Systems in the queue management [13]. The work focuses the memory management process with help of queue process. This work is helping to develop the scheduling technique for the proposed work. Maran et al. studied the wind energy location prediction between meteorological stations and this has been highly motivated for the proposed study [14].

3   The Proposed CoT Based Meteorological Data Integrating Service

The Proposed CoT based meteorological data integrating service utilize the MapReduce technique. Data center as a resource provider to handle the monitoring, execution, data storages for system generated prediction in specified cloud environment [15]. It provides efficient data integration service from the meteorological towers based on their nearest location and availability of the data. Here to achieve the time and cost constraint based on the MapReduce technique. In this proposed work, designing three major modules to access the meteorological tower information. Such as resource requestor, resource broker and resource provider [16]. The resource requestor is acting as a mobility node allocated in dynamic location based approach. In this architecture of Fig. 2, resource requestor act as a user. User have to submit their query to the resource broker. Resource Requestor are representing in mobility nodes. The mobility node allocating in dynamic manner [17]. This requestor only submit the task to the resource broker. The resource broker will forward the request to resource provider. The resource provider will take care of remaining implementation process. The resource providers supply the meteorological tower weather report to the requestor.

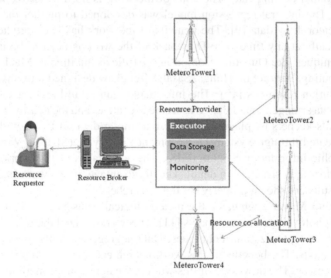

Fig. 2. Architecture for the proposed CoT based meteorological data integrating service

The resource provider implements the main three task in resource sharing. Such as executor, data Storage and monitoring. The executor executes the operational conversion based on user's requirements. For example Fahrenheit to Celsius conversion, Celsius to Fahrenheit conversion. The data storage maintains data for centralized server to provide data transformation from resource provider to resource broker. Resource allocation done by the monitoring approach. It directs the resource requestor to access data from the specified and nearest tower. The Meteorological Tower contain weather reports for every day order. Such as like temperature, wind, pressure, humidity, status, chance of precipitation. This will be the details presented in meteorological tower weather forecast. By use meteorological information, acquired from calculation, to recover the information in group procedure. Here, rehearse this methodology continuously climate to share the tower (Location based) information in incorporated worker component. This refreshed each hour out of every day. It's more valuable to recover the information in Time utilization.

Recommending this cluster based approach to resolve time constraint problem and also it can be handled both queue overflow and dynamic allocation technique. But in elastic based scheduling only handle resource allocation in priority scheduling concept and hence queue overflow may be existed. This can be solved by partitioning based cluster method. In elastic scheduling technique, data storage separately designed and resource provider only implementing the resource co allocation process. This two problems have been solved by designing resource provider with data storage, executing conversion operation, monitoring via resource allocation and resource co allocation techniques.

In elastic algorithm only evaluate based priority, in MapReduce algorithm also take care to find nearest tower location and data availability by implementing shortest energy path via partitioning based cluster approach. The study are of Tamil Nadu having met towers about 42 meteorological stations, are situated in the southeast corner of the Indian Peninsula (Fig. 3). This cluster contains group of nearest location tower in Tamilnadu (India). Example location 1 Chennai tower, location 2 Thandalam tower, location 3 Hosur tower under group a cluster. Here location 1, 2, 3 are Tamilnadu (India) regions. Through this can improve the time constraint and dynamic resource sharing efficiently.

The present study uses the met mast information have been downloaded from the website of https://www.indianclimate.com/show-data.php. and the geographical locations have been tabulated in Table 1.

3.1 Methodologies Used in Proposed Research Work

The proposed work is achieving the time and cost constraint, for allocating the resources to the user. The system generated prediction done by clustering mechanism, resource provider directs the process to co allocation based on cluster group of tower. Here scheduling done by partitioning method, so no issues about queue will exist. The proposed work implementation done in dynamic mobility node model. Meteorological tower based cloud of things service contains following tasks in step by step.

Step 1. User Base from any location submit the task through cloud portal.
Step 2. Automatic system generated prediction scheduling
Step 3. Resource Co-Allocation and Monitoring

   i.   Initialize the requestor to submit the job.
   ii.   Find the towers which are having shortest distance in cluster
   iii.   Check the Latitude and Longitude position of tower with mobility nodes coordinates.
   iv.   Compare which Latitude and Longitude tower position matching with mobility node Position.

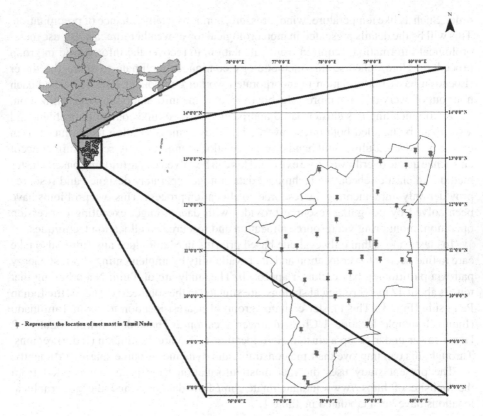

Fig. 3. Depiction of Tamil Nadu is a state in South India

v.   Take Latitude and Longitude position in ascending order and match with mobility Node position.

vi.   Using partitioning method, we can match Latitude and Longitude position going to Verify.

vii. After verifying the shortest path, based on present data's of each Tower will display.

viii. If data not found loop will exist, till data find from cluster towers (Resource Co allocation).

ix.   Repeat step vii to implement user query.

Step 4. Resource provider (Data Center) will respond to requestor (user base) via resource broker (system generated prediction).

3.2   Experimental Results of the Proposed Research Work

This section deals with the results of the proposed system and its analysis. The essential hardware requirements are cloud server/super computer, virtual machine and various sensors for the real-time implementation. The virtual machines are created through

Table 1. Places of met towers in Tamil Nadu

S.No.	Places of met towers in Tamil Nadu	Latitude (degree decimal)	Longitude (degree decimal)
1	Chennai	13.07	80.28
2	Kanyakumari	8.08	77.55
3	Thanjavur	10.78	79.17
4	Thandalam	13.15	79.95
5	Thanjavur	10.78	79.17
6	Balakrishnapuram	10.37	78.00
7	Ariyalur	11.15	79.08
8	Thoothukudi	8.80	78.18
9	Naranapuram	9.25	77.42
10	Ramanathapuram	9.37	78.87
11	Kanjirangal	9.87	78.47
12	Kannanpathy	8.18	77.48
13	Madurai	9.97	78.17
14	Balakrishnapuram	10.37	78.00
15	Periyammapatti	10.33	77.50
16	Meenaveli	10.50	78.50
17	Tirunelveli	8.73	77.73
18	Tirunelveli	8.71	77.76
19	Tiruppur	11.08	77.33
20	Thanjavur	10.78	79.17
21	Thiruvarur	10.77	79.65
22	Nagapattinam	10.77	79.82
23	Chennai	13.07	80.28
24	Chennai	13.08	80.27
25	Thandalam	13.15	79.95
26	Olaiyur	12.83	79.75
27	Chenganatham	12.92	79.18
28	Hosur	12.74	77.83
29	Kilnachipattu	12.25	79.12
30	Anichampalayam	11.95	79.53
31	Cuddalore	11.72	79.82
32	Settikarai	12.13	78.22

(*continued*)

Table 1. (*continued*)

S.No.	Places of met towers in Tamil Nadu	Latitude (degree decimal)	Longitude (degree decimal)
33	Salem	11.65	78.20
34	Odappalli Agraharam	11.33	77.77
35	Perali	11.23	78.93
36	Ariyalur	11.15	79.08
37	Nochikulam	11.12	79.07
38	Namakkal	11.22	78.22
39	Kuppanur	11.28	77.08
40	Coimbatore	11.00	77.00
41	Nagapattinam	10.77	79.82
42	Vengur	10.83	78.77

vmware tool. It plays a major role for load balancing, scheduling and resource allocation. The various sensors are wind speed and direction sensor, Humidity sensor, radiation sensor, precipitation sensor, modem and data logger. The software specification of the proposed work is front end platform as a Netbeans, programming language as a Java and Backend data base as MySQL.

The cloud infrastructure provided from CloudSim simulator. In Fig. 4, when tower location is identified process and get initiated for the smart city. Then resource broker starts the communication between resource requestor and resource provider.

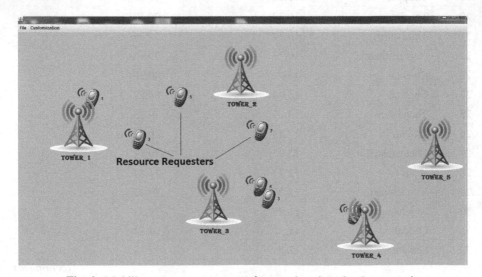

Fig. 4. Mobility resource requestor and towers locations for the smart city

Resource requestors (1–10) are initialized, and ready to submit the task to resource broker. The Resource requestors are allow to submit the task through cloud portal. The requestors can retrieve weather related data from any. The Resource broker collects the Resource requestor's requests. The Resource broker connect with resource provider for the task computation. The Resource requestor can choose the information to recover and furthermore pick which day information need to recover. For example access wind information and resource provider measures the query and recognize which tower is closest one to get to the information. This most limited energy way execution done by observing method, which one is under the piece of resource supplier. The tower 3 represents most limited one to react resource requestor 3.

The Meteorological tower represents the Data center in the cloud network. The Resource Requestor represents the User base. The Configure Simulation of Data center and User base in the cloud network. It's shown in Fig. 5. User base Configuring attributes are Name, Region, request per Hour(Hr), Data size per request(Bytes), Peak Hours start(GMT), Peak Hours end(GMT), Average peak users, Average off-peak users. Data centers Configuring attributes are Name, Region, Architecture, Operating System, Virtual Machines Cost per VMs/Hr, Memory Cost ($), Storage Cost ($), Data Transfer Cost($),Vms Count, Image Size, Memory and physical HW units have been shown in Fig. 6.

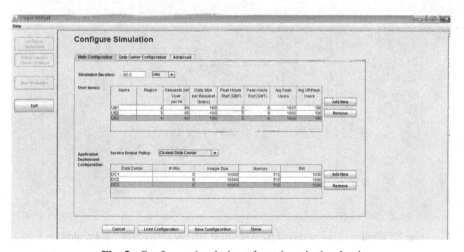

Fig. 5. Configure simulation of user base in the cloud

After calculating the shortest path of specified tower, the resource monitoring check the data. The shortest path tower is allocating data to the user in the cluster. Here tower 3 is the first shortest path in the cluster group, but it doesn't contain wind data in Fig. 7.

Based on the count of User base and Data center selects the load balancing policy for data analyses. If the count is less selects the Round Robin, throttled techniques. Else the count is high selects MapReduce technique. MapReduce is a technique to handle the massive amount of data to integrate and analyze. The MapReduce technique contains two steps one is mapping process and second one is reduce process. The mapping is a process

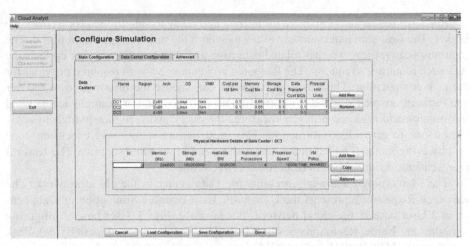

Fig. 6. Configure simulation of data center in the cloud network

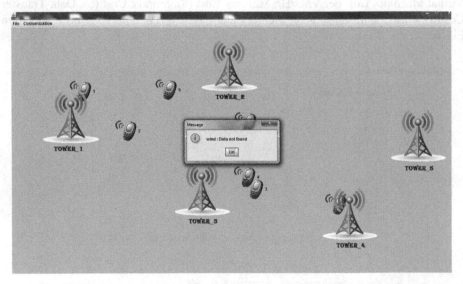

Fig. 7. Wind data not retrieved from shortest energy path tower 3 for requestor 3

to collects the unprocessed data, then split and mapping the data. The reduce process is use to sort or shuffling the data into valuable information. Apply the MapReduce technique to the cloud environment in Fig. 8. The co-allocation task has been given to the tower 5 by resource provider. Tower 5 is the next shortest one to access the wind data for requestor 3.

Resource provider retrieves the wind data from the data storage. It will validate the query for implementing the process. Example wind speed is 18 km/hr has retrieved tower 5 for requestor 3. Here cloud migration technique play a vital role for the resources in the internet are shown in Fig. 9. Executer performs conversion operation, when user wants

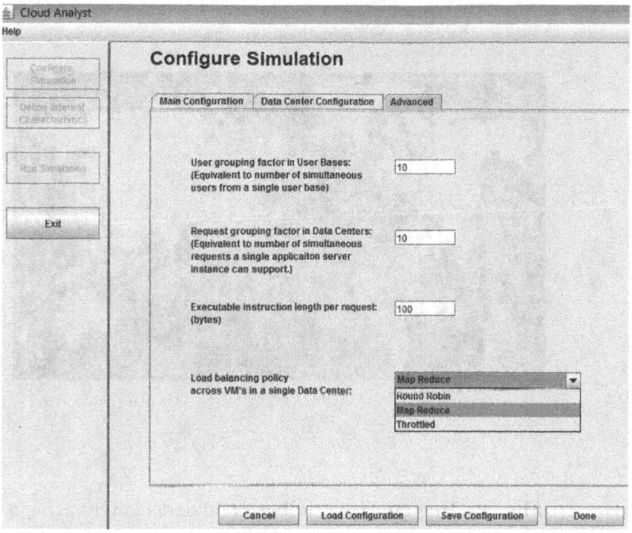

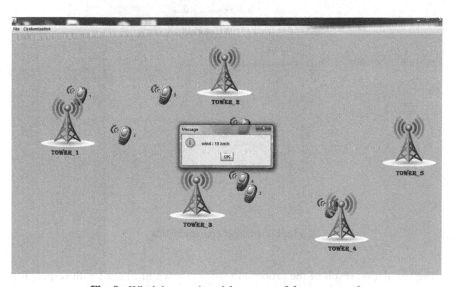

Fig. 8. Apply the MapReduce technique in the cloud network

Fig. 9. Wind data retrieved from tower 5 for requestor 3

to retrieve temperature data. Executer converts Celsius to Fahrenheit or Fahrenheit to Celsius conversion.

The Region wise Data centers (DC1, DC2, DC3) and User Bases (UB1, UB2, UB3) positions are represented in Fig. 10. In Fig. 11, The Internet Characteristics have been displayed as delay matrix and Bandwidth matrix. The available bandwidth (Mbps) between regions have been displayed for the meteorological data integration. Transmission delay (ms) between regions are displayed for the meteorological data integration.

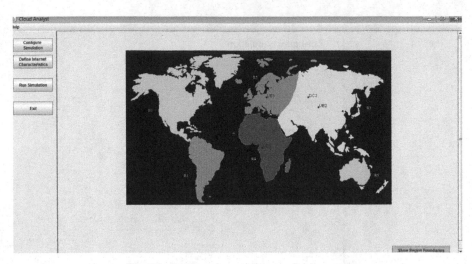

Fig. 10. Region wise user base and data center

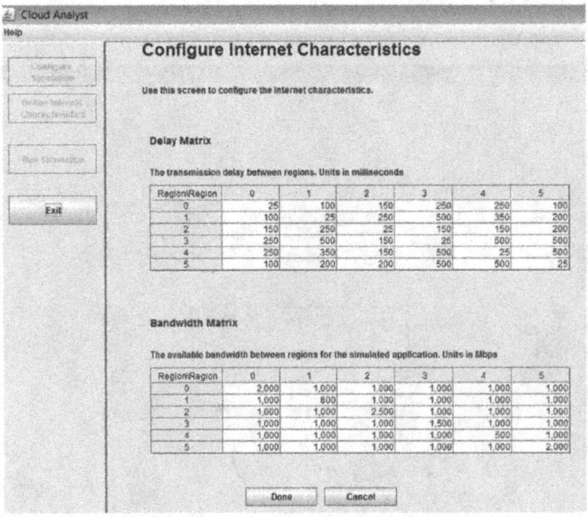

Fig. 11. Internet characteristics

The simulation result of the proposed work is shown in Fig. 12 with respect to the response time factor. Table 2 shown the Response time for User Base (UB1, UB2, UB3) by Region wise. Table 3 shown the Data center (DC1, DC2, DC3) processing time for User Base (UB1, UB2, UB3) request by Region wise. Here Overall Response Time for the User Base request is determined in Table 4. Data Center processing Time with Average, Minimum, Maximum level (units in ms) also calculated in Table 4.

The cost is the second important Quality of Service factor to analyses the meteorological data integration in Table 5. The smart city is calculate the grand total cost from Eq. 1. Summation of Virtual Machine Cost (1 to n) and VMC Data Transfer Cost (1 to

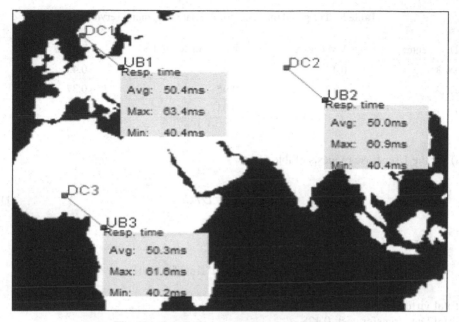

Fig. 12. Simulation result of the proposed work

Table 2. Response time for user base by region wise

User base	Average (ms)	Minimum (ms)	Maximum (ms)
UB1	50.4	40.4	63.4
UB2	50	40.4	60.9
UB3	50.3	40.2	61.6

Table 3. Data center processing time for user base request by region wise

Data centre	Average (ms)	Minimum (ms)	Maximum (ms)
DC1	0.36	0.012	0.67
DC2	0.43	0.013	0.63
DC3	0.46	0.023	0.71

Table 4. Overall response time and data center processing time for the user base request for the smart city service

Time	Average (ms)	Minimum (ms)	Maximum (ms)
Overall response time	50.2333	40.3333	61.9666
Data center processing time	0.4166	0.016	0.67

Table 5. The grand total cost for the data integrating service

Data center	VM Cost $	Data transfer cost $	Total $
DC3	0.43	0.03	0.43
DC2	0.37	0.05	0.37
DC1	0.48	0.04	0.48

n) for the User Base requests (Table 5).

$$\sum_{i=1}^{n} VMC_i + DTC_i \tag{1}$$

where VMC represents Virtual Machine cost.

DTC represents Data Transfer cost

Total virtual machine cost: 1.28$
Total Data transfer cost: 0.12$
Grand Total: 1.4$

Table 6. The performance evaluation between proposed CoT based meteorological data integrating service with existing SOA based weather data integrating application

Factors	Proposed CoT based meteorological data integrating service	Description of proposed system	Existing SOA based weather data integrating application	Description of existing system
Overall Response time	50.2333 ms	Overall Response time for User Base getting through cloud portal	67.86 ms	Overall Response time for User Base getting through web portal
Data center processing time	0.4166 ms	Virtual Machines utilized for the computing	0.71 ms	Physical Machines utilized for the computing
The grand total cost for the data integrating service	1.4$	Cloud based resource management save the cost	1.95$	Service Oriented Architecture measure the cost

(continued)

Table 6. (*continued*)

Factors	Proposed CoT based meteorological data integrating service	Description of proposed system	Existing SOA based weather data integrating application	Description of existing system
Virtual Machine cost	1.28$	VMware based virtualization cost is counted here	1.83$	Web service cost is counted here
Data transfer cost	0.12$	Internet cost for data transfer through Internet of Things (IoT)	0.23$	Internet cost for data transfer through Web Technologies
Technique used for integrating	MapReduce	If the data count is high selects MapReduce technique	Round Robin, throttled	If the data count is low select the Round Robin and medium select throttled

The Proposed CoT based meteorological data integrating service is compared with the existing SOA based weather data integrating application with respect to the various working attributes in smart city service displayed in Table 6.

4 Conclusion and Future Direction

The Proposed CoT based meteorological data integrating service is enhanced the data integration process using MapReduce technique. The proposed service simulates the user base and data center in cloud environment with region wise. The techniques utilized for data integration is data collection, monitoring, matchmaking, scheduling and resource co-allocation are given in module explanations. We investigate this approach based on tower position, tower capability, and distance from the mobility node to resource broker. Especially towers are triggered by resource providers monitoring approach. When requestors submitting the task to tower data are processed by resource provider and resource broker will transmit the request to user. The Proposed CoT based meteorological data integrating service handle user base requests to allocate resources in shortest energy path distance. The experimental results shows the efficient data integration process with respect to the time and cost. The future direction of the work is to develop as a real-world cloud environment.

Acknowledgements. The authors acknowledge that they received no external funding in support of this research work. Surendran R (40%), Tamilvizhi T (30%) and Lakshmi S (30%) conceived of the presented research work. Surendran R and Tamilvizhi T. developed the theory and performed the computations. Lakshmi S collects the related data for processing. Surendran R and Tamilvizhi

T. encouraged Lakshmi S to investigate data and supervised the findings of this research work. All authors discussed the results and contributed to the final manuscript. The authors would like to thank Chennai Institute of Technolgy and Vel Tech Multi Tech Dr.Rangarajan Dr.Sakunthala Engineering College for providing us with various resources and an unconditional support for carrying out this research work.

References

1. Alsabbagh, K.J., Alkaabi, A.A., Surendran, R.: University campus indoor navigation for android devices using augmented reality and A* Search algorithm (UCIN). In: 3rd Smart Cities Symposium (SCS 2020), pp. 257–263 (2021). https://doi.org/10.1049/icp.2021.0890
2. Heo, J., Song, K., Han, S.U., Lee, D.-E.: Multi-channel convolutional neural network for integration of meteorological and geographical features in solar power forecasting. Appl. Energy 295 (2021). https://doi.org/10.1016/j.apenergy.2021.117083
3. Sagl, G., Bernd, R., Thomas, B.: Contextual sensing: integrating contextual information with human and technical geo-sensor information for smart cities. Sensors 15(7), 17013–21703 (2015). https://doi.org/10.3390/s150717013
4. Zheng, Q., et al.: Integrating spectral information and meteorological data to monitor wheat yellow rust at a regional scale: a case study. Remote Sens. 13(2), 278 (2021). https://doi.org/10.3390/rs13020278
5. Quarati, A., et al.: Integrating heterogeneous weather-sensors data into a smart-city app. In: 2017 International Conference on High Performance Computing & Simulation (HPCS), pp. 152–159 (2017). https://doi.org/10.1109/HPCS.2017.33
6. Longo-Minnolo, G., Vanella, D., Consoli, S., Intrigliolo, D.S., Ramírez-Cuesta, J.M.: Integrating forecast meteorological data into the ArcDualKc model for estimating spatially distributed evapotranspiration rates of a citrus orchard. Agric. Water Manag. 231 (2020). https://doi.org/10.1016/j.agwat.2019.105967
7. Yadav, J.S., Misra, A., Dobhal, D.P., Yadav, R.B.S., Upadhyay, R.: Snow cover mapping, topographic controls and integration of meteorological data sets in Din-Gad Basin, Central Himalaya. Q. Int. 575–576, 160–177 (2021). https://doi.org/10.1016/j.quaint.2020.05.030
8. Farah, S., Whaley, D., Saman, W., Boland, J.: Integrating climate change into meteorological weather data for building energy simulation. Energy Build. 183, 749–760 (2019). https://doi.org/10.1016/j.enbuild.2018.11.045
9. Ji, Z., Pan, Y., Li, N.: Integrating the temperature vegetation dryness index and meteorology parameters to dynamically predict crop yield with fixed date intervals using an integral regression model. Ecol. Model. 455 (2021). https://doi.org/10.1016/j.ecolmodel.2021.109651
10. Tongkaw, S.: Management information systems and geographic information system for managing durian resources. Ann. Emerg. Technol. Comput. (AETiC) 5(5) (2021). http://dx.doi.org/https://doi.org/10.33166/AETIC.2021
11. Mayer, M.J.: Effects of the meteorological data resolution and aggregation on the optimal design of photovoltaic power plants. Energy Conv. Manag. 241 (2021). https://doi.org/10.1016/j.enconman.2021.114313
12. Maki, M., Kim, Y.: Visualizing weather radar data from volcanic eruption clouds. Data Brief 35 (2021). https://doi.org/10.1016/j.dib.2021.106942
13. Kohútka, L., Nagy, L., Stopjaková, V.: Hardware dynamic memory manager for hard real-time systems. Ann. Emerg. Technol. Comput. (AETiC) 3(4) (2019). http://dx.doi.org/10.33166/AETiC.2019.04.005

14. Maran, P.S., Ponnusamy, R., Venkatesan, R, Singh, A.B.: Wind energy location prediction between meteorological stations using ANN. GlobalNEST Int. J. **16**(6), 1135–1144 (2014). https://doi.org/10.30955/gnj.001462
15. Ewelle, R., Francillette, Y., Gouaich, A., Mahdi, G., Hocine, N.: Network aware traffic adaptation for cloud games. In: Proceedings of CloudCom-Asia 2013, International Conference on Cloud Computing and Big Data, FuZhou, China (2013). https://doi.org/10.1109/CLOUDCOM-ASIA.2013.79
16. Ewelle, R., Francillette, Y., Mahdi, G., Gouaich, A.: Network traffic adaptation for cloud games. Int. J. Cloud Comput.: Serv. Architect. (IJCCSA) **3**(5) (2013). http://dx.doi.org/https://doi.org/10.5121/ijccsa.2013.3501
17. Dixit, A., Yadav, A.K., Kumar, S.: An efficient architecture and algorithm for server provisioning in Cloud computing using clustering approach. In: 2016 International Conference System Modeling & Advancement in Research Trends (SMART), pp. 260–266 (2016). https://doi.org/10.1109/SYSMART.2016.7894532

Data Handling and Transparency Enhancement in Central Sterile Service Department

R. Surendran[1(✉)], M. L. Akashkumar[2], P. Ashwini[2], S. Indhuja[2], V. Jeevanandam[2], D. Mythrayee[2], M. Ravimukilan[2], and B. Viswa[2]

[1] Center for Artificial Intelligence and Research (CAIR), Chennai Institute of Technology, Chennai, India
surendranr@citchennai.net
[2] Department of Biomedical Engineering, Chennai Institute of Technology, Chennai, India

Abstract. Sterilization is the process of removal of impurities on the surface of an object. It is widely used in the medical field. It is a crucial department in every medical institute but it is least known to public. This paper gives an idea about security and satisfaction for patients ensuring the sterility of instruments used on them through cloud data management technology. Transparency in the sterilization is a necessity. Sterile Processing Department (SPD) is a part of a medical institute that takes care of maintaining sterilization of equipment which is commonly known as the Central Sterile Service Department (CSSD). A well-structured database system helps to handle this tedious process efficiently. Data collected from hospitals are stored in the cloud with a well-established data structure. People can get access to view the information from the cloud stored data related to them through a website/mobile app. With this system the patients are assured that they get operated with germs free equipment and the data are stored in an efficiently accessible manner.

Keywords: Sterilization · Central Sterile Service Department (CSSD) data · Cloud server · Hospital transparency · Patient satisfaction

1 Introduction

Sterilization is a broad phrase that can apply to any method of removing or killing any traces of biological/chemical contaminants [1]. This includes bacteria, fungi, viruses, and protozoans together with their reproductive structure forms that are sometimes terribly resistant. The chemical contaminant may be any by-products released by the above-mentioned contaminants which refer to life forms that are on the surface, at intervals a fluid, medications or compounds cherish buffers and culture media. Correct sterilization is well achieved with combos of heat, high pressure, filtration, chemicals, and irradiation [2].

The CSSD plays a significant role in patient safety associate degree in reducing hospital surgical infection [3]. From an infection management perspective, it's essential to make sure that the correct medical aid of surgical instrumentality is performed.

M. H. Miraz et al. (Eds.): iCETiC 2021, LNICST 395, pp. 112–125, 2021.
https://doi.org/10.1007/978-3-030-90016-8_8

If instruments are microbial contaminated, this ends up in an inflated probability of contamination and succeeding infection of the surgical wound. CSSD is being a backbone in hospitals and in other health care facilities that perform sterilization and other actions on medical devices, instruments and, other consumables; for sequent use by physicians within the working department of the hospital and also for other sterile procedure, for instance, catheterization wound sewing and, medical care during medical, surgical, maternity or, medical specialty war [4].

The CSSD is split into 5 major areas: Decontamination, Assembly and Processing, Sterilizing, Sterile storage and Distribution. The process and results done by CSSD have been recorded and stored as data which is majorly used to examine the hospital's quality [5]. The data which we are planning to provide for patients are [6],

- Method of sterility
- Sterility level
- Set name and lot number of instrument pack
- Date of events

A cloud storage system can store different type of data. Cloud-primarily based architectures had been largely followed to reinforce and simplify the layout, the development, and the deployment of records structures, for collecting, processing, results, areas, and sharing medical records, medical institution administrative records [7]. These architectures help decorate the records series process (example, the worried entities are frequently supplied with cell person interfaces to cloud offerings for collecting and handling records). Furthermore, records sharing among hospitals and sufferers are likewise benefited; the layout of these structures frequently has safety and private aspects, which can be both taken into consideration as critical [8].

The Objective of the proposed work is, the set of information that we are said to provide will be stored in the cloud from CSSD through which we are collecting and providing the information to the patient in a precise way [9]. The data stored and extracted from the cloud finally reached the patients through the websites [10].

2 Related Works

The literature survey of the proposed works is discussed here. First, Ibrahim Abdulai Sawaneh and et al. developed patient database management in computer based system. This work is to store the patient data to maintain their medical records only for official purposes. However this paper doesn't mention the transparency provided to the patients. This downside could've been easily overcome by uploading the data to the cloud [11].

Second, Debabrata Basua and et al. is about the record and preservation period of CSSD data. This article majorly notified the importance of records maintenance in CSSD which enhances the knowledge of every hospital and in charge of CSSD about the importance but it doesn't shown out for the people. However, the latter doesn't mention about providing the same to the patients, which is a determining factor affecting the patient's satisfaction and transparency [12].

Third, Ritam Dutta and et al. proposed the concept of IOT based healthcare which promoted transparency. This work concentrates on the delivering the medical records to the patients but this paper failed to deliver the complete transparency by not providing any data of CSSD [13].

Fourth, Reehan Ali Shah and et al.'s paper briefs about Intrusion Detection System (IDS), which is considered to be one of the main components in network security [14]. The article gives the statistical analysis on the infection rate due to sterilization [15, 16].

3   Central Sterile Service Department (CSSD)

Every day, several medical procedures are performed in intended facilities worldwide, with caregivers and patients hoping on the supply and use of a large variety of supplies, instruments, and equipment. These devices should be correctly cleaned, disinfected, and/ or sterilized, inspected for quality to ensure good operating condition, and out there for care within the absence of proper handling, process, and storage, these devices could become contaminated and compromise quality patient care [17].

In most tending facilities, the Central Sterile Service Department (CSSD) plays a key role in providing the things needed to deliver quality patient care. To support infection management inside the tending facility, the CSSD employee members should be well-trained, skilful and committed to "doing what's right" each step of the way [18]. This means making certain that shortcuts are created and that process and practices are systematically followed.

Consolidative reprocessing of reusable devices helps guarantee uniform standards of practice, whereas conjointly providing for improved progress (soiled, too clean, and too sterile). This also facilitates the coaching and education of skilled technicians who must be experienced with the standards, complexities, challenges, risks, and techniques related to the CSSD function. Each CSSD task should be performed in an exceedingly manner that protects the welfare and safety of patients, co-workers, and therefore the community.

Mistaking a step causes health hazards to patients. A part of Healthcare Associated Infection (HAI) is Surgical Site Infection (SSI) in which disease-causing living organisms enter into the human body directly and cause severe health infections. On an average SSI rate is around 5%-10% across different countries. SSI (Surgical Site Infection) is a part of Healthcare Associated Infection (HAI). Based on the survey conducted and research works previously done on SSI 8% result in the SSI. The report states that one-third of postoperative deaths are due to SSI. This percentage is high when seen on a large scale. 3 in 100 operations result in SSI. So in total 30,000,000 $((x/y)*z)$ patients get infected due to SSI.

This increases the length of hospital stay by 3–20 days per person. Patients have to spend extra amounts and their time. Costs of SSI is up to 10 billion dollar annually. In a growing economy the population is increasing in a rapid amount that demands many heath care services. The connection between CSSD and people makes people aware of CSSD and their importance. It also becomes the responsibility of the hospital to show the patients that the equipment used on them is 100% sterile. To reduce infections and to increase safer health service to patients, a bridge between the sterilization department and people is to be built. Storage and maintenance of records about every instrument used in hospitals are done manually by employees in local systems/ servers or in written form [19, 20].

3.1 Procedures and Maintenance of Medical Equipment in CSSD

Sterilization process have been done around the world in three different types, Steam or Autoclave sterilizer, Hydrogen Peroxide (H_2O_2), Low temperature Gas Plasma Sterilizer and Ethylene Oxide (ETO) sterilizer. In all three methods a set of all packages are exposed to chemicals that kill the microorganism. Water at high temperature is used in steam sterilization. For plasma sterilization hydrogen peroxide is ionized and used and for ethylene oxide is used in ETO machine. After a particular time limit the chemical is removed and the surface is dried.

Specific Packaging and Wrapping. This department also provides the proper set for surgeries including the patient's dress, gauss, cotton, etc. These are the works performed by CSSD apart from sterilizing the equipment. Hence they are maintaining a large record of CSSD which has a precise content of the work of CSSD in Fig. 1.

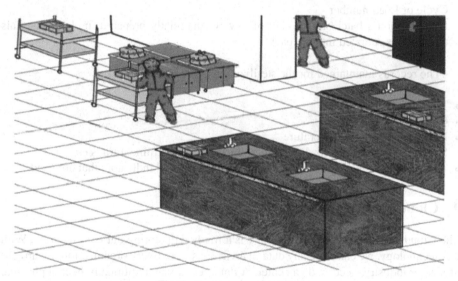

Fig. 1. Packing area in CSSD

Types of Indicators used to detect sterility: There are different classes of indicators available, in which Class I: process Indicator which is used to differentiate between processed and unprocessed units. Class V: Integrating Indicator which is a biological indicator used to detect sterility efficiently.

Types of biological indicator used for different sterilizers,

1. Steam- Bacillus stearothermophilus
2. Hydrogen Peroxide(H_2O_2) Low Temperature Gas Plasma - Bacillus stearothermophilus
3. Ethylene Oxide(ETO)- Bacillus subtilis

3.2 Data Management in CSSD

Every procedures and activities performed for every sterilized items must be documented and those records to be maintained which majorly used for inspection purposes, and also to track the process record information like: Daily production statistics to assess stock levels required for safe, continuous service, and efficient stock and cost control, All tests performed on equipment, Sterilization cycle records, Employee training records, Staff works rosters, Incident reports, Quality and procedure/ operational manual and Maintenance records [21].

Each item or pack intended for use as a sterile product must be labelled with a batch control identification which shall designate the following:

– Sterilizer identification number or code
– Date of sterilization
– Cycle or Load number
– Manufacturer's batch/ lot number of any commercially prepared implant materials that are incorporated into the pack.

The records maintained for the sterilization cycle are:

• The date of cycle
• Code of the cycle
• Exposure time and temperature
• Specific content in the load. Example, linen packs, instrument trays etc.
• The readout result of physical, chemical and biological indicators that are used.

4 Cloud Data Management Technology

The Cloud data management technology is a method of storing our data securely. With this technology, we can store any data in a virtual space. Every organization, regardless of size or industry, needs a data center. A data center has traditionally been a physical facility used by business to store information and other applications critical to their operations. We say that a data center is one, but in reality, it is often stored with technical equipment on demand. From router security and security devices to storage systems and application delivery controllers [22].

Data centers also require huge amounts of infrastructure to keep all hardware and software up to date. These installations may include ventilation and cooling systems, uninterruptible power supplies, and backup generators. A cloud data center stands out uniquely in various ways than a traditional data center. These two computer systems are not the same except that they both store data [23]. Cloud data centers are all online and are not located in a particular organization's office. When data is stored on clouds servers, it is automatically copied to multiple fragmented locations for safe storage.

We can store a wide amount of data in this virtual space and also it is possible to retain the data anywhere with the help of the internet. By using this cloud server method, there is no need of maintaining a dedicated server room for the particular organization since it is maintained by the cloud data service providers. It is possible to store any type of data in the cloud regardless of what type of data it is. By comparing the dedicated server room maintenance, Cloud data server is a best alternative to store and maintain the data with the help of a service provider which will reduce financial stress and difficulties faced while storing data by the hospital. In the medical field, there is a need for storage space to store the medical history of the patients. Also there is a need for dedicated technology for the management purpose and of course to provide transparency of impatient data for customer satisfaction. Now, cloud data management technology gives a way to fulfil these requirements.

5 Proposed Work on CSSD

This research work aims to increase the awareness about CSSD among the patients. CSSD is one of the major departments which have valuable data which is often trifled with and is not known by many patients. The information about the sterility of the surgical instrument is of the same importance as the surgery details given to a patient. So we aim to give the data to the cloud. The data is collected from the records maintained by CSSD. Usually this data is stored in the form of a CSV (Comma Separated Value) file. To transfer a CSV file to cloud server we should first understand how we are going to use the stored data. Based on the requirement we can select deployment models namely: Private, Public and Hybrid. To collect data from CSSD and provide information to patients, a hybrid type of deployment model will be beneficial. So that data used only by the CSSD department can be stored in private servers and public can be used to store data that are given to patients.

After understanding the requirement, get storage space from cloud service providers in the market and upload the data in the cloud. The information from the cloud is given to patients by creating a tab on the hospital website with proper security measures. Patients can access their sterilization report from the hospital website by logging into the portal. Once the log in details entered by the patient's matches with the server data, a detailed report is generated from the stored information. Patients can get their report once the hospital allots a particular package of sterilized materials to the patient's treatment and that data is entered in the CSV file. It's shown in Fig. 2.

5.1 Steps Involved in Proposed CSSD Data Handling

For every Surgery, the equipment has to be sterilized and then used. Each sterile Equipment set has its own Unique Lot number or a code. After Sterilization for each set precise records are maintained by the Department. From those maintained records, Data which have Useful information for the patient are selected and uploaded as CSV which makes it easier to import and export it to cloud and other platforms. The data entered in CSV file is stored in a cloud from which patients are given access to view information by logging in with their patient ID provided by the Hospital management for them as shown in Fig. 3.

The technical sequence chart for the proposed work is given in the Fig. 4 and Fig. 5.

As we all know that python is a user-friendly language, we recommend Python for this process. We all know that python is a user-friendly language, which making it a

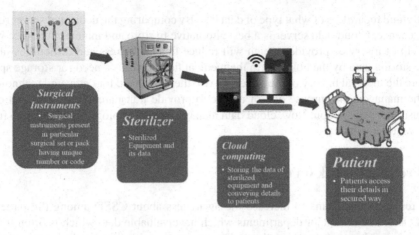

Fig. 2. Way of Approach for the proposed CSSD work

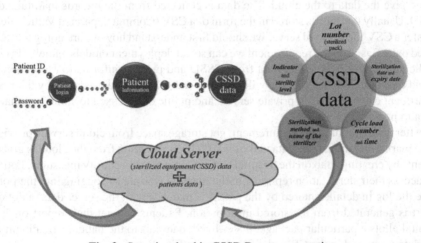

Fig. 3. Steps involved in CSSD Data transportation

reliable choice. In order to change the language from python to any other available languages like html, java, C, C++. the inbuilt functions vary drastically. If the order of execution is the same as python in any other language, a mere change in the inbuilt functions would enable the user to overcome the above-mentioned difficulties with ease. The changes mentioned in the question vary from language-to-language. Similar are the mentioned upgrades. Due to these reasons, they are not mentioned in the paper. Python has many inbuilt functions specially meant for data handling and performing mathematical operations which reduces time and gives accurate outcomes with less coding.

Algorithm for uploading CSSD data in cloud server.

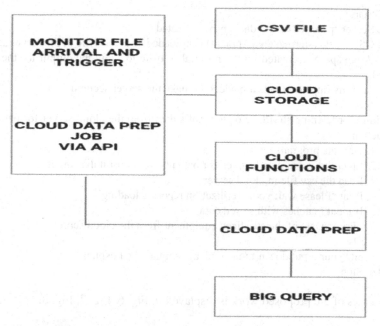

Fig. 4. Technical sequence chart for storing the data in cloud

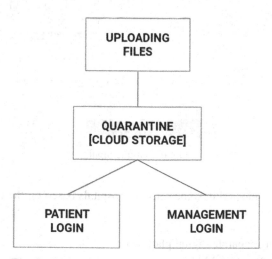

Fig. 5. Technical sequence chart for proposed work

Step1: Start
Step2: Server space for CSSD data entry is created
Step3: CSSD data (sterilized equipment) is uploaded as a CSV file in the server space.
Step4: A tab space is created on the hospital website to show the output for the data entered.
Step5: Security improvements are added to make the server secured.
Step6: Stop
Algorithm for fetching sterilized equipment's data from the cloud server for patient's satisfaction
STEP 1: Start the program
STEP 2: Enter the log in details given for patients from hospital as input
STEP 3: Read the csv file in cloud server
STEP 4: Print "Please wait your sterilization report is loading"
STEP 5: If input matches with stored data:
      Print "Data of the sterilized equipment from the cloud server."
   Else
  Print "your input doesn't match please contact the hospital"
STEP 6: Stop

Test cases of the proposed work is displayed in Fig. 6, Fig. 7, Fig. 8.

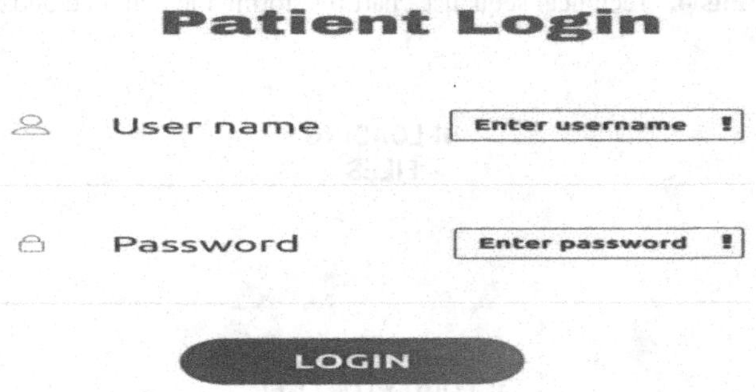

Fig. 6. Sample input

A survey was conducted in some selected hospitals based on the criteria mentioned below.

1. Hospitals having separate digital platform
2. Does the hospital have CSSD

The survey was regarding the connection between the CSSD and patients. By using some common metrics mentioned in the Fig. 9 the following results were obtained,

- Based on the survey more than half of the patients didn't know what is CSSD
- Similarly more than 65% of the respondents did not know the role of CSSD
- More than 3/4th of the respondents responded that their medical report has no details about the CSSD data

Patient details

Patient Name	-	Mr. ABC
Sex	-	Male
Age	-	55
Patient ID	-	NDGDIKCBV
Surgery	-	Laparotomy
Surgeon Name	-	Dr. XYZ
Equipment's CSSD data	-	PHD32468

CLICK HERE
See Details

Fig. 7. Sample output 1

CSSD DATA

Lot number of the Set	-	PHD32468
Sterilization Date	-	24/06/2021
Expiry Date	-	1year (if not exposed in environment)
Time of Sterilization	-	09:54:46
Sterilizer	-	Hydrogen peroxide gas Plasma sterilizer
Cycle number	-	3
Indicator	-	Biological Indicator
Indicator Name	-	Bacillus stearothermophilus
Indicator test result	-	Negative
Final Result	-	completely steriled

Fig. 8. Sample Output 2

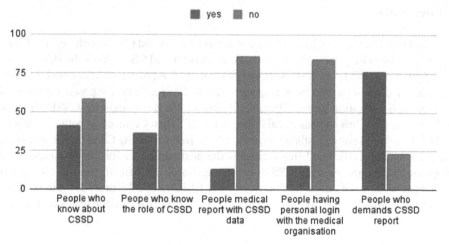

Existing CSSD process outcomes

Fig. 9. Existing CSSD process outcomes based on survey

- Only 15% of the respondents have personal login with their Medical organizations
- Nearly 75% of the respondents favored the proposed work, that is, addition of CSSD data to the already existing medical records

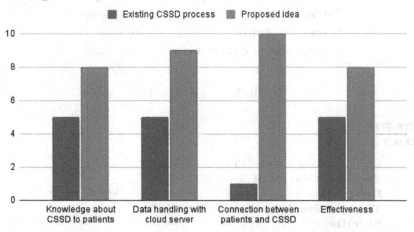

Fig. 10. Performance analysis of proposed CSSD with existing CSSD technique

The results accuracy of the proposed CSSD and Existing CSSD are measured with respect to the following Quality of Service Parameters.

- Knowledge about CSSD to patient,
- Data handling with cloud server
- Connection between patients and CSSD
- Effectiveness

The Fig. 10 depicts the Performance analysis of Proposed CSSD with existing CSSD technique. Knowledge about CSSD to patients in proposed CSSD work the skill rate is 8 out of 10. But in existing CSSD work the skill rate is 3 out of 10. Next parameter is Data handling with cloud server with respect to the utilization. The Proposed CSSD work utilized high utilization such as 9 scalability out of 10. But in existing CSSD work the utilization scale is low such as 5 scalability out of 10. Then Connection between patients and CSSD process patient satisfaction ratio 10:10. But in existing CSSD work the patient satisfaction ratio 1:10. The Effectiveness is the next parameter for the measurement of Proposed CSSD and existing CSSD technique. Based on Effectiveness the Proposed CSSD get the 8 profit out of 10. But in existing CSSD work the profit is 5 out of 10.

The data which the proposed idea to be provide can also be depicted as an Eq. (1).

$$E + P = D \tag{1}$$

Where,

E represents the Existing Data Provided to the patients.

P represents the Data to be added from the proposed idea.

D represents the final report to be provided for the patients from the proposed idea.

The Eq. 1 clearly depicts the Data handling of the proposed idea, that the data which planned to provide from the proposed idea for the for the enhancement and better bond between the patients and CSSD is the addition of Existing Data Provided to patients and the Data to be added about the CSSD in detailed manner.

Table 1. Distinguished between existing data provided to patients and data to be provided from proposed idea.

Existing data provided to patients	Data to be provide from proposed idea (Including existing data provided)
• Basic details of patients • Diagnosis report • Surgery plan • Surgeon details • Medicine details • Patient's laboratory results • Prescription report • Patient's hospital ID	• Details of surgical equipment • Quality report of instruments used • Basic information of Sterilization • Detailed report of sterility • Step by step process of sterilization • Lot number of instrument sets

Table 1 explains the major importance of Sterilization and CSSD knowledge and showed the difference between existing data provided and Data to be provided from proposed idea. From this table we clearly get to know the basic knowledge of CSSD which also increases among the people and patients. This also helps to enhance the better connection between patients and Sterilization department. Therefore, it leads to the improvement in Sterilization work than now which encourages more sterility in everywhere. This reduces the number and risk of medical error due to sterility.

6   Conclusion and Future Direction

Work done by Central Sterile Service Department (CSSD) is the basis for every single medical procedure performed in a hospital. This department ensures safety by sterilizing instruments. Letting people know about this department enhances the performance of the department. Reduces SSI to a significant amount. It creates a connectivity link between people and CSSD. The structure stated in this paper provides an effective data handling system for CSSD in a secured and gives assurance to the public. The future direction of the work is to develop as a real-world cloud environment.

Acknowledgments. The authors would like to thank Chennai Institute of Technology for providing us with various resources and an unconditional support for carrying out this study.

References

1. ANSI/AAMI/ISO 11137: Sterilization of health care products (2006)
2. Snyders, R., Sykora, C., Leone, C., Sherman, C.A., Babcock, H.: Partnering with central sterile processing department experts to advance infection prevention competency. Am. J. Infect. Control **8**(8), S20–S21 (2020)
3. Dutta, R., Chowdhury, S., Singh, K.K.: IoT-based Healthcare Delivery Services to Promote Transparency and Patient Satisfaction in a Corporate Hospital, pp. 135–151. Machine Learning and the Internet of Medical Things in Healthcare, Academic Press (2021)
4. Ross, V., Amir, A.: COVID-19 pandemic: innovative digital tool using progressive muscle relaxation to promote mental health among frontline healthcare workers. Ann. Emerg. Technol. Comput. (AETiC) **5**(5), 114–119 (2021)
5. ISO 11137–1:2006(en). Sterilization of health care products— Radiation8**8— Part 1: Requirements for development, validation and routine control of a sterilization process for medical devices (2003). https://www.iso.org/obp/ui/#!iso:std:33952:en
6. Nestman, C.S., MS, B.S, CRCST, A.C.E.: Factors Affecting the Leadership of Process Improvement Teams in Sterile Processing (2012)
7. Ran, X., et al.: Innovative applications of patient experience big data in modern hospital management improve healthcare quality. Chin. Med. Sci. J. **35**(4), 366–370 (2020)
8. Surendran, R., Tamilvizhi, T.: Cloud of medical things (CoMT) based smart healthcare framework for resource allocation. In: 3rd Smart Cities Symposium (SCS 2020), IET, pp. 29–34 (2021)
9. Alansari, Z., Soomro, S., Belgaum, M.R., Shamshirband, S.: The rise of Internet of Things (IoT) in big healthcare data: review and open research issues. Prog. Adv. Comput. Intell. Eng. Springer, Singapore (2018). https://doi.org/10.1007/978-981-10-6875-1_66
10. Mahdi, G., Gouaich, A., Michel, F.: Towards an Integrated Approach of Real-Time Coordination for Multi-agent Systems, KES-AMSTA'2010, KES-Agent and Multi-Agent Systems Technologies and Applications, 4th KES International Symposium. Gdynia, Poland (2010)
11. Shrivastava, S., Prasannaraj, P., Rana, B.K., Deepak, S.: PSA/2012/1. Scientific Operating procedures for sterilization practice in India, December (2012)
12. Pardamean, B., Rumanda, R.R.: Integrated model of cloud-based E-medical record for health care organizations. In: 10th WSEAS International Conference on E-activities (2011)
13. Sawaneh, I.A., Kamara, A., Koroma, J.H.: A computerized patient's database management system. Int. J. Comput. Sci. Inf. Technol. Res. **6**(2) (2018)
14. Shah, R.A., Qian, Y., Mahdi, G.: Group feature selection via structural sparse logistic regression for IDS, HPCC 2016. In: 18th IEEE International Conference on High Performance Computing and Communications, Sydney, Australia (2016)
15. Evans, R.P., Clyburn, T.A., Moucha, C.S., Prokuski, L.: Surgical site infection prevention and control: an emerging paradigm. Instr. Course Lect. **60**, 539–43 (2011). PMID: 21553796
16. National Collaborating Centre for Women's and Children's Health (UK). Surgical Site Infection: Prevention and Treatment of Surgical Site Infection. London: RCOG Press, October PMID: 21698848 (2008)
17. https://www.iso.org/standard/33952.html
18. Pradheep, N., Saroja, M.: a cloud computing solution for securely storing and accessing patients medical data. J. Adv. Res. Dyn. Control Syst. 12- Special Issue (2017)
19. Tamilvizhi, T., Parvatha Varthini, B.: Cessation of overloaded host by increase the inter-migration time in cloud data center. J. Theor. Appl. Inf. Technol. **95**(3), 654–660 (2017)
20. Hoefel, H.H.K., et al.: Bundles for the central sterile supply department. Am. J. Infect. Control **47**(11), 1352–1357 (2019)

21. Basu, D., et al.: The importance of paper records and their preservation period in a central sterile supply department: an experience from a oncology center in eastern India. J. Infect. Pub. Health **10**(5), 685–687 (2017)
22. Ali, B., Alshurooqi, R.S.: Mobile-based pressure sore prediction and prevention system (PSPPs). In: 3rd Smart Cities Symposium (SCS 2020), IET, pp. 415–420 (2021). https://doi.org/10.1007/978-981-10-6875-1_66
23. Vizhi, T., Varthini, B.P.: Online vaccines and immunizations service based on resource management techniques in cloud computing. Biomed. Res. (India), (Special Issue 1), S392–S399 (2016)

AI, Expert Systems and Big Data Analytics

Data Mining Approach Improving Decision-Making Competency Along the Business Digital Transformation Journey: A Literature Review

Hyrmet Mydyti[✉] and Arbana Kadriu

CST Faculty, South-East European University, Tetovo, Republic of Macedonia
{hm28315,a.kadriu}@seeu.edu.mk

Abstract. Advanced analytics and artificial intelligence are drivers of deep analysis and change in the perspective of businesses' digital transformation. Data mining, as an essential part of artificial intelligence, is a powerful digital technology, which provides guidance for businesses in terms of analyzing information and predicting in business. The key advantage of the application of the data mining approach in business is the impact by improving customers' experience and decision-making. The aim of this research is to present a theoretical model to understand the researchers' perspectives on data mining application in different business areas and digital transformation, and the discussion of some benefits and challenges of the data mining application in improving decision-making along the digital transformation of businesses. Moreover, this paper analyzes how the implementation of data mining techniques in business can lead to an increased efficiency and business productivity along their digital transformation journey.

Keywords: Advanced analytics · Digital transformation · Data mining in business · Decision-making

1 Introduction

Businesses are striving to adapt their strategies to the digital era, by incorporating novel technologies in their business models, which places more significance on the subject of processes and operations management, and, more essentially assesses their businesses' success of becoming digital [62, 81].

Advanced analytics (AA) and artificial intelligence (AI) are powerful digital technologies, which provide guidance for businesses, guidance on analyzing information, predicting and monitoring processes in business [83]. The analytics systems and intelligent applications used by businesses prove the importance of result delivery in improving decision-making and productivity, efficiency and effectiveness [5].

Data mining (DM), as a confluence of statistics and machine learning (ML), is the process of sorting through a high volume of information stored in repositories, corporate

© ICST Institute for Computer Sciences, Social Informatics and Telecommunications Engineering 2021
Published by Springer Nature Switzerland AG 2021. All Rights Reserved
M. H. Miraz et al. (Eds.): iCETiC 2021, LNICST 395, pp. 129–146, 2021.
https://doi.org/10.1007/978-3-030-90016-8_9

databases, and data warehouses to identify correlations, patterns, and trends and set relationships through data analysis [55, 67]. Through the DM approach, businesses will alleviate the process of reducing costs and enhancing customer experience along their digital transformation (DT) journey [8, 74]. Businesses will become more customer-oriented by advancing their services and saving their customers' time by strengthening their processes [12]. The issue of DM approach delivering linkages between businesses and customers has prompted to be highly significant for this research.

This research aims to analyze how the implementation of DM approach in businesses can lead to an improved decision-making and increased efficiency. The theoretical contribution and practical implication is to understand the researchers' insights and perspectives on DM along the business DT. We place two research questions: (i) RQ1. Which techniques and tools can be helpful if a business thinks about starting to use DM aiming to improve decision-making? (ii) RQ2. Which business areas have used and benefited from DM techniques along the business DT? Both questions have been answered using the literature review approach. After the introduction, the methodology for the analysis of DM research and studies is presented, followed by perspectives on DT, DT technologies, on advanced and big data analytics (BDA) techniques, on DM applications in business areas, benefits and challenges of applying DM, conclusion and recommendations on future work.

2   Methodology

The performed study covers the ensuing steps: perspectives on the DT, identification of DT technologies, perspectives on the DM and other advanced and big data analytics techniques, identification of DM application areas and identification of benefits and challenges of applying DM (Fig. 1).

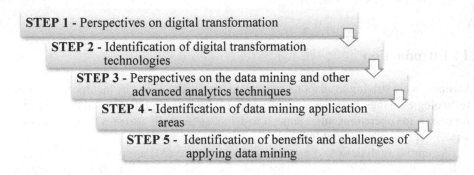

Fig. 1. Methodology workflow

3 Perspectives on Digital Transformation

3.1 Digital Transformation

DT encourages the integration of digital technologies and digital capabilities in innovative business models [68]. Certainly, the role of the digital maturity model (DMM), covering business dimensions, as an approach to empowering DT of businesses by evaluating the situation of the business transformation journey is a very important facet [14]. Agile has become a driving framework in the DT of businesses.

Reis et al. [65] outline DT as the practice of novel digital technologies with the aim of enabling main business enhancements such as improving customer experience, simplifying operations or developing new business models. Accordingly, DT surpasses justly digitizing resources and outcomes in value and incomes being produced.

Deloitte [14] emphasizes that one of the elements keeping the communications industry back from expansive growth in DT is the lack of a clear roadmap. The DMM is a useful means to enable guidance for a clear path throughout the transformation journey. In addition, China Mobile asserts that the DMM will be very helpful and, as a result, strengthens decision-making.

Morakanyane et al. [49] note two fundamental DT drivers such as digital capabilities and digital technologies. At the foundation of all DT attempts, are digital technologies. Digital technologies construct opportunities that businesses leverage These transformational opportunities have the power to transform business models, operational processes and customer experiences. Thus, businesses benefit from the impact of DT.

Orfanidis [54] hints at the digital capabilities as analytical capabilities, business and IT integration, unified data and processes, and efficient delivery of solutions as the foundations contributing to the formation of digital capabilities in businesses. Morakanyane et al. [49] hint at the digital technologies such as mobile technologies, internet of things (IoT), cloud technologies, BDA, etc. as technologies that businesses adopt to improve their daily operations.

DT is considered as an evolutionary process since it changes with time, and the impacts bring a major change to the business. Similarly, digital technologies as fundamental drivers of DT are evolving. The main impact of DT is value creation. This value is accomplished by both the business and its customers [11, 49].

Assessing Progress of the Business Digital Transformation. The DMM enables decision-makers to give a view on matters of digital strategizing to evaluate and implement the required change to the target areas [4].

The results show that the DMM is to assess the digital capabilities mostly across some common business dimensions, such as customers, strategies, technologies, operations, organization and culture. The consulted papers on identifying most common dimensions of DT have been included above in Table 1.

The strategy, in the perspective of DT concentrates on how the business changes to grow its competitive strength through digital delivering in facility [80]. The customer experience concentrates on the need of tackling customers' demands, and benefits as a foundation for evolving digital service offerings [56]. Technology advances the success of strategy by supporting to collect, protect, analyze and utilize data to respond the

Table 1. Dimensions of digital transformation

Industry/field of study	Strategies	Customers	Technologies	Operations	Organizations and culture
Telecommunications [80]	√	√	√	√	√
SME [42]	√		√		√
Business [21]	√	√	√	√	√
Corporate [19]	√	√	√	√	√
Telecommunications [14]	√	√	√	√	√

demands of clients at low cost and expenses [29]. The operations dimension focuses on the capacities that bolster the service provision. Enhanced maturity within this context proves a better digitized and manageable operation [76]. The organization and culture dimension outlines as an organizational culture with governance and talent processes to bolster improvement along the DMM curve [56].

Driving Framework in Business' Digital Transformation. Agile, the modern approach, has become a driving framework in the DT of businesses. Agile serves as a unique tool to drive DT as it simplifies how technology is used for handling the operations of the business. Agile methodology is the guiding beacon to revolutionize the whole business [1, 77]. Gunasekaran et al. [25] highlight that agile provides stability and flexibility, continuous improvement, risk reduction, great communication and engagement, transparency and high quality.

O'Regan [51] introduces agile as a popular lightweight software development methodology. Agile claims to be more reactive to customer demands than traditional methods and its supporters consider that it leads in higher quality and productivity, and faster time to market and enhanced customer satisfaction.

3.2 The Future of Digital Transformation and Advanced Analytics

Davenport et al. [13] claim that in the future, many segments, such as business models, customer service options, and customer behaviors will be influenced and transformed by AI. AI intelligence will enable e.g., online retailers to predict and know customers' preferences and ship items to customers without an official order; as a result, AI will transform business strategies, business models, and customer behaviors and will be used in areas such as analytics and predictive behaviors.

Makridakis [40] asserts the impact of DT on businesses will be significant, resulting in well interconnected businesses with decision-making according to the exploitation of big data and strengthened, competition among businesses. In general, AI technologies will influence how businesses operate. In addition, DT of businesses has significant impact on different aspects of society, such as our lives and work, our shopping, our entertainment habits and our employment patterns.

McCormick et al. [45] assume how AI technologies will be assimilated into analytics practices, giving business users remarkable access to powerful insights that drive action. Digital technologies, AI, big data, and IoT, will grow businesses' access to data, broaden the variety of data that can be analyzed, and advance the level of sophistication of the resulting insight. An insights-driven business exploits and applies data and analytics at each possibility to distinguish its products and customer experiences.

4   Digital Transformation Technologies

Ziyadin et al. [38], list digital technologies as in Table 2 that change business models. Wiesböck and Hess [84] refer to technologies – social, mobile, analytics, and CC technologies as digital technologies. Hausberg et al. [28] consider the major technological areas, which enable DT. Those areas include, cyber-physical systems, IoT, cloud computing (CC), big data, AI, augmented and virtual reality. Schwertner [69] highlights that maturing digital businesses are focused on integrating digital technologies. The use of analytics empowers business decision-making and the dynamism of decision-making has to adapt due to altering needs and transforming technologies [78]. Telegescu [79] outlines that businesses have possibilities to enfold the advantages that the technologies of the digital economy bring. Finally, the results show that BDA is one of accelerators of DT of businesses. The consulted papers in identifying potential DT technologies have been included in Table 2.

Table 2. Digital transformation accelerators.

Author/s	Big data analytics	IoT	Cloud	Mobile	Social networks
Ziyadin *et al.* [38]	√	√		√	√
Wiesböck and Hess [84]	√		√	√	√
Hausberg *et al.* [28]	√	√	√		
Schwertner [69]	√	√	√	√	√
Telegescu [79]	√	√	√	√	

4.1   Cloud Technologies

Mazumdar and Alharasheh [44] present the key attributes of CC such as on-demand self-service through a secure portal, scalability and elasticity, pay per use, ubiquitous access and location-independent resource pooling. The on-demand self-service attribute is introduced as an independent service, without interacting with service providers in provisioning server, network, and storage capabilities. Scalability and elasticity attributes are introduced as increasing or reducing resources elastically to maintain cost efficiencies.

Neware and Khan [50] define CC as a model for offering adequate, on-demand network connection to a shared pool of configurable resources and introduce CC's three major service models. 1) Infrastructure-as-a-Service is addressed as an on-demand service of virtualization by offering virtual machine, storage infrastructure and network. 2) Platform-as-a-Service builds application or settings to build application by offering virtual machine, operating system, application and development structure. 3) Software-as-a-Service offers on-demand cloud-based foundation for software to the end user, as a whole package.

Quinn et al. [61], through a survey, show how cloud technology contributed to decision-making and improved decision-making in comparison to previous systems. The authors assert that CC provides benefits for decision-making, lowers cost, and alleviates systems administration.

Lastly, Benlian et al. [3] highlight how, on a societal and economic level, CC is an enabler of the DT of industries. CC offers the infrastructure that has driven other key digital trends comprising mobile computing, the IoT, big data, and AI, thus disrupting current business models, and powering DT.

4.2 Internet of Things

Pflaum and Gölzer [57] affirm that smart products, which are at the heart of the IoT, drive the future DT of business and change its business model.

Zeinab and Elmustafa [48] elaborate the IoT as a novel technology, which affords numerous applications to join things to things and humans to things. The applications enabled through the IoT include smart healthcare, homes, energy, cities and environments. The authors consider two major challenges of the IoT, and they are as follows: the coexistence with different networks and big data size of the IoT. The combination of data from several resources with the IoT makes possible the development of applications and advanced services that can combine situation and context awareness into the decision-making components.

Coetzee and Eksteen [10] provide predictions of the future of the IoT, the impact of the IoT on society and an overview of the challenges and highlight the fact that trust and privacy are likely to be the major obstacles in the IoT uptake. The key challenge areas are categorized as follows: 1) privacy, identity management, security and access control; 2) standardization and interoperability; 3) data deluge. Several interesting applications as identified are environment monitoring; intelligent environments; retail, logistics and supply chain management; and healthcare. The IoT is presented as a potential and as a supporter in DT processes.

4.3 Big Data Analytics

Elgendy and Elragal [17] refer to big data as datasets that are not only big, but also high in variety and velocity. More importantly, decision makers can gain valuable insights from such big data, ranging from day-to-day actions, which can be provided using BDA. BDA is the implementation of AA techniques on big data. Several advanced data analytics have been elaborated, such as social media analytics, sentiment analysis, advanced data visualization, etc. BDA provides opportunities in areas, such as fraud detection, customer intelligence, and supply chain management. Moreover, its advantages deliver to various domains.

Memon et al. [46] introduce BDA as a method for looking at big data to reveal hidden patterns, incomprehensible relationship and other important data that can be utilized on enhanced decisions. In addition, Hadoop is elaborated as an open source distributed processing framework that manages data processing and big data storage. Predictive analytics is emphasized as a subsequent operation whereupon it utilizes a range of measurable, displaying, information-mining, and ML strategies and verifiable information, along these lines allowing experts to make forecast customer behavior and other future developments.

Dremel et al. [15] consider that the DT of businesses includes establishing BDA capabilities and that the deployment of the establishment is a challenging process. BDA enable evidence-based decisions for digital business opportunities. Business benefit from the potential of BDA and BDA support evidence based decision-making and enable new digital services.

5 Advanced and Big Data Analytics Techniques Empowering Business Decision-Making

Elgendy and Elragal [18] present how BDA techniques can be implemented, in the context of DT, to enable business transformation and, specifically, to improve decision-making by uncovering hidden insights, and beneficial knowledge. The main aim of the decision makers of the business is to enhance decision-making, insights, and knowledge through the application of BDA techniques.

The authors, in their study [64, 58, 82, 70, 23], provide several advanced analytics (AA) techniques. Finally, the results show that DM, ML, and NLP are the key techniques of big data and AA of DT of the businesses. The consulted papers in identifying potential advanced and BDA techniques have been included in Table 3.

Table 3. Analysis on advanced analytics techniques

Authors	Machine learning	Text mining (NLP)	Data mining	Social network analysis	Visual analytics	Web mining	Statistics
Vivekananth & Baptist [82]	√	√	√	√			
Sadiku et al. [70]	√	√	√		√	√	
Galetsia et al. [23]	√	√	√	√	√	√	√
Rehman et al. [64]	√	√	√				√
Prabhu et al. [58]	√	√	√				

5.1 Data Mining

Reddy [63] presents DM as a knowledge discovery process (KDD) by analyzing huge amounts of data from different views and turning them into valuable information affecting different areas of human life, and incorporating business, science, etc.

Siguenza-Guzman et al. [73] categorize functions, or models, of DM based on the task done: association, classification, clustering, and regression. Three DM analysis techniques have been considered: classical statistics, AI, and ML. Unlike other techniques, DM benefits additionally include extracting patterns/trends, and predicting behavior. The authors describe the mining process as an interactive sequence of steps. The first step takes place the integration of data belonging to different sources and formats. In the second step, the cleansing process is applied. Additionally, the transformation of data into an appropriate format is applied. In the third step, knowledge is extracted from the transformed data. Lastly, knowledge is visualized to the user.

Sharma et al. [72] elaborate the implementation of DM projects by pursuing the KDD. The KDD process consists of a number of stages, such as business understanding, data understanding, data preparation, modelling, evaluation and deployment. In the modelling (DM) phase, different techniques are designated and applied. The evaluation phase is described as consisting of thoroughly evaluating the model and reviewing the steps that it accomplishes the business goals. Lastly, the deployment model is described as a formation of the model and usually is not the end of the project.

Data Mining Tools as Modern Solutions. Gergin et al. [24] point out that data science and DM tools are the modern solutions that the businesses are using in this DT age. Businesses improve the cost efficiency of quality control processes with the application of DM methods. Data are processed on DM tools for understanding and inspecting the patterns and relationships. The results on identifying potential DM tools and their advantages have been included in Table 4.

Table 4. Data mining tools [16, 33, 35, 36]

Data mining tool: type	Advantages
Weka (Java): ML	Easy to use – easy user interface, supports numerous DM tasks
Rapid Miner (Java): Statistical Analysis; DM; Predictive Analysis	Visualization - user-friendly GUI, enormous flexibility, offers procedures (such as attribute selection and outlier detection)
R (C, Fortran, R): Statistical Computing	Strong choice for DM tasks, very fast implementation of many machine learning algorithms, better graphics, has specific data types
Orange (C++, Python, C): ML; DM; Data visualization	Better debugger, shortest scripts, poor statistics

5.2 Machine Learning

ML is the study of computer algorithms and statistical models to execute tasks without explicit instructions, such as by using pattern recognition and inference [52]. The implementation of data-intensive ML techniques can be noticed in science, technology and commerce, as a result contributing to more evidence-based decision-making [34].

Simon et al. [75] introduce the classification of ML in two categories, such as supervised learning (SL) and unsupervised learning (UL). Accordingly, the authors tackle deep learning and big data as important fields. "Deep learning algorithms extract complex data patterns, across a hierarchical learning process by analyzing and learning vast reserves of unsupervised data (big data)".

Bastanlar and Ozuysal [2] introduce the classification of ML tasks when one considers the desired output of a machine-learned system. UL techniques comprise only the input values in the training data, and the learning algorithm comprehends hidden structure in the training data dependent to them. SL techniques demand the value of the output variable for each training sample to be acknowledged.

5.3 Natural Language Processing

NLP is defined as a field of AI, computer science and linguistics preoccupied with the computers - human languages interacts [20].

NLP is vital because it helps us to construct models and processes which take chunks of information as input in the form of voice or text or both and manipulates them as per the algorithm inside the computer. Thus, the output of an NLP system processes speech as well as written text [32]. NLP applications compose numerous areas of studies, such as NLP text processing and summarization, machine translation, speech recognition, AI and expert systems, and so forth [2].

Friedman et al. [22] point out how NLP systems are becoming advanced to ease decision-making, besides supporting information and relations extraction. In addition to NLP techniques, through a method make NLP applications enable decision-making.

6 Data Mining Applications in Different Business Domains

The major goal of the overview of DM applications is to understand the researchers' perspectives on DM implementation in different domains and DT. DM is implemented in different categories of businesses and impacts driving DT in different businesses [63]. The study of the application of DM is to alleviate the process of comprehending businesses in refining their strategies to a new technology epoch. As a result, a number of research papers are selected to help understand and explain DM in business domains of a) Retail, b) E-commerce, c) Banking and d) Manufacturing.

6.1 Data Mining in Retail

Chen et al. [9] present an analysis to help businesses better understand their customers and as a result convey customer-centric marketing more successfully. The authors demonstrated a case study in how business intelligence for an online retailer is built by tools of

DM techniques to obtain competitive advantages on the market. The study facilitates the process of understanding consumers in the perspective of profitability, and implements appropriate decision-making and marketing strategies, as e result accelerates DT efforts. Association analyses were supportive in the context of establishing customer-buying patterns.

Castelo-Branco et al. [7] build a body of knowledge, so that a project can utilize the techniques related with DM in retail sales, at the same time present concepts as market basket analysis, association rules and cross-selling and up-selling. The DM implementation success stories are also introduced, as follows: 1) The Hewlett-Packard analytics team implemented a manually driven pilot in the online store and call center. Ultimately, the pilot gave importance to the analytics and data-driven decision-making at Hewlett-Packard. 2) The Swedish interior giant IKEA featured image recognition and augmented reality and resulted in increased customer satisfaction and fewer returned products. 3) Macy, the upmarket department store, utilizes big data to provide a more intelligent customer experience. 4) Amazon Go is the technology that is assumed to guide the approach to the future of AI in retail. The essential concept behind is that it resembles a store that blossoms on the principle of no checkout requests. 5) The Starbucks CTO proposed to combine the transaction evidence with other inputs, like weather, promotions, etc. in order to provide better personalized service.

Kaur and Jagdev [37] research the influence of changes brought in the retail sector by big data. It is highlighted that retail is entirely reliant on BDA. The mining of customers analytics is to increase profits, increase growth and be competitive, whether it is in-store or online. Through digital technologies, as a fundamental driver of DT, retailers make well-informed decisions using online data. Next, it is demonstrated how ML takes big data to gather, to utilize and to predict important insight about customers spending patterns and how these patterns experience changes. Big data is intelligent to directly affect sales by collecting data about consumer's exact spending habits. For example, Amazon responds to the competitive market promptly because of its analytical platform, which provides dynamic pricing, and compared to other retailers, it makes this change about every 3 months. Similarly, Metro Group retailers use retail analytics to identify movement of goods within the stores to enable real time information to concerned store personnel and customers for their ease of use. Furthermore, Staples use Hadoop and big data technologies to predict sales by processing around 10 million data transactions per week across 1100 retail outlets in the US.

6.2 Data Mining in e-commerce

Ismail et al. [31] present the DM process for e-commerce. Benefits and challenges of DM are the topic within the paper. The tackled benefits of DM in e-commerce are related to planning, forecasting, basket analysis, segmentation, etc. The tackled e-commerce DM challenges are related to spider identification, data transformations, etc. Herein the concept of DM in e-commerce is elaborated as an integration of statistics, databases and AI with some subjects with the intention of better decision-making. CC, as a key of technology in the age of DT, in e-commerce is considered to effectively utilize resources and reduce costs for companies embracing efficient DM. Additionally, some common

DM tools are described in detail. The end product of DM builds a possibility for decision makers to be capable to pursue their buying customers' patterns, need trends and locations, bringing in the effective way of the strategic decision for the advancement and the revenue of the business.

Zhao [6] studies big data algorithms and their implementations in e-commerce to deliver some recommendations to e-commerce businesses along the implementation of big DM. In the age of DT, big DM perform an important role in the improvement of c-commerce and it is the future of global e-commerce. The challenges of ecommerce applications are presented such as the enhancement of DM algorithms, the enhancement of mobile data and social network mining. Mobile e-commerce is presented as fast developing and changing consumers' behavior and habits. Similarly, social network-related e-commerce is presented as a novel significant e-business model. The presented e-commerce models use big data technology, eliminate risks, analyze market state, make strategies, increase profits, etc. In the paper, eBay is introduced as a model of the largest online business website and DM is the priority. EBay's big data platform comprises of three layers such as the data platform, the data integration and the data access layer. In the end, the presented goals of big DM algorithms in e-commerce are predominantly for: 1) optimization of the platform to advance the customer e-shopping experience; 2) enhancement of the capacity of CRM to improve decision-making; 3) provision of personalized services to advance the e-sales; 4) provision of value-added service.

6.3 Data Mining in Banking

Preethi and Vijayalakshmi [59] study the different DM techniques that can be practiced in the banking area to improve its performance and reduce costs. The authors consider handling enormous transactional data and making decision is an essential task; on the other hand, manual and conservative processing of decision-making is retarding, time consuming and error prone. In this situation, DM techniques offer an effective form of processing and decision-making. In the paper, two areas of banking application tackled are CRM and fraud detection. In addition, DM, by involving processes makes it possible to use the information in applications such as fraud detection, market analysis, production control, science exploration, etc. A CRM system is mainly used by banks to build brand value and find and understand their customers' needs. In this case, DM techniques are used to discover the new customers by using clustering techniques and to retain the customers by using Apriori algorithms. Furthermore, algorithms are another topic that has been tackled. Fraud detection is the next important area elaborated since fraudulent actions are very concerning for banks and most banks are utilizing a hybrid approach to detect fraud patterns. In the end, in the context of DT, it is concluded that by implementing data-mining techniques in data processing and decision-making, banks increase their profit tremendously.

Hasheminejad and Khorrami [27] review DM techniques utilized for analyzing bank customers consequently to designate more effective marketing strategies. Elaboration is performed for certain DM techniques, which are used to support the businesses to make decisions. CRM is considered having the aim to increase the business relationships with customers in this paper. The study of the analysis on customers by implementing DM will be easier. Importance is given to revealing the customers and their demands, as a pillar of DT. Through customer clustering, banks can detect the customers' crucial attributes. Customer clustering is highlighted to be a facilitator on directing the implementation of design marketing strategies for each group of customers. A conduction of research on data sets of recent studies of different researchers is performed. DM techniques are reviewed and summarized in order to identify customers' behavior, which results in the banking industry gaining a competitive advantage.

6.4 Data Mining in Manufacturing

Harding and Shahbaz [26] review applications of DM in manufacturing. This paper has a target to exclusively represent the relation of DM to the manufacturing industry and how DM is becoming important in the face of DT. DM is applied to support decision-making processes. The study in this paper has essentially focused on algorithm applications. An in-depth study has been conducted related to the applications in areas such as manufacturing systems, decision support systems, etc.

Oliff & Liu [53] present the utilization of DM techniques and the advancement of their usage in Industry 4.0 ready factories. Hence, the methodology contoured embraces the principles of DM and utilizes them to help decision-making with regard to quality. Advanced data analytics and ML, as an integral part of DT, are crucial digital technologies and DM and knowledge discovery for utilization of enormous amount of data to comprehend the manufacturing processing are highlighted in the paper. Algorithms are the next subject matter. A study is conducted with the intention to elaborate the best way of utilization of DM to advance assembly and quality control processes and to apply into current systems without drawback. Most of the algorithms are based on Rule Based Learning where those function by means of mathematical relationships.

Dai et al. [11] bring an overview and discuss the demands and challenges of BDA in manufacturing IoT (MIoT). The analytics of MIoT, as a key driver of DT, offers benefits in manufacturing processes. Subsequently, data analytics plays a significant role in extracting information, estimating the upcoming events and predicting the increment of products. Consumer behavior prediction has a vital role in the manufacturing area. The life cycle of BDA for MIoT comprises of the three stages. The challenges of data analytics tackled include: 1) data temporal and spatial correlation, 2) efficient DM schemes and 3) privacy and security. This paper also develops a system prototype in order to prove the feasibility of distributed computing models in MIoT.

7   Benefits of Applying Data Mining

DM adoption is beneficial with regard to driving business digitalizing of processes as DM enables predictive analytics, improves decision-making, increases profitability, enables risk mitigation, and signifies customer behavior [68]. DT makes possible novel business models that depend on smart data analytics, which are applied to obtain new insights and better digitalized decision-making [66]. The study of the decision-making benefit of DM is to ease the process of encouraging businesses in adapting their strategies to a new digital epoch.

7.1 Improvement of Decision-Making

Milovic and Milovic [47] tackle the context of prediction in two phases such as the learning phase and the phase of decision-making. The phase of decision-making by people is usually considered not qualitative when there is a huge amount of data to be classified. As a result, insights obtained with the usage of DM practices can be useful to take effective decisions that will enhance the success of an organization. Pulakkazhy and Balan [60] assume that useful information is hidden within the volume of data, which can be utilized for decision-making processes if they are revealed. Businesses that apply DM techniques immensely benefit since interesting patterns and knowledge can be mined. Ltifi et al. [39], in their paper, propose a model with visual DM methods for supporting dynamic DM. Moreover, the authors note the importance of trends such as visualization, DM and dynamic decision-making. Integration of visual DM techniques in real-time decision-making is crucial for treating compound, complicated and temporal data, and application of DM techniques allows digitalizing the processes. As a result, decision makers are able to visually predict trends in the temporal data and their behaviors. Manita et al. [41] demonstrate the increasing interest of digitalization in businesses and how digital technology affects businesses. Moreover, the paper brings out the significance of implementing digital strategies to provide regulators with the necessary modifications in the context of DT. Data analytics and DM improve the effectiveness of decision-making and enable to predict the performance of businesses with a higher level of confidence.

8 Challenges and Limitations of Applying Data Mining

A few research papers studied will ease the process of revealing the challenges and limitations of applying DM in businesses. The study intends to contribute an approach on how to apply DM by taking into account the limitations coped with.

Zain and Rahman [43] list the five common challenges and disadvantages of applying DM such as technology, skills, inconsistent or missing data as well as privacy and data security. Poor technology utilized in DM prompts the poor handling the data, differently powerful technology prompts the more effective the DM processes as well as can avoid the problems regarding technology. Skills are crucial to handle and manage the vast amount of data, consequently the DM application. Inconsistent data or missing data could give a big and many negative impacts towards businesses. DM is a violation to privacy and a risk to data security due to the fact that it is a threat through the objective of preserving statistics secured and guarding against the intrusion on privacy.

Sharma et al. [71], in their paper list three limitations of DM as follows: security and privacy issues, and misusage of/unreliable information. Businesses collect information about their customers in many ways and the possibility of violating privacy of its users is possible. Security is considered a high-risk challenge since data are collected and the probability of hacking the collected data is a serious matter for businesses. And, lastly, the misuse of information/inaccurate information is considered to be very harmful and cause serious consequences in case it will be used for decision-making by unethical people.

Ikenna et al. [30] list challenges faced with implementing DM in a business as follows: problem of poor data quality, employee empowerment, data integrity and security issues and complexity of integration. DM techniques empower managerial decision-making processes in a business. The authors consider that applying DM techniques to a business problem entails disposal of high quality data, which are usually primary data produced within the business functions. Moreover, finding a DM expert for a DM project within a business can present a challenge. Furthermore, integrity and security are considered crucial challenges with any data collection that is shared and utilized in a business. Finally, complexity of integration is considered a critical issue because the ability to effectively integrate DM projects into the business processes is a difficult task.

9 Conclusions

An inclusive research of data mining has been carried out, and different researchers' perspectives, insights and overviews of domains of application of data mining approach have been provided, together with several important aspects of benefits and challenges of data mining along the business digital transformation journey.

The paper demonstrates advantages and impact of business digital transformation assessing progress - maturity model, and most common digital transformation dimensions. Moreover, the IoT, cloud and big data analytics, as the best suited digital transformation technologies, have been presented as accelerators of digital transformation of businesses. Herewith, data mining, machine learning and natural language processing are the main techniques of big data and advanced analytics of digital transformation of the businesses have been considered. In addition, Weka, RapidMiner, Orange and R have been outlined as important data mining tools.

More importantly, the paper introduces advanced analytics and big data techniques tools by demonstrating their significance and digital transformation as the necessary trend, which influence businesses. The challenges of applying data mining are as follows: technology, skills, problem of poor data quality, misuse of information/inaccurate information, complexity of integration as well as data security, and privacy. The benefits of data mining include facilitating the process of streamlining decision-making, increasing efficiency and business productivity and enhancing customer experience along their digital transformation journey. The data mining technology is being adopted in many domains of businesses for its benefits. The main business domains where data mining is being implemented include retail, e-commerce, banking and manufacturing.

This paper helps businesses in particular, as key beneficiaries, and managers, to understand the positive aspects of data mining along their business digital transformation. Our future research goal is to conduct a case study, based on empirical studies, collect and analyze data, and obtain feedback from a business case study on using the advantages of the data mining techniques and approach in improving decision-making competency along the digital transformation journey.

References

1. Balashova, E., Gromova, E.: Russian industrial sector in the conditions of the 4th industrial revolution. In: IOP Conference Series: Materials Science and Engineering, vol. 404, p. 012014. IOP Publishing (2018)

2. Baştanlar, Y., Özuysal, M.: Introduction to machine learning. In: Yousef, M., Allmer, J. (eds.) miRNomics: MicroRNA Biology and Computational Analysis. MMB, vol. 1107, pp. 105–128. Humana Press, Totowa, NJ (2014). https://doi.org/10.1007/978-1-62703-748-8_7
3. Benlian, A., et al.: The transformative value of cloud computing: a decoupling, platformization, and recombination theoretical framework. J. Manag. Inf. Syst. **35**(3), 719–739 (2018)
4. Boström, E., Celik, C.: Towards a maturity model for digital strategizing - a qualitative study of how an organization can analyze and assess their digital business strategy. Dpt. of informatics, UMEA Universitet. Academic Press (2017)
5. Bughin, J., et al.: Artificial intelligence - The next digital frontier?. https://apo.org.au/node/210501. Accessed 21 May 2021
6. Zhao, X.: A study on the application of big data mining in E-commerce. In: 2018 IEEE 4th ICCC, pp. 1867–1871. IEEE (2018)
7. Castelo-Branco, F., Reis, J.L., Vieira, J.C., Cayolla, R.: Business intelligence and data mining to support sales in retail. In: Rocha, Á., Reis, J.L., Peter, M.K., Bogdanović, Z. (eds.) Marketing and Smart Technologies. SIST, vol. 167, pp. 406–419. Springer, Singapore (2020). https://doi.org/10.1007/978-981-15-1564-4_38
8. Chen, J., et al.: Systems of Insight for Digital Transformation - Using IBM Operational Decision Manager Advanced and Predictive Analytics. IBM Redbooks, USA (2015)
9. Chen, D., et al.: Data mining for the online retail industry - a case study of RFM model-based customer segmentation using data mining. J. Database Mark. Cust. Strategy Manage. **19**(3), 197–208 (2012)
10. Coetzee, L., Eksteen, J.: The Internet of Things-promise for the future - an introduction. In: IST-Africa Conference Proceedings, pp. 1–9. IEEE, Botswana (2011)
11. Dai, et al.: Big data analytics for manufacturing internet of things - opportunities, challenges and enabling technologies. Enterp. Inf. Syst. **14**(9–10), 1279–1303 (2020)
12. Dias, J., et al.: Introducing the next-generation operating model. Introducing the Next-generation Operating Model. McKinsey and Company, New York, 41 (2017)
13. Davenport, T., Guha, A., Grewal, D., Bressgott, T.: How artificial intelligence will change the future of marketing. J. Acad. Mark. Sci. **48**(1), 24–42 (2019). https://doi.org/10.1007/s11747-019-00696-0
14. Deloitte: Digital Maturity Model - Achieving digital maturity to drive growth. https://www.tmforum.org/wp-content/uploads/2018/08/Deloitte-DMM.pdf. Accessed 21 May 2021
15. Dremel, C., et al.: How AUDI AG established big data analytics in Its DT. MIS Q. Exec. **16**(2), 81–100 (2017)
16. Dušanka, D., et al.: A comparison of contemporary data mining tools. In: IS 2017, 4(6). Serbia (2017)
17. Elgendy, N., Elragal, A.: Big data analytics: a literature review paper. In: Perner, P. (ed.) ICDM 2014. LNCS (LNAI), vol. 8557, pp. 214–227. Springer, Cham (2014). https://doi.org/10.1007/978-3-319-08976-8_16
18. Elgendy, N., Elragal, A.: Big data analytics in support of the decision-making process. Procedia Comput. Sci. **100**(2016), 1071–1084 (2016)
19. Eremina, Y., et al.: Digital maturity and corporate performance - the case of the baltic states. JOItmC **5**(3), 54 (2019)
20. Fabian, R., Alexandru-Nicolae, M.: Natural language processing implementation on Romanian ChatBot. In: SMO 2009. WSEAS, Hungary (2009)
21. Felch, V., et al.: Maturity models in the age of Industry 4.0 - Do the available models correspond to the needs of business practice?. In: HICSS, pp. 5165–5174 (2019)
22. Friedman, C., et al.: Natural language processing - state of the art and prospects for significant progress, a workshop sponsored by the national library of medicine. J. Biomed. Inform. **46**(5), 765–773 (2013)

23. Galetsi, P., Katsaliaki, K., Kumar, S.: Big data analytics in health sector - theoretical framework, techniques and prospects. Int. J. Inf. Manage. **50**, 206–216 (2020)
24. Gergin, Z., et al.: Data Mining Approach for Quality Control Process Improvement. (2019)
25. Gunasekaran, A., et al.: Agile manufacturing - an evolutionary review of practices. Int. J. Prod. Res. **57**(15–16), 5154–5174 (2019)
26. Harding, A., Shahbaz, M., Kusiak, A.: Data mining in manufacturing - a review. J. Manuf. Sci. Eng. Acme **128**, 969–976 (2006)
27. Hasheminejad, H., Khorrami, M.: Data mining techniques for analyzing bank customers - a survey. Intell. Decis. Technol. **12**(3), 303–321 (2018)
28. Hausberg, P., et al.: Research streams on digital transformation from a holistic business perspective - a systematic literature review and citation network analysis. J. Bus. Econ. **89**(8–9), 931–963 (2019)
29. Hie, P.: Impact of transforming organizational culture and digital transformation governance toward digital maturity in Indonesian banks. Int. Rev. Manag. Mark. **9**(6), 51–57 (2019)
30. Ikenna, O., et al.: Review of data mining as a tool for organization's growth and productivity. IJCSMC **9**(3), 284–290 (2014)
31. Ismail, M., et al.: Data mining in electronic commerce - benefits and challenges. Int. J. Commun. Netw. Syst. Sci. **8**(12), 501 (2015)
32. Jain, A., et al.: Natural language processing. J. Comput. Sci. Eng. **6**(1), 161–167 (2018)
33. Janoščová, R.: Mining Big Data in WEKA. In: 11th International workshop on Knowledge Management, pp. 29–39. Slovakia (2016)
34. Jordan, I., Mitchell, M.: Machine learning - trends, perspectives, and prospects. Science **349**(6245), 255–260 (2015)
35. Jovic, A., et al.: An overview of free software tools for general data mining. In: 37th MIPRO, pp. 1112–1117. IEEE, Croatia (2014)
36. Kaur, K., Dhiman, S.: Review of data mining with Weka tool. Int. J. Eng. Comput. Sci. **4**(8), 41–44 (2016)
37. Kaur, R., Jagdev, G.: Big data in retail sector - an evolution that turned to a revolution. Int. J. Res. Stud. Comput. Sci. Eng. **4**(4), 43–52 (2017)
38. Ziyadin, S., Suieubayeva, S., Utegenova, A.: Digital transformation in business. In: Ashmarina, S.I., Vochozka, M., Mantulenko, V.V. (eds.) ISCDTE 2019. LNNS, vol. 84, pp. 408–415. Springer, Cham (2020). https://doi.org/10.1007/978-3-030-27015-5_49
39. Ltifi, H., et al.: Enhanced visual data mining process for dynamic decision-making. Knowl. Based Syst. **112**, 166–181 (2016)
40. Makridakis, S.: The forthcoming AI revolution - Its impact on society and firms. Futures **90**, 46–60 (2017)
41. Manita, R., et al.: The digital transformation of external audit and its impact on corporate governance. Technol. Forecast. Soc. Change **150**, 119751 (2020)
42. Williams, et al.: Digital maturity models for small and medium-sized enterprises - a systematic LR. In: ISPIM Conference Proceedings, pp. 1–15. ISPIM, Italy (2019)
43. Zain, M.S.I.M., Rahman, S.A.: Challenges of applying data mining in knowledge management towards organization. Int. J. Acad. Res. Bus. Soc. Sci. **7**(12), 405–412 (2017)
44. Mazumdar, A., Alharahsheh, H.: Insights of trends and developments in cloud computing. SARJET 1(3). South Asian Research Publication (2019)
45. McCormick, J., et al.: https://dmcny.org/wp-content/uploads/attachments/Forrester_Predictions_2017_-Artificial_Intelligence_Will_Drive_The_Insights_Revolution.pdf. Accessed 29 May 2021
46. Memon, A., et al.: Big data analytics and its applications. AETiC **1**(1), 45–54 (2017)
47. Milovic, B., Milovic, M.: Prediction and decision making in health care using data mining. IJPHS **1**(2), 69–78 (2012)

48. Zeinab, M., Elmustafa, A.: Internet of things applications, challenges and related future technologies. World Sci. News **2**(67), 126–148 (2017)
49. Morakanyane, R., et al.: Conceptualizing digital transformation in business organizations - a systematic review of literature. In: 30th Bled eConference, vol. 21, p. 427–444. Slovenia (2017)
50. Neware, R., Khan, A.: Cloud computing digital forensic challenges. In: 2018 Second ICECA, pp. 1090–1092. IEEE (2018)
51. O'regan, G.: Concise Guide to Software Engineering. UTiCS. Springer, Cham (2017). https://doi.org/10.1007/978-3-319-57750-0
52. OECD: Artificial intelligence in Society. https://ec.europa.eu/jrc/communities/sites/jrccties/files/eedfee77-en.pdf/. Accessed 29 May 2021
53. Oliff, H., Liu, Y.: Towards industry 4.0 utilizing data mining techniques - a case study on quality improvement. Procedia CIRP **63**(2017), 167–172 (2017)
54. Orfanidis, P.: Prominence of big data in the digital transformation era. School of Economics, Business Administration and Legal Studies, Thessaloniki – Greece (2018)
55. Palmer, A., et al.: Data mining - machine learning and statistical techniques. In: Funatsu, K. (Ed.) Knowledge-Oriented Appl. in Data Mining, pp. 373–396 (2011)
56. Paschou, T., Rapaccini, M., Peters, C., Adrodegari, F., Saccani, N.: Developing a maturity model for digital servitization in manufacturing firms. In: Anisic, Z., Lalic, B., Gracanin, D. (eds.) IJCIEOM 2019. LNMIE, pp. 413–425. Springer, Cham (2020). https://doi.org/10.1007/978-3-030-43616-2_44
57. Pflaum, A., Gölzer, P.: The IoT and digital transformation - toward the data-driven enterprise. IEEE Pervasive Comput. **17**(1), 87–91 (2018)
58. Prabhu, R., et al.: Big data analytics. In: Big Data Analytics - Systems, Algorithms, Applications, pp. 1-23. Springer, Singapore (2019).https://doi.org/10.1007/978-3-662-43720-9_14
59. Preethi, M., Vijayalakshmi, M.: Data Mining in Banking Sector. Int. J. Adv. Netw. Appl. **8**(5), 1–4 (2017)
60. Pulakkazhy, S., Balan, S.: Data mining in banking & its applications - a review. J. Comput. Sci. **9**(10), 1252–1259 (2013)
61. Quinn, M., et al.: The effects of cloud technology on management accounting and business decision-making. Financ. Manage. **10**(6), 1–12 (2014)
62. Rachinger, et al.: Digitalization and its influence on business model innovation. J. Manuf. Technol. Manag. **30**(8), 1143–1160 (2019)
63. Reddy, C.: A review on data mining from past to the future. Int. J. Comput. Appl. **15**(7), 19–22 (2011)
64. Rehman, H., et al.: The role of big data analytics in industrial Internet of Things. Future Gener. Comput. Syst. **99**, 247–259 (2019)
65. Reis, J. et al.: Digital transformation - a literature review & guidelines for future research. In: WorldCIST'18, pp. 411–421. Springer, Cham. (2018).
66. Roedder, N., et al.: The digital transformation and smart data analytics - an overview of enabling developments and application areas. In: IEEE Big Data 2016, pp. 2795–2802. IEEE, Washington (2016)
67. Rohanizadeh, S., Bameni, M.: A proposed data mining methodology and its application to industrial procedures. J. Ind. Eng. **4**, 37–50 (2009)
68. Saeed, T.: Data mining for small and medium enterprises - a conceptual model for adaptation. Intell. Inf. Manag. **12**(05), 183 (2020)
69. Schwertner, K.: Digital transformation of business. Trakia J. Sci. **15**(1), 388–393 (2017)
70. Sadiku, N., Adebo, O., Musa, M.: Big data in business. Int. J. Adv. Res. Comput. Sci. Softw. Eng. **8**(1), 160–162 (2018)
71. Sharma, B., et al.: Review on data mining - its challenges, issues and applications. Int. J. Curr. Eng. Sci. Res. **3**(2), 695–700 (2013)

72. Sharma, S., Osei-Bryson, K., Kasper, G.: Evaluation of an integrated knowledge discovery and data mining process model. Expert Syst. Appl. **39**(13), 11335–11348 (2012)
73. Siguenza-Guzman, et al.: Literature review of data mining applications in academic libraries. J. Acad. Librariansh. **41**(4), 499–510 (2015)
74. Sima, et al.: Influences of the Industry 40 revolution on the human capital development and consumer behavior - a systematic review. Sustainability, **12**(10), 4035 (2020)
75. Simon, A., et al.: An overview of machine learning and its applications. Int. J. Electr. Sci. Eng. **1**(1), 22–24 (2016)
76. Srivastava, U., Gopalkrishnan, S.: Impact of big data analytics on banking sector - learning for Indian banks. Procedia Comput. Sci. **50**, 643–652 (2015)
77. Betz, C., et al.: The impacts of digital transformation, agile, and DevOps on future IT curricula. In: SIGITE 2016, p. 106. ACM, New York (2016)
78. Teichert, R.: Digital transformation maturity - a systematic review of literature. Acta Univ. Agric. et Silvic. Mendelianae Brun. **67**(6), 1673–1687 (2019)
79. Telegescu, T.: IT in the workspace - the need for digital transformation. In: Proceedings of the International Conference on Business Excellence, vol. 12, pp. 952–965. Sciendo (2018)
80. Valdez-de-Leon, O.: A digital maturity model for telecommunications service providers. Technol. Innov. Manag. Rev. **6**(8), 19–32 (2016)
81. Verhoef, C., et al.: Digital transformation - a multidisciplinary reflection and research agenda. J. Bus. Res. **122**, 889–901 (2019)
82. Vivekananth, P., Baptist, A.: An analysis of big data analytics techniques. Int. J. Eng. Tech. Mgmt. Res. **5**(5), 17–19 (2015)
83. West, M., Allen, R.: https://www.brookings.edu/research/how-artificial-intelligence-is-transforming-the-world/. Accessed 29 May 2021
84. Wiesbock, F., Hess, T.: Understanding the Capabilities for Digital Innovations from a Digital Technology Perspective. Arbeitsbericht. WIM, München (2018)

An Event-Level Clustering Framework for Process Mining Using Common Sequential Rules

Zeeshan Tariq[1]([✉])(iD), Darryl Charles[1], Sally McClean[1], Ian McChesney[1],
and Paul Taylor[2]

[1] School of Computing, Ulster University, Jordanstown, UK
{zeeshan,dk.charles,si.mcclean,ir.mcchesney}@ulster.ac.uk
[2] Applied Research, Ipswich, BT, UK
paul.n.taylor@bt.com

Abstract. Process mining techniques extract useful knowledge from event logs to analyse and improve the quality of process execution. However, size and complexity of the real-world event logs make it difficult to apply standard process mining techniques, thus process discovery results in spaghetti-like models which are difficult to analyse. Several event abstraction techniques are developed to group-up low-level activities into higher level activities, but abstraction ignores the low level critical process details in the real-world business scenarios. Also, trace clustering techniques have been extensively used in literature to cluster the processes executions which are homogeneous in nature, but event-level clustering is not yet considered for process mining. In this paper, a novel framework is proposed to identify event-level clusters in a business process log by decomposing into several sub-logs based upon the similarity of the sequences between events. Our technique provides clustering without abstraction of very large complex event logs. Proposed algorithm Common Events Identifier (CEI) is applied on a real-world telecommunication log and the results are compared with two well-known trace clustering techniques from the literature. Our results achieved high accuracy of clustering and improved the quality of resulting process models using the given size and complexity of the event log. We further demonstrated that the proposed techniques improved process discovery and conformance results for a given event log.

Keywords: Process mining · Process discovery · Trace clustering · Rule-based mining · Process analytics · Business processes · Sequence mining

1 Introduction

Collections of business processes enable organizations to operate efficiently and achieve their operational goals. A business process is a combination of activities performed by organizations to serve the needs of their internal or external

© ICST Institute for Computer Sciences, Social Informatics and Telecommunications Engineering 2021
Published by Springer Nature Switzerland AG 2021. All Rights Reserved
M. H. Miraz et al. (Eds.): iCETiC 2021, LNICST 395, pp. 147–160, 2021.
https://doi.org/10.1007/978-3-030-90016-8_10

customers [3]. These activities are recorded in the form of event logs and later utilized by businesses to assess the execution quality of their processes, resulting in identification of the possible improvement areas [19]. The complexity of organisation's business processes has also evolved with the growing diversity of the business environment in recent times. Execution of such processes lead to the generation of unstructured and variable event data which is prone to various inadequacies [23]. Proactive identification of these inefficiencies is critical in competitive business environments for maintaining alignment of an organisation's activities with its business goals.

Process mining is a set of tools and techniques used to discover, analyse and improve business processes [25]. Among other components, process discovery is one of the integral research area of the process mining domain. Control flow models of the process such as petri nets, helps in analysing the way process is executed and evaluate the dispensaries between ideal process model and generated event log [20]. Discovered models from the real world events are generally unstructured and exhibit a spaghetti-like pattern having low model quality [20]. Things become further complicated where the number of events in the process is extensively large and the outcome of the process directly affects the financial aspect of the organisation, such as customer churn out rate in telecommunication sector. A recent focus of research is in development of the techniques for trace clustering for identifying clusters in the large event logs with lowest level of events recorded, results in spaghetti-like process models. Clustering techniques are mostly based on the similarity of traces within an event log [16]. Generally, techniques focused on trace clustering neglect the business perceptive of the process while dealing with real-world logs [21].

Event logs may contain very low level of process details, event-abstraction techniques are developed to group the low-level events into high level events [17], but these techniques tend to ignore the activities which are meaningful for analysis at lower abstraction level. When a real-world process execution is recorded, there may be similar activities existing in the log which reflects that there exists a common behaviour in the process execution which is reflected in all of the recorded traces. The importance of the identification of this common behaviour is elevated where number of events per trace is exponentially large and business process is composed of several sub-processes. Also, such discovery eliminates possible performance overheads due to presence of such "always occurring" similar events in a competitive business environment. Our approach is presented in Fig. 1, presenting that raw complex log with large number of events is decomposed into several sub-logs. In Fig. 1, sub-figure (a) shows a spaghetti-like process model of the services diagnostic process, for the customers at a telecommunication firm. The event log contains several subcategories of traces and clusters of events which are common in all the traces. When common events are identified and segregated from the log, several sub-logs are created as a result of this event-level segmentation. Sub-figures (b) & (c) are the segments of the traces with common events while sub-figure (d) presents the remaining portion

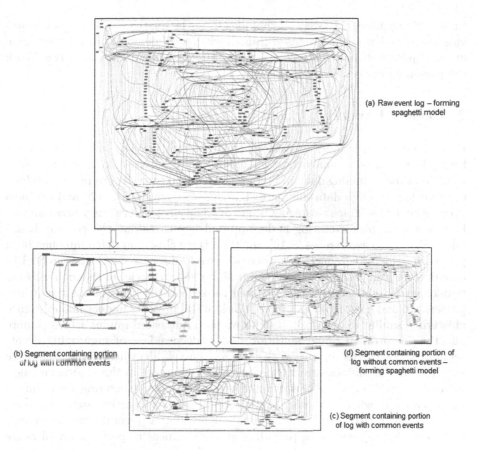

(a) Raw event log – forming spaghetti model

(b) Segment containing portion of log with common events

(d) Segment containing portion of log without common events – forming spaghetti model

(c) Segment containing portion of log with common events

Fig. 1. Event log segmentation as a result of common events identification.

of the log with events with similarity in association rules higher than the defined threshold.

Our contributions in this paper are summarised as follows:

- We investigated the event-level clustering for the complex event logs where number of events are exponentially large. Solutions such as trace clustering and event abstraction, provides decomposition of an event log but clustering of low level abstracted events are not considered.
- A novel approach for the clustering of the event log is presented for identification of the similarity in the events through the sequential rule-based mining technique. An algorithm Common Events Identifier (CEI) is proposed to identify the portion of the process log having similar sequential rules, referred in this paper as Common Event Segment (CES).
- We conducted several experiments to evaluate the proposed technique on a real-world telecommunication data. We also compared the results with other well-known trace clustering techniques from the literature, ActiTraC proposed by Song et al. [7] and NoHiC by Tariq et al. [21].

In Sect. 2, we discussed several techniques from the related research, Sect. 3 provides an overview of the proposed framework, Sect. 4 demonstrates the outcome of the experiments and related discussions. Finally, Conclusion and Future Work are presented in Sect. 5.

2 Related Work

Process mining techniques are developed to discover process models from event logs which assists in analysing and enhancing the quality of process execution [20]. Process mining domain bridges the gap and provides ground for analysis of event logs through data mining techniques, as mentioned in [2], and business process analytics. Trace clustering is one of a key research area in process mining in which a complex event log is decomposed by discovering the clusters based on similarity of cases/traces [8,16]. In [16] a trace clustering technique has been proposed to identify frequent sequence patterns to discover the clusters in healthcare dataset using domain experts input about subcategories of the main process trunk. Several clustered traces are then ranked on the basis of their sequence patterns to find most frequent traces. Work of [16] presents understandable trace clustering, similar to our work, instead we used rule based mining which is more affective in terms of implementation and understanding of underlying event-sequences. Furthermore, our work is based on self-identification of difference subcategories of business process based on the difference in the sequential rules. In another work on trace clustering, a tree-based trace clustering technique is proposed in [6] where the process is clustered using a iterative approach using a DWS (Disjunctive Workflow Schema) algorithm. A general trace clustering techniques is proposed in [5] providing an environment to perform broad range of process centric analysis to indicate correlation in several process characteristics, such as control-flow, data-flow time resources and conformance. Abstraction techniques analyses event logs with very low level of abstraction by converting low-event events into high level events. Authors of [17] proposed a methodology to initially discover the Local Process Models(LPM) at higher abstraction level of events. Authors showed that the composite of LPM models with high-level activities resulted in improved fitness and precision of discovered model.

Rule-base mining is used for finding interesting sequence patterns among the events through extraction of sequential patterns [14]. In [21], authors presented rule-based mining for segregation of different classes in business process data, in order to support clustering of cases based on agglomerative approach. A rule based algorithm is proposed in [9] to address the problem of missing unique identifiers in the event log. Proposed algorithm in [9] use varying threshold of similarity between events to combine the events in a group. We also use rule based mining in this paper but our focus is to group those events which are in the form of a sequence thus not disturbing the underlying flow of the business process.

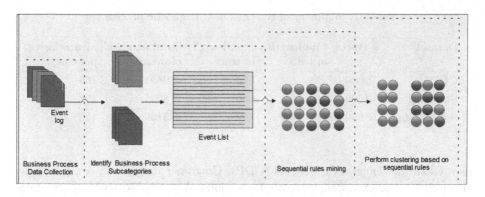

Fig. 2. Proposed framework for the identification of common events cluster

3   Methodology

This paper presents a solution for identification of common events existing in the lengthy heterogeneous business processes. These events are present in the logs as a cluster of similar activities performed during all the traces. Business processes in modern corporations encompassing a variety of process subcategories Subcategories of the process are referred to as independent groups of the instances which are a part of a business process. Organizations allow these hybrid categories of instances in a business process to manage diverse business scenarios in a highly competitive business environment. Event logs contain these subcategories as different classes of traces. Irrespective of occurrence and duration,it is possible that different subcategories of the business process instances contain several such events which are common across all subcategories of the business process.

We project that identification of these clusters does two main roles, (i) decomposing the extensively large logs into sub-logs, thus making the discovery phase more effective, (ii) common events in logs may be serious processing overhead and should be considered for several process enhancement measures, such as compression, time reduction or replacing them with automated systems.

3.1   Framework for Common Events Identification

The framework proposed in this paper is composed of four stages starting with the collection of raw event log, presented in Fig. 2. We discuss stages of our framework through a case study of a call centre process at BT, one of the leading telecom firms in the UK. Details of each stage are as follows:

Event Log. Events are the activity performed by a resource within a scope of a process instance at the given time stamp [5]. We used a real-world event log of a call centre setup at BT. Customers contact the organisation (BT) for the solution of their service-related queries through a semi-automated chat service, termed

Table 1. Summary of the customer diagnostic process log

Dataset	Traces	Min length of trace	Max length of trace	Total number of events	Mean classes per case
CDP	2000	5	660	489804	169
Subcategory A	1000	13	660	276635	178
Subcategory B	1000	5	302	213169	159

as a Customer Diagnostic Process (CDP). Customer diagnostics are performed through a series of system generated questions. A similar scenario of sequential questions is presented in [18]. The flow of the process for CDP is presented in Fig. 3. Each instance is labelled with a unique Case_ID. Event details are abstracted with numbers IDs for privacy regulations. Initial preprocessing of the data is performed, which includes the removal of duplicate instances and exclusion of uncompleted logs. Details of the CDP log is mentioned in Table 1.

Identification of Business Process Subcategories. Event log from organizational information systems generally include instances belonging to several subcategories. These subcategories can be identified through several ways, such as by exploring the broad characteristics of process instances or getting direct information from domain experts. In our dataset, customers interacting with CDP belong to two subcategories, Broadband customers and PSTN customers. Table 1 presents the details of these subcategories.

Event List. The event list is a tabular view of cases with their associated events, represented as L. The first column of L represents the case unique_id, and the remaining columns present the events performed in sequential order. Each row of L represents the execution of a complete instance. For simplicity, we are only considering traces where starting event for all the cases is restricted to single class.

Sequential Rules Mining. This stage generates the sequential rules for the given events under certain performance metrics using the Apriori algorithm. Sequential rule-based mining technique is used to identify the frequent subsequences of events in all the cases of the considered portion of the log. Rules are extracted for each of the subcategories of the CDP through the Apriori algorithm [1] using R. Rules are extracted using the mandatory performance metrics

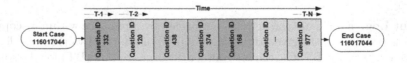

Fig. 3. Sample diagnostic process with labelled events

such as support, confidence and lift. Apriori learns the rule in the form of $\Rightarrow$, which means that every time X (event) appeared in the given unique process then Y (event) appeared at least once in that given sequence and X is always followed by Y.

To validate the performance of the rules, the following three metrics are used:

- **Support:** A measure of the applicability of a rule used. Let X and Y are two events, N_X be the number of instances for which X holds & N_Y be the number of instances for which Y holds then *Support* of a rule X $\Rightarrow$ Y is the proportion of cases which holds for both X and Y. Higher support shows more applicability of the approach. If N is total number of cases then Support of a rule is defined as (1).

$$Support(X \Rightarrow Y) = N_{X \wedge Y}/N \tag{1}$$

- **Confidence:** It is worth of the rule with respect to the reliability within the given dataset. A value of the confidence closest to 1 qualifies extent of the given rule's worth to be represented with maximum confidence. Confidence of a rule is defined as (2).

$$Confidence(X \Rightarrow Y) = N_{X \wedge Y}/N_X \tag{2}$$

- **Lift:** It is the measure of positive correlation between X and Y. A value of lift closer to 1 indicates that X and Y are more positively correlated & independent to each other. Lift of a rule is defined as (3).

$$Lift(X \Rightarrow Y) = N_{X \wedge Y}N/N_X N_Y \tag{3}$$

Sample of sequential rules generated for CDP are presented in Table 2. The process of identifying the frequent subsequences using the TraMineR package [12] implemented in the R tool is; First the Time Stamped Event (TSE) format of event log is created along with event sequence objects. Then frequent subsequences among the events are generated and sequential rules are extracted based on threshold values of *Support*, *Confidence* and *Lift*. Finally, discriminating sub-sequences are identified, which shows level of inheritance of rules in a defined cohort of data. Frequent subsequences of events occurring in the traces of subcategory-A are not necessarily the same as those which exists in the subcategory-B.

Algorithm for Common Events Identification. We proposed an algorithm Common Events Identifier (CEI) for the discovery of clusters with common events in a given process log. CEI consists of 4 steps, where Step-1 concerns with the preparation of the process log. Consider a process log α having events e forming an event list L. In Step-2, L is traversed with the single step increment, given as window size n, and sequential rules for the events corresponding to L are extracted. i is pointer for the starting column of the L. The value of window n increases with every iteration following the sliding window principle. In

Table 2. Sample rules generated from the CDP process log with the values of *Support*, *Confidence* and *Lift*

	Rules	Support	Confidence	Lift
1	{1332} ⇒ {1442}	0.8131	0.9737	1.0124
2	{1442} ⇒ {108}	0.6949	0.8942	1.0928
3	{1005} ⇒ {1004}	0.6932	0.8920	1.0884
4	{1005} ⇒ {1002}	0.6932	0.8920	1.0884
5	{1198} ⇒ {1887}	0.6876	0.9833	1.3772
6	{103} ⇒ {1093}	0.6837	0.9857	1.4139
7	{21} ⇒ {100}	0.6837	0.9808	1.4139
8	{11} ⇒ {220}	0.6837	0.9808	1.4139

Step-3, we considered the generated sequential rules at each iteration for evaluation of the Pearson residual correlation [12] using Chi-square test. Correlation is detected between different cohorts of rules generated by CBA algorithm. A fixed threshold of 10% correlation is considered to distinguish the commonality of rules between the cohorts. We kept the low value of threshold to make sure that slightest difference in rules between cohort is effectively detected. Finally, Step-4 identifies the columns in the event list which are a part of the Common Events Segment (CES). Discrimination residual represents the frequency of occurrence of any specific subsequence.

All test runs are performed on a desktop computer with an Intel Core-i5-8th Gen processor running at 1.80 GHz, 16 GB of RAM, Windows 10 Enterprise (64-bit), and a 64-bit version of Java 8 with 8 GB of RAM assigned to the Java virtual machine. Time to run single iteration varied from 0.7 s to maximum of 33 mins depending upon the length of trace.

Dissimilarity in the cohorts is identified as a Pearson residual value P between -1 and $+1$. If P increases to the certain threshold ($P = 0.1$) all e in the list L till γ will be marked as CES. Algorithm stops when task list L reaches to an end.

Iteration of CEI on CDP Event Log. Findings from the iterations of CEI on customer diagnostic process log are as follows:

1st iteration: $i = 1$, $n = 2$, $P = 0$, where i is indicating the 1st column of the event list L, n is starting from 2 as to consider first two columns of events. Support minimum threshold is kept at default value of 0.2.

2nd iteration: $i = 1$, $n = 3$, $P = 0$. Several new sequential rules are generated during the 2nd iteration of CEI but all these rules are mutually common between Broadband and PSTN cases.

3rd iteration: At the end of the 3rd iteration, $i = 1$, $n = 3$, $P = 0$. The value of n keeps on increasing as a sliding window grows until the value of P increase from the set threshold.

Algorithm 1: High-level pseudo-code description of the Common Events Identifier (CEI) Algorithm

---

Step-1: For an event log α

$i=1$(start of α);

$n=2$ (initializing with 2nd column in the event list);

$e=$Set of events in each column between i and n;

Step-2: If ($e=$NULL)

Exit,

else Generate sequential rules for e;

Step-3: Evaluate the Pearson residual correlation P of the Chi-square test;

if *(correlation value of $P \neq 0$)* then

   | $max = n$-1;

   | Cs (start of cluster) = event in the list at position i;

   | Ce (end of cluster) = event in the list at position max;

   | $i= n$;

   | $n= i+1$;

else

   | until $n \neq$ End of event list;

   | $n= n+1$;

end

Step-4: Common Events Cluster = Events between Cs and Ce

Go to *Step-2* (for discovery of further clusters)

Similarly, algorithms traverse the event list L and compare the resulting rules with minimum threshold of correlation.

CES marking As CEI continues to traverse L, at the end of 106th iteration the value of $n = 107$, $P = +0.1$. Results from the cohort analysis show the discrimination is identified, as the value of P is > 0.1. This presents that a set of sequence rules now exists within n columns of the event list which discriminate between cohorts. Portion of the log with common events is identified as CES.

4   Results and Discussion

This section presents the results of the proposed framework. The quality of the clustering process is evaluated and later we showed the accuracy of the log segments (sub-logs) generated as a result of clustering. We performed the quality assessment of identified clusters in comparison with other well-known techniques from the literature. In this section, firstly, the weighted Shannon Entropy [15] to measure the change in entropy of the CES as compared to the rest of the process log. Secondly, Classification based on Association (CBA) [13] technique to measure the quality of the discovered clusters. We presented CBA results with performance metrics, such as accuracy, precision, sensitivity and the F-measure.

4.1   Measuring the Quality of Clusters

To measure the quality of the generated clusters, we used two methods. The first method is the weighted Shannon entropy [10], to measure the entropy of the event list L. The second method is to measure the prediction accuracy of the discovered clusters using Classification based on Association rules (CBA) [11].

Entropy Change Between the Event. Shannon's Information Entropy is the average rate at which information is produced by a stochastic source of data [15]. The entropy H is calculated for list L as value of randomness between activities of each column. Entropy H is a probability p of an activity i appearing in the given column of a event list. The formula of Shannon entropy is given by (4):

$$H = \sum_{i=1}^{m} p_i log_2 p_i \qquad (4)$$

Figure 4 shows the graph of the weighted Shannon's entropy calculated for columns of the event list L. Change in the entropy Entropy H reflects the change in randomness as observed in Fig. 4. Increase in the Entropy H is an indicator for the decluttering of events in the log. Portion of the log with minimum randomness is the segment with common events, thus event log is divided into two sub-logs, one with common events and other with remaining events.

Clustering Accuracy. As a result of clustering, process lag is decomposed into several segments. We compared the association rules between different segments of the process log through the CBA technique [13] implemented in R. Results are presented in the Table 3 which shows that the overall accuracy of the classification of segments is above 90% for all the traces where minimum support for the generated rules is greater than or equal to 30%. The value of confidence is set as a default in CBA (80%). On average, 95% accuracy is achieved with two variations of testing and training data sets, which suggests that clusters are well segregated. An average sensitivity of around 90% presents the accuracy of the discrimation of rules between events of different segments. The F1 measure varies between 91.7% and 98.8% for all support and testing percentage scenarios presenting high precision and recall values.

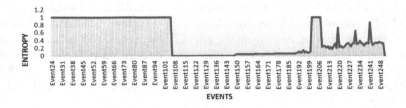

Fig. 4. Shannon Entropy calculated for the events in the process log

Table 3. Accuracy of the identified clusters

Parameters			Results		
Support	Training data	Testing data	Accuracy	Sensitivity	F1 Measure
30%	80%	20%	97.22%	94.00%	97.14%
35%	80%	20%	98.12%	96.20%	98.00%
40%	80%	20%	94.40%	88.80%	94.11%
45%	80%	20%	94.40%	88.80%	94.11%
30%	85%	15%	98.80%	97.60%	98.80%
35%	85%	15%	92.35%	84.71%	91.70%
40%	85%	15%	96.47%	87.70%	91.00%
45%	85%	15%	95.88%	91.76%	95.00%

4.2   Comparison with Other Trace Clustering Techniques

To evaluate the impact of our technique on the process discovery, we generated process models for all the sub-logs using heuristic miner three quality criterion of process models, as mentioned in [24], fitness f, Coefficient of connectivity(CNC) & Coefficient of network complexity (CNC_k), are compared with the clustering results of other techniques from the literature. Results from the Algorithm CEI is compared with two clustering techniques from the literature, Trace clustering (ActiTraC) [7] and NoHiC [21].

For ActiTraC, we kept the default settings as implemented in the ProM 6.10 plugin *ActiTraC Clustering*. We compared the results of clustering based on 3 quality criteria of process discovery which are, fitness of model (f), Coefficient of connectivity(CNC), Avg Degree of Connectivity(CD), and Coefficient of network complexity (CNC_k) detailed in [24]. Fitness *fitness* gauge the quality of the process model by measuring the events mismatch when the event log is replayed with the discovered process model [4]. A process model is said to have perfect *fitness* if it allows replay of all the traces in the process log at the given petri net model. Equation (5) presents the fitness f of the process log σ on petri net η.

$$f(\sigma, \eta) = 1/2(1 - m/c) + 1/2(1 - r/p) \tag{5}$$

where m = missing tokens, c = number of consumed tokens, r = number of tokens remaining after replay,p = total number of tokens produced.

Figure 5 shows two comparison plots. In, Fig. 5a overall fitness of raw CDP log is 77%, which is elevated to 86% with the segregation of log into common events clusters and remaining portion of trace. This increase in fitness is due to the segregation of events between different segments/sub-logs. Portion of the log with common events results with higher fitness value. NoHiC and ActiTrac discovered 4 clusters each, but average fitness of models is yet slightly lower than CEI, 83% and 81% respectively. Decrease in CNC from 1.63 to 1.36 by CEI is shown in Fig. 5b which evident the impact on complexity of the log. There

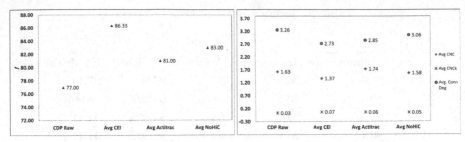

(a) Comparison of average fitness f (b) Comparison of CNC, CD & CNC_k

Fig. 5. CDP raw is the process log without any clustering. CEI outperformed for several criterion including fitness Coefficient of Connectivity(CNC), Avg Degree of Connectivity(CD) & Coefficient of Network Complexity(CNC_k)

is a slight increase in the value of CNC_k as those segments emerged from the log which got high graph network complexity, depicting that events with more randomness are segregated in a sub-log. Raw log has CD of 3.26 presenting high level of connectivity in comparison to the average fragmented logs. Average of CEI has CD lowest among all which is 2.73 but this is an average of fragments' CD ranging from 2.0 (for cluster with common events) to 4.4 (most fuzzy part of the log). Yet, lowest average CD presents the better precision of the resulting process models.

5   Conclusion

Event data extracted from real-life business processes is very large and highly unstructured. Discovery of such processes lead to the complicated patterns which are difficult to understand with traditional process mining techniques. In this paper we proposed a framework to simplify the event log by decomposing it into manageable segments. Our technique discovers the clusters of the common events within a business process log thus allowing large log to be fragmented into easy manageable portions. We demonstrated through real-world case study that our technique improved the process discovery. We achieved high accuracy of clustering using our proposed algorithm CEI and compared the results with other techniques from the literature. We also presented the accuracy of clusters through entropy calculation of event log and cohort-based analysis using CBA algorithm. For future, we will extend our work in two dimensions (i) conformance analysis of the identified log segments, and (ii) incorporating further complexities in the event log, such as, multiple start/finish classes and trace misalignments.

Acknowledgment. This research is supported by the BTIIC (BT Ireland Innovation Centre) project, funded by BT and Invest Northern Ireland.

References

1. Aggarwal, C.C., Bhuiyan, M.A., Hasan, M.A.: Frequent pattern mining algorithms: a survey. In: Aggarwal, C.C., Han, J. (eds.) Frequent Pattern Mining, pp. 19–64. Springer, Cham (2014). https://doi.org/10.1007/978-3-319-07821-2_2
2. Ashraf, N., Ahmad, W., Ashraf, R.: A comparative study of data mining algorithms for high detection rate in intrusion detection system. Ann. Emerg. Technol. Comput. (AETiC), pp. 2516–0281 (2018). Print ISSN: 2516-0281
3. Borgianni, Y., Cascini, G., Rotini, F.: Business process reengineering driven by customer value: a support for undertaking decisions under uncertainty conditions. Comput. Ind. **68**, 132–147 (2015)
4. Buijs, J.C.A.M., van Dongen, B.F., van der Aalst, W.M.P., et al.: On the role of fitness, precision, generalization and simplicity in process discovery. In: Meersman, R. (ed.) OTM 2012. LNCS, vol. 7565, pp. 305–322. Springer, Heidelberg (2012). https://doi.org/10.1007/978-3-642-33606-5_19
5. De Leoni, M., van der Aalst, W.M., Dees, M.: A general process mining framework for correlating, predicting and clustering dynamic behavior based on event logs. Inf. Syst. **56**, 235–257 (2016)
6. de Medeiros, A.K.A., Guzzo, A., Greco, G., van der Aalst, W.M.P., Weijters, A.J.M.M., van Dongen, B.F., Saccà, D.: Process mining based on clustering: a quest for precision. In: ter Hofstede, A., Benatallah, B., Paik, H.-Y. (eds.) BPM 2007. LNCS, vol. 4928, pp. 17–29. Springer, Heidelberg (2008). https://doi.org/10.1007/978-3-540-78238-4_4
7. De Weerdt, J., Vanden Broucke, S., Vanthienen, J., Baesens, B.: Active trace clustering for improved process discovery. IEEE Trans. Knowl. Data Eng. **25**(12), 2708–2720 (2013)
8. Delias, P., Doumpos, M., Grigoroudis, E., Matsatsinis, N.: A non-compensatory approach for trace clustering. Int. Trans. Oper. Res. **26**(5), 1828–1846 (2019)
9. Djedović, A., Karabegović, A., Žunić, E., Alić, D.: A rule based events correlation algorithm for process mining. In: Avdaković, S., Mujčić, A., Mujezinović, A., Uzunović, T., Volić, I. (eds.) IAT 2019. LNNS, vol. 83, pp. 587–605. Springer, Cham (2020). https://doi.org/10.1007/978-3-030-24986-1_47
10. Eskov, V., Eskov, V., Vochmina, Y.V., Gorbunov, D., Ilyashenko, L.: Shannon entropy in the research on stationary regimes and the evolution of complexity. Mosc. Univ. Phys. Bull. **72**(3), 309–317 (2017). https://doi.org/10.3103/S0027134917030067
11. Filip, J., Kliegr, T.: Classification based on associations (CBA)-a performance analysis. Tech. rep, EasyChair (2018)
12. Gabadinho, A., Ritschard, G., Studer, M., Mueller, N.: Mining sequence data in r with the traminer package. University of Geneva, A User's Guide. Department of Econometrics and Laboratory of Demography (2011)
13. Hahsler, M., Johnson, I., Kliegr, T., Kucha, J.: Associative classification in r: arc, arulesCBA, and rCBA. R J. **9**(2) (2019)
14. Lim, A.H., Lee, C.S.: Processing online analytics with classification and association rule mining. Knowl.-Based Syst. **23**(3), 248–255 (2010)
15. Lin, J.: Divergence measures based on the Shannon entropy. IEEE Trans. Inf. Theory **37**(1), 145–151 (1991)
16. Lu, X., Tabatabaei, S.A., Hoogendoorn, M., Reijers, H.A.: Trace clustering on very large event data in healthcare using frequent sequence patterns. In: Hildebrandt, T., van Dongen, B.F., Röglinger, M., Mendling, J. (eds.) BPM 2019. LNCS, vol.

11675, pp. 198–215. Springer, Cham (2019). https://doi.org/10.1007/978-3-030-26619-6_14

17. Mannhardt, F., Tax, N.: Unsupervised event abstraction using pattern abstraction and local process models. arXiv preprint arXiv:1704.03520 (2017)

18. Onik, M.M.H., Al-Zaben, N., Hoo, H.P., Kim, C.S.: A novel approach for network attack classification based on sequential questions. Ann. Emerg. Technol. Comput. (AETiC), pp. 1–14 (2018). Print ISSN:2516–0281

19. Rojas, E., Munoz-Gama, J., Sepúlveda, M., Capurro, D.: Process mining in healthcare: a literature review. J. Biomed. Inform. **61**, 224–236 (2016)

20. Rudnitckaia, J.: Process mining: Data science in action, pp. 1–11. University of Technology, Faculty of Information Technology pp (2016)

21. Tariq, Z., Khan, N., Charles, D., McClean, S., McChesney, I., Taylor, P.: Understanding contrail business processes through hierarchical clustering: a multi-stage framework. Algorithms **13**(10), 244 (2020)

22. Tax, N., Sidorova, N., Haakma, R., van der Aalst, W.M.P.: Event abstraction for process mining using supervised learning techniques. In: Bi, Y., Kapoor, S., Bhatia, R. (eds.) IntelliSys 2016. LNNS, vol. 15, pp. 251–269. Springer, Cham (2018). https://doi.org/10.1007/978-3-319-56994-9_18

23. Taylor, P., Leida, M., Majeed, B.: Case study in process mining in a multinational enterprise. In: Aberer, K., Damiani, E., Dillon, T. (eds.) SIMPDA 2011. LNBIP, vol. 116, pp. 134–153. Springer, Heidelberg (2012). https://doi.org/10.1007/978-3-642-34044-4_8

24. Thaler, T., Ternis, S.F., Fettke, P., Loos, P.: A comparative analysis of process instance cluster techniques. Wirtschaftsinformatik **2015**, 423–437 (2015)

25. van der Aalst, W., et al.: Process mining manifesto. In: Daniel, F., Barkaoui, K., Dustdar, S. (eds.) Business Process Management Workshops, BPM 2011. LNBIP, vol. 99, pp. 169–194. Springer, Heidelberg (2012). https://doi.org/10.1007/978-3-642-28108-2_19

Fuzzy Logic Enabled Stress Detection Using Physiological Signals

Shabbar Naqvi[1]($\boxtimes$), Aamir Zeb Shaikh[2], Talat Altaf[3], and Saurabh Singh[4]

[1] Department of Computer Systems Engineering, Balochistan University of Engineering and Technology, Khuzdar, Pakistan
shabbar@buetk.edu.pk
[2] Department of Electronic Engineering, NED University of Engineering and Technology Karachi, Karachi, Pakistan
[3] Department of Electrical Engineering, Sir Syed University of Engineering and Technology, Karachi, Pakistan
[4] Department of Industrial and Systems Engineering, Dongguk University Seoul, Seoul, South Korea

Abstract. Stress is attributed as the natural response of body towards unwanted and challenging conditions of society and environment. The consequences of stress are in general very harmful. However, in some specific situations, stress can be highly serious to the human health as it impacts the cardiovascular system in addition to other body sub systems. Timely Detection of stress through physiological sensors may help in arresting the disease. As the stress results in change of heart rate, skin conduction, temperature, blood pressure and oxygen levels, hence, measurement and assessment of these parameters is useful in deciding the stress levels into a candidate. In this paper, a fuzzy logic based automatic stress detection system is designed to timely detect the patients passing through this silent killer disease. The physiological signals of human body are used to assess the current state of person. The parameters used for the purpose are heart rate, Galvanic Skin Response (GSR), and temperature. The fuzzy logic is an exciting branch of artificial intelligence that is used to make useful decisions under uncertain and incomplete input knowledge. A synthetic data set of 500 patients is also developed to train and test the proposed architecture. The algorithms used for this purpose are Hill Climbing (HC) and Simulated Annealing (SA) for fuzzy membership functions training. The results show that Simulated Annealing gives a testing accuracy of 89% in comparison to Hill climbing with 81% accuracy. Future work is directed towards using new methods like type-2 fuzzy logic and deep learning etc.

Keywords: Stress detection · Fuzzy logic · Physiological signals

1 Introduction

Stress is one of the largest prevalent harmful silent killer diseases in the world. Sometimes, the consequences of stress can be fatal if it is not diagnosed and treated timely and

M. H. Miraz et al. (Eds.): iCETiC 2021, LNICST 395, pp. 161–173, 2021.
https://doi.org/10.1007/978-3-030-90016-8_11

efficiently. There are many diseases caused by hyper stress. It increases the chances of cardiovascular disease that may increase the mortality rate [1]. This is in addition to the COVID-19 patients trying for suicide [2]. However, these precious lives can be saved if the disease is treated timely. Cannon's research study shows that when a person passes through a threatening like situation, his or her body responds in the form of flight- fly fashion [3]. Hence, his or her body produces higher respiratory rate and activates bigger blood flow that requires more oxygen level [4, 5]. Additionally Dr. Rosalind Picard of Massachusetts Institute of Technology published an exciting book in the field of Affective Computing. This book introduces the connection of physiological changes of human body with emotional state [6]. Hence, the changes in human body directly affects the mental state of a person.

Stress has become an integral part of the modern life and society. There are many events in which one cannot escape from its detrimental effects. These include truck drivers travelling for long hours on highways, social pressure due to employment and unemployment, candidates passing through tough recruitment assessments and interviews, students preparing for examinations, patients suffering from COVID-19 disease and flight-phobia patients travelling on commercial flights [7].

However, it is an important fact that stress results in various variations in human body. These variations can be assessed through diagnostic tests. Hence, timely evaluation and diagnosis of disease may recommend in taking useful decisions regarding treatment of patient. This will also save the precious human lives. Some of the testing procedures include Trier Social Test, Stroop color-word inference test, Montreal imaging stress task, cold pressor test, sing a song stress test [7].

Furthermore, human vital signs can be evaluated through physiological sensors that can be attached on a human body in non-invasive fashion. These sensors can sense the required parameters periodically and compare those with pre-set threshold regarding presence or absence of risky stress levels. Once, the values rise above the threshold, the information can be transmitted to the subject as well as medical consultant who would provide suitable consultation to manage the given situation and avoid any fatal mishap.

The vital signs used by various researchers for making suitable decisions include heart rate, breathing rate, temperature, humidity, speech, blood pressure, galvanic skin response, photoplethysmogram, electrocardiogram, electromyogram. The researchers formulate the binary problem of presence or absence of stress for a patient. Different artificial intelligence based algorithms are used by authors to make intelligent decisions in diversified fields, these include fuzzy logic, genetic algorithm, and neural networks, support vector machine (SVM), Naïve Bayes, and Decision Tree etc. [8–12].

Fuzzy logic is an exciting area of Artificial Intelligence that uses incomplete or imprecise information to come up with better decisions. This paper uses parameters i.e. Galvanic skin response (GSR), heart rate and temperature to predict the mental state of a person. The parameters are fed to a Fuzzy Inferencing System. The motive behind selection of the parameters is that the literature shows that two parameters are sufficient to identify the mental state of a candidate most of the time [13]. These include GSR and heart rate. However, the third parameter will give additional reliability in decision making process in which fuzzy inferencing system with imprecise data might be useful. The results are fused using fuzzy logic algorithm. Additionally, 500 synthetic data set elements are also used to train and test the system. Two algorithms are used for training and testing purpose. These include Hill Climbing (HC) and Simulated Annealing (SA) algorithms which have been used to train the fuzzy membership function parameters for finding optimal values. The results show that SA performs better than HC Algorithm.

The rest of the paper is organized as follows. Section 2 presents the related work done by other researchers to detect the presence or absence of risky stress levels. Section 3 presents the proposed setup whereas Sect. 4 provides results with its discussion. Section 5 is the last section which concludes the paper and also provides future direction.

2 Related Work

Several researchers have demonstrated the significance of the automated systems for identification of risky and normal stress levels [14–17]. These researchers collect the physiological information from subjects and formulate the problem of classification whether the person is going through abnormal stress levels or not. The decisions are computed through several algorithms. This section presents a brief review of the work done by the researchers.

In [18], authors use electrocardiogram(ECG), GSR and respiratory rate (RESP) signals to detect the presence of Stress into a human being. As the previous observations based on recent research describe that the physiological signals contain pivotal information about the mental state of a person. Hence, the extracted data is processed to extract useful information. The processing includes detection of R peaks or when decomposing the GSR signal. Additionally RESP signal is used to identify the stress level of the people. Hence, the improvement results in better performance in comparison to other systems. This research work uses image processing techniques to provide useful decisions regarding the presence of disease.

In [13], researchers use heart rate and GSR levels of a candidate to detect the stress levels. Additionally, they claim that these two parameters are sufficient to segregate between normal and stressed patients. The database is also developed to test the proposed system. The database contains 80 females in the age bracket from 19 to 32 years. The database acquisition is based on physiological experiments carried out by doctors. The key benefit offered by the proposed setup is that it is a non-invasive system. The authors use fuzzy logic to decide the presence or absence of disease. The proposed scheme is computationally efficient and highly accurate. The proposed setup gives an accuracy of 99.5% using 10 s to extract the stress template and 7 s to detect stress on an individual using two physiological signals and GSR measured only during two tasks.

In [19], authors use respiratory rate, heart rate variability, oxygen saturation and temperature to formulate a stress level detection system. The proposed system is designed using fuzzy logic architecture. The wearable sensors are used to collect vital signs of the human being which are exploited in the next phase to detect the disease in candidates. The performance of the proposed setup shows good results.

In [14], researchers measure heart rate, GSR and breathing rate to design an intelligent system for discrimination of relaxed state and stressed state of a human being. The proposed system uses fuzzy logic model to decide the state of a person. The benefits of the developed system includes computational efficiency under low budget requirements.

The proposed system is implemented using an Arduino and Raspberry Pi Boards. The data collection is completed through Arduino while data processing task is performed through Raspberry Pi board. Identification of stress is achieved on F1 score of 91.5% and relaxation at 96.81%. The processing time is 20 s sliding window. The proposed system is also validated on 42 persons.

In [20], researchers formulate the stress detection system for long-time computer users. It is observed that the long usage of screen time typically induces stress into a user. The physiological data collected for the purpose is heart rate and GSR. The final decision is devised using fuzzy logic. The proposed system is implemented for the faculty and students of Computer science department at U C San Carlos. The proposed system gives an accuracy of 72%.

In [21], authors model a fuzzy logic based stress detection system for travelers. Two inputs are considered, these include speed and traffic density. The inputs are used to model six driving postures i.e. idle, journey, high urban workload, low urban workload, high non-urban workload and low non-urban workload. The proposed system is validated using real –world data collected from eight participants.

In [22], authors have used fuzzy inferencing to model the stress faced by students during COVID-19 in University education. Three types of factors including controllable, intermediate and uncontrollable have been defined. Mamdani type inferencing with Triangular membership functions has been used. Results have been divided into three categories called reflecting short term, medium term and long-term stress management schemes for university students with a focus on far flung Universities of Pakistan. It has been concluded that fuzzy system can model students stress in an efficient manner.

The literature review shows that identifying stress using automated intelligent systems is an important area of research and there is need to investigate various soft computing methods. In this research, a fuzzy logic-based system with membership functions training through HC and SA algorithms for stress recognition using physiological sensors has been developed.

In the next section, the proposed system is elaborated along with the required results and discussion.

3   Proposed Fuzzy Based Stress Detection System

This section presents the proposed setup for identification of stress through physiological sensors. The signals of interest for the proposed system are assumed as heart rate, GSR and temperature. These parameters are fed to a fuzzy Mamdani system. Each of the inputs is distributed in three levels i.e. low, medium and high. The results are decided into the binary classification issue i.e. stressed or normal. The stress identification factors are now elaborated.

Heart Rate
Heart Rate measures the breathing rate of a person. Studies show that this parameter is significantly related to the detection of stress levels in a human body [23]. Heart rate displays the heart activity when Autonomous Nervous System (ANS) reacts to cope up with increasing demands of the human body. Hence, it is dependent on the stimuli

which initially provoked the body. The value of heart rate above 50 shows the candidate is healthy. If the value comes out to be 14–25, it is attributed as slightly stressed and 2–15 with hyper stressed.

Galvanic Skin Response
Skin temperature is also one of the key parameters to detect the mental health of a person. It is also known as Electro Dermal Activity (EDA). It measures the skin conductance [24, 25]. Typically, GSR electrodes are connected to a human being to measure the sweat levels of a person. Hence, GSR indicates the healthy human being by showing lower GSR levels and higher levels for person being stressed.

Temperature
The literature shows that the body temperature is also a pivotal parameter to detect the mental state of person in connection with other parameters. The average body temperature of an individual is around 36–37 °C. Hence, a change in human being can be arrested as the temperature changes from the listed levels.

The FIS consists of three input variables Heart Rate, GSR and Temperature. Each of these variables has three membership functions low, medium, and high. The output of the system is Normal or Stressed based on two membership function values. Mamdani type Inferencing has been used and based on the type of parameter, triangular or Trapezoidal membership functions have been used. Centroid defuzzification method has been used. Figure 1 shows the proposed setup for identification of stressed person through physiological sensors. Different Physiological sensors as available in the literature might be used for obtaining reliable data. After computing machine has determined the diagnosis using fuzzy system, the result is sent to patients and consultants. This can help consultants to understand the case better and also taking patients into confidence for future plan regarding treatment if stress is confirmed by the system.

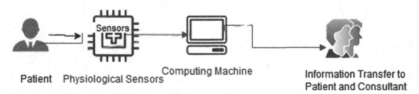

Patient   Physiological Sensors   Computing Machine   Information Transfer to
                                                            Patient and Consultant

Fig. 1. Shows the proposed setup.

Figures 2, 3 and 4 show the input levels of sensors fed to the System. The output levels of the proposed system are shown in Fig. 5.

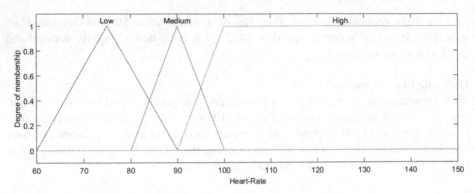

Fig. 2. Shows the heart rate levels for FIS system

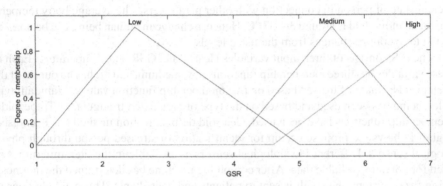

Fig. 3. Shows the GSR levels

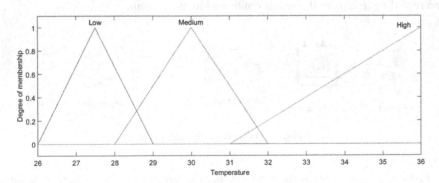

Fig. 4. Shows the temperature levels

The proposed system is implemented through following procedural steps to reach out to the Stressed or Normal Conditions of a person. These steps are elaborated in Fig. 6. It can be seen that once fuzzy inferencing system (FIS) has been evaluated with HC and SA algorithms, accuracy acceptability is determined. It is acceptable only when the current result is better than the previous result, otherwise the system goes back to the previous position in both cases of HC and SA [26].

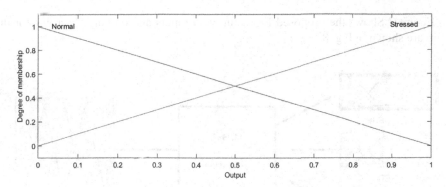

Fig. 5. Shows output levels

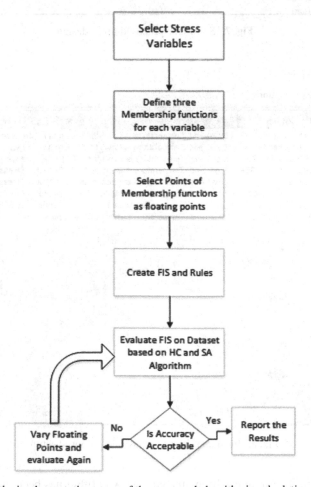

Fig. 6. Shows the implementation steps of the proposed algorithmic calculation of stress levels.

Figure 7 Shows the proposed FIS setup with inputs and output. The rules for the setup are shown in Fig. 8.

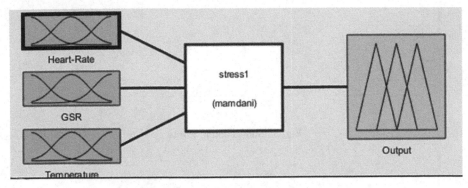

Fig. 7. Shows the proposed fuzzy design

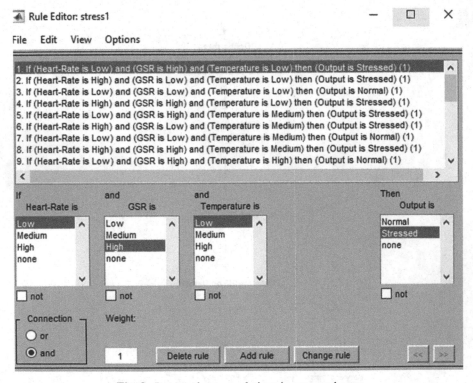

Fig. 8. Input and output relations in proposed setup

Once the basic system has been created, HC Algorithm has been used to train the membership functions. For this purpose, Floating Points have been used which are corners of the membership functions for each variable. These floating points have been given random values in incremental and decremented manner to find the optimal value of the membership function suitable to the system. Each time an increment or decrement is made, system is evaluated and accuracy is compared and if found better then it is further incremented or decremented in the direction the accuracy is improving in the Hill Climbing fashion followed by SA algorithm. The system stops after 1000 iterations or if value does not improve for the 10 consecutive iterations which might indicate a local optimal solution. Figure 9 shows the optimum connections for proposed setup.

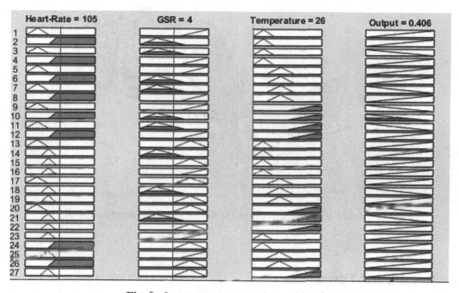

Fig. 9. Input output connections with rules

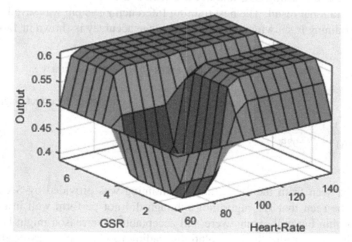

Fig. 10. Surface view of the proposed system with GSR and heart rate

Figure 10 shows the surface view of the output for the proposed setup. Clearly indicating the fact that under the condition that both of these inputs rise the probability of person being stressed is increase. Similarly, the similar outcome can be seen for the other input connections and the output. However, the results are similar as expected (Fig. 11).

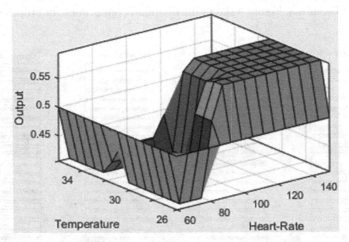

Fig. 11. Surface view of the proposed system with temperature and heart rate

4   Results and Discussion

The data set contains 500 synthetic entries towards various connections. The dataset has been divided into training and testing data. 60% data points were used for training and remaining 40% for testing. HC and SA algorithms are used to determine the optimal peak for the rational result. The best training Inferencing system was saved. The result of the best training is shown in terms of percentage accuracy is shown in Table 1:

Table 1. Training result in terms of percentage accuracy

Type	Percentage correct diagnosis	Percentage incorrect diagnosis
Training (HC)	81%	19%
Training (SA)	92%	8%

It can be seen from the Table that best training was provided by SA algorithm. It can also be seen that HC algorithm although did not perform well in comparison to SA algorithm but still results were still acceptable. The reason might be ability of SA algorithm to consider the bad solutions leading to good solutions on the basis of probability [26]. The results of the testing data have been shown in Table 2:

Table 2. Testing result in terms of percentage accuracy

Type	Percentage correct diagnosis	Percentage incorrect diagnosis
Testing (HC)	80%	20%
Testing (SA)	89%	11%

It can be seen from Table 2 that testing data results are also in line with the training data. SA algorithm was able to provide higher accuracy in terms of stress diagnosis. HC algorithm had higher percentage of incorrect diagnosis. These results also reaffirm the results of the literature that in certain cases, SA algorithm performs better as compared to HC when the results are likely to converged into local optimal solution [27]. However, to get more confidence in the results, different fitness functions, temperatures are required to be investigated.

5 Conclusion and Future Work

Stress is a silent killer. However, this disease can be detected through assessing a change in vital signs of a person. These vital signs can be detected through physiological sensors. In this paper, a Fuzzy Inferencing system is proposed and implemented that takes three input variables and decides the presence of presence or absence of risky stress levels in a human body. Mamdani inferencing scheme has been used with triangular membership functions. To find the optimal values of membership function parameters, HC and SA algorithms have been used. Floating point membership parameters have been identified and trained. The final output of the proposed system classifies the case as normal or stressed. The results suggest that the proposed system can be highly useful in the modern age, there are many events in which stress is increased and we most of the people passing through this disease are unable to identify. The testing efficiently shows that the SA algorithm results in better performance in comparison to the HC algorithm. In future, more real time datasets would be obtained and compared with the existing system in addition to using type-2 fuzzy logic and deep learning to investigate the level of complexities in the datasets as type-2 fuzzy logic has shown to provide better results in case of high level of complexity. Different fitness functions and temperatures would also be investigated for SA algorithm. Besides that, noninvasive sensors shall be used to gather vital signs of persons stress and integrate them in the current system.

Acknowledgment. Dr. Shabbar Naqvi would like to thank the administration of Balochistan University of Engineering and Technology Khuzdar, Balochistan, Pakistan for providing resources to complete the research.

References

1. Cohen, B.E., Edmondson, D., Kronish, I.M.: State of the art review: depression, stress, anxiety, and cardiovascular disease. Am. J. Hypertens. **28**(11), 1295–1302 (2015). https://doi.org/10.1093/ajh/hpv047

2. Liu, Y., Cao, L., Li, X., Jia, Y., Xia, H.: Awareness of mental health problems in patients with coronavirus disease 19 (COVID-19): a lesson from an adult man attempting suicide. Asian J. Psychiatr. **51**, 102106 (2020). https://doi.org/10.1016/j.ajp.2020.102106
3. Coan, J.A., Allen, J.J.B.: Frontal EEG asymmetry as a moderator and mediator of emotion. Biol. Psychol. **67**(1), 7–50 (2004). https://doi.org/10.1016/j.biopsycho.2004.03.002
4. Poon, C.-S., Siniaia, M.S.: Plasticity of cardiorespiratory neural processing: classification and computational functions. Respir. Physiol. **122**(2–3), 83–109 (2000)
5. Sadati, S.M.S., Qureshi, F.U., Baker, D.: Energetic and economic performance analyses of photovoltaic, parabolic trough collector and wind energy systems for Multan, Pakistan. Renew. Sustain. Energy Rev. **47**, 844–855 (2015). https://doi.org/10.1016/j.rser.2015.03.084
6. Picard, R.W.: Affective Computing. MIT Press, Cambridge (2000)
7. Can, Y.S., Arnrich, B., Ersoy, C.: Stress detection in daily life scenarios using smart phones and wearable sensors: a survey. J. Biomed. Inform. **92**, 103139 (2019). https://doi.org/10.1016/j.jbi.2019.103139
8. Ghulam, M., Yannick, F., Abdelkader, G., Michel, F., Hocine, N.: Level of detail based AI adaptation for agents in video games. In: 5th International Conference on Agents and Artificial Intelligence (ICAART) (2013).https://doi.org/10.1007/978-3-642-29966-7
9. Mahdi, G., Gouaich, A.: Interval based integrated real-time coordination for multi-agent systems. In: Proceedings of the 3rd International Conference on Agents and Artificial Intelligence - Volume 1: ICAART, pp. 664–669, (2011) https://doi.org/10.5220/0003188406640669
10. Baloch, S.A., Shaikh, A.Z.: Fuzzy logic enabled spectrum access scheme for cognitive radio applications. In: International Conference on Innovations in Computer Science (2018)
11. Baloch, S.A., Shaikh, A.Z., Ahmed, A.: Survey on fuzzy logic enabled cognitive radio. In: International Conference for Emerging Technologies in Computing, pp. 190–196 (2018)
12. Ahmed, M., Naqvi, S., Ali, I., Uddin, S., Shaikh, A.Z.: A fuzzy inferencing system for highlighting the complexities involved in electronic surveys with emotions. Int. J. Comput. Sci. Netw. Secur. **19**(10), 6–14 (2019)
13. de Santos Sierra, A., Avila, C.S., Casanova, J.G., del Pozo, G.: A stress-detection system based on physiological signals and fuzzy logic. IEEE Trans. Ind. Electron. **58**(10), 4857–4865 (2011). https://doi.org/10.1109/TIE.2010.2103538
14. Zalabarria, U., Irigoyen, E., Martinez, R., Larrea, M., Salazar-Ramirez, A.: A low-cost, portable solution for stress and relaxation estimation based on a real-time fuzzy algorithm. IEEE Access **8**, 74118–74128 (2020). https://doi.org/10.1109/ACCESS.2020.2988348
15. Chen, J., Abbod, M., Shieh, J.-S.: Pain and stress detection using wearable sensors and devices—a review. Sensors, **21**(4) (2021). https://doi.org/10.3390/s21041030
16. Albertetti, F., Simalastar, A., Rizzotti-Kaddour, A.: Stress detection with deep learning approaches using physiological signals. In: Lecture Notes of the Institute for Computer Sciences, Social Informatics and Telecommunications Engineering, pp. 95–111 (2020)
17. Durán-Acevedo, C.M., Carrillo-Gómez, J.K., Albarracín-Rojas, C.A.: Electronic devices for stress detection in academic contexts during confinement because of the COVID-19 pandemic. Electronics, **10**(3) (2021). https://doi.org/10.3390/electronics10030301
18. Salazar-Ramirez, A., Irigoyen, E., Martinez, R., Zalabarria, U.: An enhanced fuzzy algorithm based on advanced signal processing for identification of stress. Neurocomputing **271**, 48–57 (2018). https://doi.org/10.1016/j.neucom.2016.08.153
19. Lakshmi, B., Boban, E., Sulphikar, N., Aparna, T.M., Dhanya, S., Anjaly, S.V.: Mental stress calculation using fuzzy logic algorithm. Int. J. Appl. Eng. Res. **15**(1), 35–43 (2020)
20. Ceniza, A., Cantara, A.: Stress sensor prototype: determining the stress level in using a computer through validated self-made Heart Rate (HR) and Galvanic Skin Response (GSR) sensors and fuzzy logic algorithm. Int. J. Eng. Res. Technol., **5**(3) (2016)

21. Dobbins, C., Fairclough, S.: Detecting and visualizing context and stress via a fuzzy rule-based system during commuter driving. IEEE Int. Conf. Pervasive Comput. Commun. Workshops (PerCom Workshops) **2019**, 499–504 (2019). https://doi.org/10.1109/PERCOMW.2019.873 0600

22. Karim, S., et al.: A fuzzy inferencing system for stress management of university students in COVID-19 for Pakistan. In: 2nd International Conference on Computational Sciences and Technologies, 17–19 December 2020 (INCCST 2020), MUET Jamshoro, pp. 5–10 (2020)

23. de Santos Sierra, A., Ávila, C.S., del Pozo, G., Casanova, J.G.: Stress detection by means of stress physiological template. In: 2011 Third World Congress on Nature and Biologically Inspired Computing, pp. 131–136 (2011). https://doi.org/10.1109/NaBIC.2011.6089448

24. Shi, Y., Ruiz, N., Taib, R., Choi, E., Chen, F.: Galvanic Skin Response (GSR) as an index of cognitive load. In: CHI 2007 Extended Abstracts on Human Factors in Computing Systems, New York, NY, USA: Association for Computing Machinery, pp. 2651–2656 (2007)

25. Zhai, J., Barreto, A.: Stress detection in computer users based on digital signal processing of noninvasive physiological variables. Int. Conf. IEEE Eng. Med. Biol. Soc. **2006**, 1355–1358 (2006). https://doi.org/10.1109/IEMBS.2006.259421

26. Naqvi, S.: Modelling FTIR Spectral Data with Type-I and Type-II Fuzzy Sets for Breast Cancer Grading, Ph. D. Thesis, The University of Nottingham for the Degree of Doctor of Philosophy. The University of Nottingham (2014)

27. Suman, B., Kumar, P.: A survey of simulated annealing as a tool for single and multiobjective optimization. J. Oper. Res. Soc. **57**, 1143–1160 (2006)

The Auxiliary Parametric Sensitivity Method as a Means of Improving Project Management Analysis and Synthesis of Executive Elements

Serhii Kostiuchko[1] , Mykola Polishchuk[1] , Oleg Zabolotnyi[1(✉)] ,
Anatolii Tkachuk[1] , and Boguslaw Twarog[2]

[1] Lutsk National Technical University, 75, Lvivska street, Lusk 43018, Ukraine
volynasi@gmail.com
[2] Rzeszów University, 1, Pigonia street, 35-310 Rzeszów, Poland

Abstract. To write differential state equations of investigated actuating devices in the needed Cauchy's normal form, we must abandon the traditional theory of electrical circuits for the theory of electromagnetic circuits. In this work, the known and developed new mathematical models for the analysis of special states have been involved. For solving this problem, it is necessary, at first, to construct a mathematical model of the actuating device. This model is based on the construction of a monodromy matrix, and simulation of transient and steady-state processes at the same time. To make the numerical analysis more convenient, differential equations for models of electromechanical state are written down in Cauchy's normal form. The algorithm involves the study of transient and stationary processes by decomposing them into constituent parts using the mathematical apparatus of the classical theory of nonlinear differential equations, which are calculated in a relatively simple way. The transitional process is obtained as a result of the differentiation of state equations for given initial conditions. We obtain a steady-state process by the initial conditions that exclude transient response. Such conditions we receive by the iterative Newton method. The proposed method of auxiliary variation equations allowed bypass procedure of differentiation of matrix coefficients over the argument that ensured the possibility of the algorithm application of the method of parametric sensitivity. The method of analysis can be spread to more complex nonlinear systems, such as electric motors.

Keywords: Asynchronous motor · Auxiliary parametric sensitivity · Project management · Transition process

1 Introduction

The tasks that solve the problem of improving the management of projects of analysis and synthesis of technical computerized systems are characterized by the use of gradient methods, which leads to the problem of constructing matrices of parametric sensitivity [1, 2]. When the gradients (rows of such a matrix) of certain variables in the field that characterizes the constant values of the parameters allow accelerating the procedure of

M. H. Miraz et al. (Eds.): iCETiC 2021, LNICST 395, pp. 174–184, 2021.
https://doi.org/10.1007/978-3-030-90016-8_12

designing variational differential equations to the optimal level [3, 4]. Since the main current engineering problem is to develop a mechanism for creating differential equations that on the one hand determine the physical state of a particular electrodynamic system, and on the other hand they are variational. Therefore, a method for constructing auxiliary variational equations of parametric sensitivity is proposed [5, 6].

The auxiliary model of parametric sensitivity is a modern apparatus of classical nonlinear differential equations theory, which creates preconditions for facilitating the calculation and modeling of electromagnetic processes. This makes it possible to determine all stages of the analysis of electromagnetic systems: the calculation of transient and stable processes of a real physical system, the determination of static stability of processes and the parametric sensitivity of this system. Thus, in this case, the auxiliary model of parametric sensitivity is a kind of generalized auxiliary model of sensitivity to the initial conditions of the physical system.

This proposed method has been carefully tested in the most complex practical problems of project management analysis and synthesis of electromagnetic nonlinear technical systems [1, 7].

2 Literature Review

The system of differential equations of the physical system in vector form has the form [8, 9]

$$\frac{d\mathbf{x}}{dt} = f_1(\mathbf{x}, \boldsymbol{\lambda}, t); \quad 0 \le t \le \infty, \tag{1}$$

where $f_1(\mathbf{x}, \boldsymbol{\lambda}, t)$: t – certain periodic function, $\mathbf{x} = (x_1, x_2, \ldots, x_n)$; $\boldsymbol{\lambda} = (\lambda_1, \lambda_2, \ldots, \lambda_n)$ – vectors that characterize the constant parameters of the system.

It must be assumed that there is a periodic solution of the system of differential Eqs. (1) in the form $x(t) = x(t + T)$. Taking into account the initial conditions, $\mathbf{x}(0)$ becomes possible to enter directly into the batch solution, without taking into account the transient reaction of the system. In the periodicity equation, they will be an argument [9]

$$f(\mathbf{x}(0)) = \mathbf{x}(0) - \mathbf{x}(\mathbf{x}(0), T) = 0 \tag{2}$$

If we analyze Eqs. (1), (2), it is clear that they constitute a two-point T-periodic boundary value problem for nonlinear differential equations for determining the state of a physical system.

The obtained nonlinear transcendental Eq. (2) must be solved using Newton's iteration method.

$$\mathbf{x}(0)^{s+1} = \mathbf{x}(0)^s - f'\left(\mathbf{x}(0)^s\right)^{-1} f\left(\mathbf{x}(0)^s\right) \tag{3}$$

Equations in the form of Jacobi matrices $f'(\mathbf{x}(0))$ is obtained by differentiation $x(0)$ of the objective function (see Eqs. 2) [10]

$$f'(\mathbf{x}(0)) = \mathbf{E} - \boldsymbol{\Phi}(T) \tag{4}$$

where

$$\Phi(T) = \frac{\partial \mathbf{x}(\mathbf{x}(0), t)}{\partial \mathbf{x}(0)}\bigg|_{t=T} \tag{5}$$

Expression (5) can be called a matrix of monodromy and use it in the future. This matrix is obtained from the calculations of the equation of the first variation by differentiating expression (1) on $\mathbf{x}(0)$:

$$\frac{d\Phi}{dt} = \frac{\partial f(\mathbf{x}, t)}{\partial \mathbf{x}}\Phi. \tag{6}$$

Together with expression (6) it is necessary to integrate expression (1) on the s-th iteration of Newton's formula using a regulated time interval. Completion of the iteration process is confirmed by the given accuracy of the periodic solution of these equations [11, 12].

Parameter Φ (5) is a matrix of sensitivity to the initial conditions of the system. Thus, the rows of the obtained matrix determine the gradient of a certain one variable in the space of initial conditions, and the columns of the matrix - the sensitivity of the total set of obtained variables to one initial condition. Therefore, the study of the above differential equation is a prototype of the model of sensitivity to the initial conditions of real electromagnetic physical systems [13, 14].

The obtained eigenvalues of the monodromy matrix (5) characterize the static stability of the studied physical process (under regulated conditions). The calculation of parametric sensitivity is usually recommended by variational methods (based on Newtonian iterations (3)) [15].

Differentiation by λ we obtain a matrix of parametric sensitivities

$$\mathbf{S} = \frac{\partial \mathbf{x}}{\partial \lambda} \tag{7}$$

The element of matrix λ can be any constant parameter of the system under study. Differentiating (1) by λ we obtain a linear parametric equation [16]

$$\frac{d\mathbf{S}}{dt} = \frac{\partial f_1(\mathbf{x}, \lambda, t)}{\partial \mathbf{x}}S + \frac{\partial f_1(\mathbf{x}, \lambda, t)}{\partial \lambda} \tag{8}$$

In a stable state, $\mathbf{x}(0) = \mathbf{x}(T)$, therefore, Eq. (8) also has a $\mathbf{S}(t)$ periodic solution.

The complexity, in this case, is caused by partial derivatives of $\mathbf{x}$ and λ in the right part (6), (8). In order to implement the selected strategy, it is proposed to use a matrix of auxiliary parametric sensitivities of parameter χ for some vector $\mathbf{y}$:

$$\chi = \frac{d\mathbf{y}}{d\lambda}; \quad \mathbf{S} = \mathbf{A}\chi, \tag{9}$$

where $\mathbf{A}$ is the matrix that determines the coefficients for Eq. (1) [1].

According to new vector $\mathbf{y}$ we form the equation of state [9]:

$$d\mathbf{y}/dt = f_2(\mathbf{x}, \lambda, t) = f_3(\mathbf{y}, \lambda, t) \tag{10}$$

f_2 – the periodic function of the parameter t.

After differentiating expression (10) by λ and taking into account the results of expressions (5), (6), we obtain the following [2]

$$\frac{d\chi}{dt} = \frac{\partial f_3(\mathbf{y}, \lambda, t)}{\partial \mathbf{x}}\chi + \frac{\partial f_3(\mathbf{y}, \lambda, t)}{\partial \lambda} \tag{11}$$

This equation has a periodic solution $\chi(t)$.

Replacing $\mathbf{x}$ with $\mathbf{y}$ should be done so that Eq. (10) is simpler than Eq. (1). Such substitution will be valid in the case when the relationship between the values of $\mathbf{x}$ and $\mathbf{y}$ is established [17].

Therefore, if we assume that $\lambda = \chi(0)$, then (11) turns into a homogeneous expression

$$\frac{d\chi}{dt} = \frac{\partial f_2(\chi, \lambda, t)}{\partial \mathbf{x}}A\chi \tag{12}$$

from will describe the sensitivity models of the system to its initial conditions (6).

The result of solving Eq. (3) will be the periodic solution of Eq. (11). In the process of solving Eqs. (1), (3), and (11), a periodic solution of the equations of state of the system in the form of a matrix (5) was obtained.

In order to continue the distribution on the column and implement the record in the form of a vector matrix (9) it is necessary to take into account

$$\chi = \left(\chi_1, \chi_2, \dots, \chi_m\right) \tag{13}$$

where m is the number of elements that make up the vector of constant parameters of the expression $\lambda = (\lambda_1, \lambda_2, \dots, \lambda_m)$, $2\,\lambda = \text{const.}$ Moreover

$$\chi_i = d\mathbf{y}/\partial \lambda_i, \quad i = 1, 2, \dots, m \tag{14}$$

are vectors of parametric sensitivities of vector elements $\mathbf{y}$ to individual constant parameters.

The condition of the periodic solution of the differential Eq. (11) is written analogously to (2)

$$F\left(\chi_i(0)\right) = \chi_i(0) - \chi_i\left(\chi_i(0), T\right) = 0, \quad i = 1, 2, \dots, n \tag{15}$$

Equation (15) can be solved using Newton's iteration method, but because expression (11) is a linear equation, the solution is greater than one iteration. In the case of zero approximation (3) will look like

$$\chi_i(0) = F'\left(\chi_i(0)\right)^{-1}\chi_i(T), \quad i = 1, \dots, n. \tag{16}$$

The resulting Jacobi matrix should be expressed in terms of the known matrix, and in our case $\Phi(T)$, which is obtained by calculating the periodic equation $x(t) = x(t + T)$

$$F'\left(\chi_i(0)\right) = \mathbf{E} - \Phi(T) \tag{17}$$

Using the initial conditions found in (16) and integrating (11), and making the transition (9) from $S_i(0)$ to $\chi_i(0)$, we find the periodic solution $\chi(t) + \chi(t+T) = 0$. In accordance with expression (9), we find the sensitivity S.

The transformation of functions of continuous variables into functions of discrete variables is carried out by explicit or implicit methods. When using implicit methods of the Jacobi matrix, the basic equation and the goal equation coincide.

For a practical demonstration, let's take the example of an executive three-phase asynchronous motor of a computerized control system.

3   Researches Methodology

Equation (1) of the electromagnetic state of the electric motor is written as [1, 2]

$$\frac{d\mathbf{i}}{dt} = \mathbf{A}(\mathbf{u} - \Omega'\Psi - \mathbf{R}\mathbf{i}), \tag{18}$$

where

$$\begin{array}{|c|}\hline \lambda_S \\\hline \lambda_R \\\hline\end{array},\ \lambda = \mathbf{u}, \Psi, \mathbf{i};\quad \mathbf{A} = \begin{array}{|c|c|}\hline \mathbf{A}_S & \mathbf{A}_{SR} \\\hline \mathbf{A}_{RS} & \mathbf{A}_R \\\hline\end{array};$$

$$\Omega' = \begin{array}{|c|c|}\hline & \\\hline & \Omega \\\hline\end{array};\quad \mathbf{R} = \begin{array}{|c|c|}\hline \mathbf{R}_S & \\\hline & \mathbf{R}_R \\\hline\end{array}. \tag{19}$$

Here $\mathbf{i}_k = (i_{kA}, i_{kB})_t$, $k = S, R$ – columns of phase currents of a stator winding and the converted currents of a rotor winding; $\Psi_k = (i_{kA}, i_{kB})_t$, $k = S, R$ – columns of the corresponding phase full flux couplings; $\mathbf{u}_k = (u_{kA}, u_{kB})_t$, $k = S, R$ – columns of phase voltages of the stator winding; $\mathbf{A}_S$, $\mathbf{A}_{SR}$, $\mathbf{A}_{RS}$, $\mathbf{A}_R$ – matrices

$$\mathbf{A}_S = \alpha_S(1 - \alpha_S\mathbf{G}); \quad \mathbf{A}_{SR} = \mathbf{A}_{RS} = -\alpha_S\alpha_R\mathbf{G};$$
$$\mathbf{A}_R = \alpha_R(1 - \alpha_R\mathbf{G}), \tag{20}$$

where $\mathbf{G}$, Ω – matrices.

$$\mathbf{G} = \begin{array}{|c|c|}\hline T + b_A i_A & b_B i_A \\\hline b_A i_B & T + b_B i_B \\\hline\end{array},\quad \Omega = \frac{\omega}{\sqrt{3}}\begin{array}{|c|c|}\hline -1 & -2 \\\hline 2 & 1 \\\hline\end{array}. \tag{21}$$

moreover

$$b_A = b(2i_A + i_B); \quad b_B = b(i_A + 2i_B); \quad b = \frac{2}{3}\frac{R - T}{i_m^2}; \tag{22}$$

$$R = \frac{1}{\alpha_S + \alpha_R + \rho}; \quad T = \frac{1}{\alpha_S + \alpha_R + \tau}. \tag{23}$$

In expression (23) τ, ρ – inverse static and differential inductances, they are found by the characteristic of magnetization (idling) of the motor as:

$$\tau = \left[\frac{\psi_m(i_m)}{i_m}\right]^{-1}; \quad \rho = \left[\frac{d\psi_m(i_m)}{di_m}\right]^{-1} \tag{24}$$

where i_m is the modulus of the spatial vector of magnetizing currents

$$i_m = 2\sqrt{(i_A^2 + i_A i_B + i_B^2)/3}; \quad i_A = i_{SA} + i_{RA}; \quad i_B = i_{SB} + i_{RB}. \tag{25}$$

In the absence of saturation, the magnetization characteristic degenerates into a straight line $i_m = \alpha_m \psi_m$, where α_m is the reverse main inductance, and matrix (21) according to (23) into a diagonal one, which greatly simplifies Eqs. (1).

$$\mathbf{G} = \frac{1}{\alpha_S + \alpha_R + \alpha_m} \begin{array}{|c|c|} \hline 1 & \\ \hline & 1 \\ \hline \end{array}, \tag{26}$$

In this case, we get the simplest of all known mathematical model of an induction motor; $\mathbf{R}_S$, $\mathbf{R}_R$ – resistance matrices and α_S, α_R, – reverse dissipation inductances of the stator and rotor windings; r_S – resistance of stator phases; r_R – reduced resistance of the rotor winding; Ω – angular velocity matrix ω.

$$\mathbf{R}_s = \begin{array}{|c|c|} \hline r_S & \\ \hline & r_S \\ \hline \end{array}; \quad \mathbf{R}_R = \begin{array}{|c|c|} \hline r_R & \\ \hline & r_R \\ \hline \end{array}, \tag{27}$$

The components of the actual electromagnetic quantities of the rotor and stator windings of an induction motor can be found by

$$\psi_{kj} - \frac{1}{\tau}(i_{Sj} + i_{Rj}) + \frac{1}{\alpha_k} i_{kj}, \quad j = A, B; \quad k = S, R. \tag{28}$$

The equation of the mechanical state of an electric motor in a computerized control system has the form

$$\frac{d\omega}{dt} = \frac{p_0}{J}(M_E - M(\omega)), \quad M_E = \sqrt{3} p_0(\psi_{SA} i_{SB} - \psi_{SB} i_{SA}), \tag{29}$$

where $M(\omega)$ is the mechanical moment of an induction motor; p_0 – the number of pairs of magnetic poles of an induction motor; J – moment of inertia of the engine (on a shaft); M_E – the electromagnetic moment of the system as a whole.

The mathematical A-model of this device is described by the system of differential Eqs. (18), (29). With its help, we can calculate transient and stable processes. The practical use of this model requires knowledge of certain technical characteristics of the object under study.

4   Results

The formation of columns of unknowns is as follows

$$\mathbf{x} = (\mathbf{i}, \omega)_t; \quad \mathbf{y} = (\mathbf{\Psi}, \omega)_t. \tag{30}$$

The differential Eq. (1) corresponding to $\mathbf{y}$ has the form

$$\frac{d\mathbf{\Psi}}{dt} = \mathbf{u} - \Omega' \mathbf{\Psi} - \mathbf{R}\mathbf{i}, \quad \mathbf{i} = \mathbf{L}^{-1}\mathbf{\Psi}, \tag{31}$$

where L^{-1} – the inverse matrix of static inductors.

$$
L^{-1} = T
\begin{array}{|c|c|c|c|}
\hline
\alpha_S(\alpha_R + \tau) & & -\alpha_S\alpha_R & \\
\hline
& \alpha_S(\alpha_R + \tau) & & -\alpha_S\alpha_R \\
\hline
-\alpha_S\alpha_R & & \alpha_R(\alpha_S + \tau) & \\
\hline
& -\alpha_S\alpha_R & & \alpha_R(\alpha_S + \tau) \\
\hline
\end{array}
\tag{32}
$$

We write the monodromy matrix similarly to expression (9)

$$
\Phi = (Az, w)_t, \tag{33}
$$

where

$$
z = \frac{\partial \Psi}{\partial x(0)}; \quad w = \frac{\partial \omega}{\partial x(0)}. \tag{34}
$$

Variation equations for calculating submatrices (34) are determined by differentiation by $x(0)$ of the equations of the electromechanical state of an induction motor under the control of a computerized system (29), (31).

Differentiating expression (31), we obtain

$$
\frac{dz}{dt} = -(\Omega' + RA)z - \frac{\partial \Omega'}{\partial \omega} w\Psi. \tag{35}
$$

Performing differentiation operations on $x(0)$ of expression (29), it was obtained

$$
\frac{dw}{dt} = \frac{p_0}{J}\left(\sqrt{3}p_0(\tfrac{\partial \Psi_{SA}}{\partial x(0)} i_{SB} + \Psi_{SA}\tfrac{\partial i_{SB}}{\partial x(0)} - \tfrac{\partial \Psi_{SB}}{\partial x(0)} i_{SA} - \Psi_{SB}\tfrac{\partial i_{SA}}{\partial x(0)}) - \frac{\partial M(\omega)}{\partial \omega} w\right. \tag{36}
$$

Derivatives $\partial\Psi_{SA}/\partial x(0)$, $\partial\Psi_{SB}/\partial x(0)$, $\partial i_{SA}/\partial x(0)$, $\partial i_{SB}/\partial x(0)$ are elements of the matrices z, Az, so they are known.

Thus, the construction of the monodromy matrix of an induction motor requires, in conjunction with (18), (29), the integrations of the equations of the first variation (35), (36).

The equation of parametric sensitivities is obtained similarly to (35), (36) if we replace by λ.

$$
\frac{d\chi}{dt} = -(\Omega' + RA)\chi - \frac{\partial \Omega'}{\partial \omega} w\Psi + F; \quad \chi = \frac{\partial \Psi}{\partial \lambda};
$$

$$
F = \frac{\partial U}{\partial \lambda} + RL^{-1}\frac{\partial L}{\partial \lambda} i - \frac{\partial \Omega}{\partial \lambda}\Psi - \frac{\partial R}{\partial \lambda} i. \tag{37}
$$

$$
\frac{d\eta}{dt} = \frac{p_0}{J}\left(\frac{\partial M_E}{\partial \lambda} - \frac{\partial M(\omega)}{\partial \omega}\eta\right) + p_0(M_E - M(\omega))\frac{\partial(1/J)}{\partial \lambda};
$$

$$
\frac{\partial M_E}{\partial \lambda} = \sqrt{3}p_0(\xi_{SA}i_{SB} + \Psi_{SA}S_{SB} - \xi_{SB}i_{SA} - \Psi_{SB}S_{SA}). \tag{38}
$$

The matrix of static inductances of an induction motor L has the form [2, 9]

$$
\mathbf{L} =
\begin{array}{|c|c|c|c|}
\hline
l_S + l_\tau & & l_\tau & \\
\hline
& l_S + l_\tau & & l_\tau \\
\hline
l_\tau & & l_R + l_\tau & \\
\hline
& l_\tau & & l_R + l_\tau \\
\hline
\end{array},
\tag{39}
$$

In this case $l_S = 1/\alpha_S$, $l_R = 1/\alpha_R$ – inductance of dissipation of windings of a stator and a rotor; $l_\tau = 1/\tau$ – basic static inductance.

The matrix of parametric sensitivities S in our case repeats the expression (33)

$$
\mathbf{S} = (\mathbf{A}\chi, \eta)_t,
\tag{40}
$$

5 Conclusions

In order to formulate an application problem related to an induction motor, you need to write columns of unknown values of expression (30) in extended form, as follows

$$
\mathbf{x} = (i_{SA},\ i_{SB},\ i_{RA},\ i_{RB},\ \omega)_t; \qquad \mathbf{y} = (\Psi_{SA},\ \Psi_{SB},\ \Psi_{RA},\ \Psi_{RB},\ \omega)_t.
\tag{41}
$$

Derivatives λ from the elements of column $\lambda = (\lambda_1, \lambda_2, \ldots, \lambda_n)$ must be carried out according to the rules of differentiation of complex functions because they can be functions from the parameters of the system.

The use of formulas (1)–(17) allows for practical analysis. The analysis of the transient process is carried out by simultaneous integration of the system (1), (11) on a time interval $[0, \infty]$.

In practical implementation, this equation corresponds to the system of differential Eqs. (18), (29), (37), (38).

In the process of performing the iteration, the integration of differential Eqs. (1) and (12) was performed in parallel. The resulting system corresponds to a system of differential Eqs. (18), (29), (35), (36) by which it is possible to determine the parametric sensitivity of the physical system.

In the process of analysis of stationary parametric sensitivity, formula (16) is used in one iteration. On it, differential Eqs. (1), (11), which correspond to a specific system of differential Eqs. (18), (29), (37), (38), are subject to joint integration at time step $[0, T]$. As a result, we find periodic time functions of the set currents, angular velocity, and their parametric sensitivities to a set of constant parameters. The obtained results in the form of periodic solutions of equations are not convenient for practical use, so it is necessary to convert them to the form root mean square values:

$$
\mathbf{S} = \sqrt{\frac{1}{T} \int_0^T \mathbf{S}(t)^2 dt}.
\tag{42}
$$

Table 1. Full RMS sensitivities

	r_S	r_R	U_m	J	l_R	l_S
ω	1.26	2.29	$1.22 \cdot 10^{-3}$	$3.29 \cdot 10^{-4}$	59.27	46.96
M_E	37.30	1.95	$5.18 \cdot 10^{-2}$	$1.44 \cdot 10^{-2}$	2085.60	2117.50

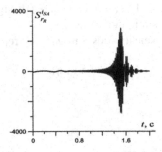

Fig. 1. The result of modeling the transient parametric current sensitivity on the stator of the motor to the resistance of the winding of its rotor

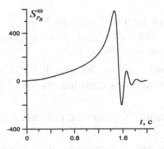

Fig. 2. The results of modeling the transient parametric sensitivity of the angular velocity of an induction motor to the resistance of its rotor winding

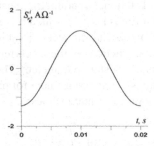

Fig. 3. The results of modeling the stable parametric sensitivity of the stator current of an induction motor to the resistance of its rotor winding

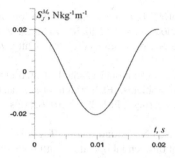

Fig. 4. Stable parametric sensitivity of the electromagnetic moment to the moment of inertia of

Figures 1–4 show the results of simulation of a model induction motor, a table of total RMS sensitivities (42) of angular velocity and electromagnetic moment in the corresponding constant parameters is developed (Table 1).

The method of auxiliary parametric sensitivity creates the preconditions for practical access to gradient methods to the problems of project management analysis and synthesis of nonlinear computerized systems with multipolar elements, as it removes the problem of constructing variational equations.

Thus, further research will focus on a more detailed description of the method of parametric sensitivity and the development of algorithms for its application. It is also planned to apply the developed provisions in practice in computerized control systems for electric motors. Control systems based on this method must have increased productivity and flexibility of setting the operating modes of electric motors.

References

1. Tchaban, V.: Mathematical Modeling in Electrical Engineering. Taras Soroka Publishing House, Lviv (2010)
2. Tchaban, V., Kostiuchko, S., Tchaban, Z.: Auxiliary model of parametric sensitivity. Comput. Probl. Electr. Eng. **2**(2), 105–111 (2012). http://nbuv.gov.ua/UJRN/CPoee_2012_2_2_19
3. Saltelli, A., Marivoet, J.: Non-parametric statistics in sensitivity analysis for model output: a comparison of selected techniques. Reliab. Eng. Syst. Saf. **28**(2), 229–253 (1990). https://doi.org/10.1016/0951-8320(90)90065-U
4. Nacer, M.L., Kherfane, H., Moreau, S., Saad, S.: Robust observer design for uncertain lipschitz nonlinear systems based on differential mean value theorem: application to induction motors. J. Control, Autom. Electr. Syst. **32**(1), 132–144 (2020). https://doi.org/10.1007/s40313-020-00658-w
5. Caiza, G., Garcia, C.A., Naranjo, J.E., Garcia, M.V.: Assessment of engineering techniques for failures simulation in induction motors using numerical tool. In: Iano, Y., Arthur, R., Saotome, O., Kemper, G., Padilha França, R. (eds.) BTSym 2019. SIST, vol. 201, pp. 307–319. Springer, Cham (2021). https://doi.org/10.1007/978-3-030-57548-9_28
6. Mamis, M.S.: Lumped-parameter-based electromagnetic transients simulation of non-uniform singlephase lines using state variable method. IET Gener. Trans. Distrib. **14**(23), 5626–5633 (2020). https://doi.org/10.1049/iet-gtd.2020.0454
7. Bremer, J., Pang, Q., Yang, H.: Fast algorithms for the multi-dimensional Jacobi polynomial transform. Appl. Comput. Harmon. Anal. **52**, 231–250 (2021). https://doi.org/10.1016/j.acha.2020.01.004

8. Farhi, S.E., Sakri, D., Goléa, N.: Control and observation of induction motor using first-order sliding mode. In: Bououden, S., Chadli, M., Ziani, S., Zelinka, I. (eds.) ICEECA 2019. LNEE, vol. 682, pp. 63–76. Springer, Singapore (2021). https://doi.org/10.1007/978-981-15-6403-1_5

9. Kostiuchko, S., Tchaban, V.: Variational Method of auxiliary equations in nonlinear systems analysis and synthesis problems. IEEE 20th International Conference on Computational Problems of Electrical Engineering, CPEE 2019 (2019). https://doi.org/10.1109/CPEE47179.2019.8949123

10. Mirzoev, K.A., Konechnaya, N.N., Safonova, T.A., Tagirova, R.N.: Generalized Jacobi matrices and spectral analysis of differential operators with polynomial coefficients. J. Math. Sci. **252**(2), 213–224 (2020). https://doi.org/10.1007/s10958-020-05154-9

11. Allaire, G., Dapogny, C., Jouve, F.: Shape and topology optimization. Handb. Numer. Anal. **22**, 1–132 (2021). https://doi.org/10.1016/bs.hna.2020.10.004

12. Stechlinski, P., Barton, P.I.: Nonsmooth hessenberg differential-algebraic equations. J. Math. Anal. Appl. **495**(1), 124721 (2021). https://doi.org/10.1016/j.jmaa.2020.124721

13. Pan, Y., Cai, G., Zhang, W.: High-precision flux linkage observation of induction motor at low switching frequency. J. Power Electr. **21**(2), 396–404 (2021). https://doi.org/10.1007/s43236-020-00208-2

14. Liu, G., Wang, Y., Chen, Q., Xu, G., Song, C.: Multiobjective deterministic and robust optimization design of a new spoke-Type permanent magnet machine for the improvement of torque performance. IEEE Trans. Ind. Electr. **67**(12), 10202–10212 (2020). https://doi.org/10.1109/TIE.2019.2962472

15. Xia, J., Yang, Z., Yang, B.: Parametric sensitivity analysis of maintainability design. In: 8th International Conference on Reliability, Maintainability and Safety, pp. 525–555 (2009). https://doi.org/10.1109/ICRMS.2009.5270131

16. Kassis, M.T., Tannir, D., Toukhtarian, R., Khazaka, R.: Moments-based parametric sensitivity analysis of X-parameters. Packag. Manuf. Technol. **9**(12), 2451–2464 (2019). https://doi.org/10.1109/TCPMT.2019.2947588

17. Painen-Paillalef, J.V., Aros-Oñate, N.H.: Parametric sensitivity analysis of an induction machine with predictive control. Conference on Electrical, Electronics Engineering, Information and Communication Technologies (CHILECON), pp. 1–7 (2019). https://doi.org/10.1109/CHILECON47746.2019.8988055

Predicting Diabetes Using Diabetes Datasets and Machine Learning Algorithms: Comparison and Analysis

Bekim Fetaji[1]([⊠]) [iD], Majlinda Fetaji[2] [iD], Mirlinda Ebibi[1], and Maaruf Ali[3] [iD]

[1] Informatics/Computer Sciences, Mother Teresa University, Skopje, Republic of Macedonia
{bekim.fetaji,mirlinda.ebibi}@unt.edu.mk
[2] Computer Sciences, South East European University, Skopje, Republic of Macedonia
m.fetaji@seeu.edu.mk
[3] Computer Engineering, Epoka University, Vorë, Tiranë, Albania
maaruf@ieee.org

Abstract. The performance of three popular machine learning algorithms to predict diabetes based upon using three diabetes datasets is presented. Two of the datasets are from the public domain and the third is composed from a research study group. The J48, Random Forest and Naïve Bayes machine learning algorithms were evaluated. Machine Learning (ML) is used to both analyse and make predictions from data that is simply too voluminous for humans to process. This is especially true with medical data where the use of machine learning and data analytics is still in its infancy. More specifically this research investigates the application of ML algorithms on the growing data from the healthcare industry on the global diabetes epidemic. The performance of ML algorithms to predict diabetes is lacking. This paper provides an analysis of the challenges of machine learning in this field and covers this gap in the research.

Keywords: Machine learning · Diabetes · Diabetes prediction · J48 · Random forest · Naïve Bayes · ML · Healthcare · Datasets · Data analytics

1 Introduction

Machine Learning (ML) [1] has risen rapidly [2] to become one of the most important branches of Artificial Intelligence (AI) and IT with myriad of applications. ML can be defined generally as algorithms that computers are programmed with so that they can learn from the available inputs or in response to external data. ML is usually used for tasks beyond human capabilities such as: analysing large complex datasets, Big Data or making predictions based on the available data analysed.

ML is used for "automated detection of meaningful patterns in data" [2]. Applications [3] of ML include: image and speech recognition, medical diagnosis, learning associations, predictions, classifications etc.

M. H. Miraz et al. (Eds.): iCETiC 2021, LNICST 395, pp. 185–193, 2021.
https://doi.org/10.1007/978-3-030-90016-8_13

Recently interest has grown of the application of ML for the study of diabetes [4]. This approach deals with the creation of techniques and algorithms that facilitate computers to acquire knowledge and procure intelligence that relies on previous experience. ML represents a member of AI heavily associated with statistics [1]. Here, the system would be capable of recognising and understanding the data related to the input, such that it could make predictions and decisions by depending on that data. One of the most important issues in healthcare recently is dealing with Diabetes. Diabetes represents a well-known metabolic disease that could adversely affect the complete body system. Usually, type two diabetes onset occurs in middle age and rarely in old age. However, incidences of diabetes are also identified in children. Diabetes is driven by multiple etiologic factors such as sedentary lifestyle, food habits, body weight and genetic susceptibility. An undiagnosed diabetes could cause the levels of blood sugar to become very high. This condition is known as hyperglycaemia and could lead to complications such as: cardiac arrest, stroke, diabetic foot ulcer, neuropathy, nephropathy and retinopathy. Hence, diabetes detection at the earliest stage is central to enhance the patient related QOL (quality of life) and extend life expectancy [5].

2 Literature Review

Machine Learning as a concept was pioneered and introduced by the American computer scientist in the field of artificial intelligence and computer gaming, Arthur Samuel, in 1959 [6]. In his paper [6] he actually stated, "Programming computers to learn from experience should eventually eliminate the need for much of this detailed programming effort."

Since 1959 there has been continuous development in the field of ML especially in categorisation and classification of learning and learning algorithms. There are many approaches employed by ML including memorisation, extraction of information and learning by example. It differs from traditional software engineering by instead of providing instructions about the function f (as in traditional software engineering), the computer is provided input x and output y and is expected to determine or predict the function f using what has been provided [i.e., $Y = f(x)$, which can be understood as Output $=$ function(Input)]. Machine learning programs learn through reasoning to solve a problem from examples, rules and information. It can also learn to generalise and help with issues of uncertainty with the use of statistics and probability-driven techniques. Models can also learn from previous computations or experiences to produce subsequent reliable and repeatable decisions and results [5].

Currently selecting effective algorithms for a specific application is a very difficult decision due to the sheer diversity of these algorithms. The decisions of the systems that use ML are made when the machine is able to learn from the data provided as an input and provide prediction as an outcome through pattern matching and data analysis. "A central challenge in building a machine-learning model is assembling a representative, diverse data set" [7]. Choosing the best algorithm depends on many factors such as: performance, speed, accuracy, data used for training, etc. Several databases in the field of biomedical sciences were searched extensively to identify articles that employ ML in healthcare, specifically in diabetes: PubMed, IEEE Xplore, ACM digital library, the DBLP Computer Science Bibliography, etc.

ML is a diverse field. A range of algorithms are given in [8]. However, there are four important types of Machine Learning Algorithms [9]:

1. Supervised Learning
2. Unsupervised Learning
3. Semi-supervised Learning
4. Reinforcement Learning.

Since semi-supervised learning is similar to supervised learning, it will not be covered in this systematic literature review (SLR) - the focus will be on the other three algorithms. This SLR will provide a short description of the three main types of ML algorithms, though the research will be focusing on Supervised Learning and its use cases. Supervised learning is one of the most popular machine learning type and it is widely used on cases with precise demand on mapping between the input and output data.

In the case of supervised learning, the dataset is labelled where the operator providing a dataset knows the correct answer and the algorithm makes predictions based on identified patterns. The categories of algorithms that fall under the supervised learning category include classification, regression and forecasting [10]. According to [5], "The term supervised means that the "machine" (the system) learns with the help of something—typically a labeled (sic) training data". Some of the application types where supervised learning is used are, viz.: fraud detection, email and spam detection, diagnostics, image classification, risk assessment and score prediction.

3   Research Methodology

The research methodology encompassed fundamental research that covered analyses of different ML algorithms for diabetes prediction using the three diabetes datasets. Applied research was then used to test the hypothesis. The main objective of the research study was to investigate the performance of the machine learning algorithms on predicting diabetes and the possibilities of this approach and its applications in improving healthcare.

3.1   Research Methodology and Hypothesis

The research hypothesis was: Using three different machine learning algorithms for three different diabetes datasets will give us more comparable results and increase insight on different machine learning algorithms and their performances.

This research focused on supervised learning algorithms especially on classification algorithms, which were:

- J48
- Naïve Bayes
- Random Forest.

The evaluation of the algorithms proceeded by comparing the results and performance of each algorithm on a specific dataset. All the above algorithms were implemented in WEKA (Waikato Environment for Knowledge Analysis) [4]. WEKA was developed in New Zealand by the University of Waikato. It consists of a collection of algorithms and tools for data mining and machine learning implemented in the JAVA language.

The data collection, processing and analysis of the result were performed using WEKA for this research. The diabetes datasets that have been used for testing were the:

1. UCI Diabetes [11] - this dataset is from AIM'94. It has been used in 29 research projects.
2. Pima Indians Diabetes Dataset [12] - this dataset predicts "the onset of diabetes based on diagnostic measures" [12]. It has been used in 184 projects.
3. Kosovo Dataset [13] - it has been used in a PhD thesis on Data Science and Machine Learning and two further research projects.

4   Results

This section presents the results for all three algorithms using the three diabetes datasets. The first dataset to experiment with was the UCI Diabetes Dataset [11]. After loading the dataset and running the experiment, the results shown below, in Tables 1–3 , were obtained. The speed performance of analysing the dataset is the same for all three algorithms, which is one second. All the tables show the accuracy of the results for each one of the three algorithms performed on the breast-cancer dataset.

For this type of application and data the best performing algorithm is the J48 (Table 1) followed by Naïve Bayes algorithm (Table 2) and the least performing one was the Random Forest algorithm (Table 3).

Table 1. Results for J48 algorithm.

J48 algorithm	Results
Correctly classified instances	216 (75.5%)
Incorrectly classified instances	70 (24.5%)
Kappa statistic	0.2826
Mean Absolute Error (MAE)	0.3676
Root Mean Squared (RMS) error	0.4324
Relative absolute error	87.86%
Root relative squared error	94.61%
Total number of instances	100,000

Table 1 correctly classified 216 instances or 75.5% for the J48 algorithm.

Table 2. Results for Naïve Bayes algorithm.

Naïve Bayes - algorithm	Results
Correctly classified instances	205 (71.7%)
Incorrectly classified instances	81 (28.3%)
Kappa statistic	0.2857
Mean absolute error	0.3272
Root mean squared error	0.4534
Relative absolute error	78.21%
Root relative squared error	99.18%
Total number of instances	100,000

Table 3. Results for random forest-algorithm.

Random forest - algorithm	Results
Correctly classified instances	199 (69.6%)
Incorrectly classified instances	87 (30.4%)
Kappa statistic	0.1736
Mean absolute error	0.3727
Root mean squared error	0.4613
Relative absolute error	89.09%
Root relative squared error	100.9%
Total number of instances	100,000

The Naïve Bayes algorithm performance on correctly classified instances is: 205 or 71.7%.

The Random Forest performance on correctly classified instances is: 199 or 69.6%.

The second dataset to experiment with was the Pima Indians Diabetes Database [12]. After loading the dataset and running the experiment, the results shown in Tables 4–6 were produced. For the Pima Indians dataset [12], the best performing algorithm is the Random Forest algorithm (Table 4) followed by the J48 algorithm (Table 5) and the least performing was the Naïve Bayes algorithm (Table 6).

The correctly classified instances are 19,301 or 96.5% for the Random Forest Algorithm.

The J48 algorithm performance on correctly classified instances is: 17,596 or 88.0%.

The Naïve Bayes performance on correctly classified instances is: 12,823 or 64.2%.

The third dataset to experiment with was the Kosovo Diabetes dataset [13]. After loading the dataset and running the experiment, the results produced are given in Tables 7, 8, 9. For the Kosovo dataset [13], the best performing algorithm is the Naïve Bayes

Table 4. Results for random forest-algorithm.

Random forest-algorithm	Result
Correctly classified instances	19301 (96.5%)
Incorrectly classified instances	699 (3.5%)
Kappa statistic	0.9637
Mean absolute error	0.0131
Root mean squared error	0.0622
Relative absolute error	17.65%
Root relative squared error	32.4%
Total number of instances	768

Table 5. Results for J48-algorithm.

J48 -algorithm	Result
Correctly classified instances	17596 (88.0%)
Incorrectly classified instances	2404 (12.0%)
Kappa statistic	0.875
Mean absolute error	0.0105
Root mean squared error	0.0903
Relative absolute error	14.24%
Root relative squared error	46.94%
Total number of instances	768

Table 6. Results for Naïve Bayes-algorithm

Naïve Bayes-algorithm	Result
Correctly classified instances	12823 (64.1%)
Incorrectly classified instances	7177 (35.9%)
Kappa statistic	0.6268
Mean absolute error	0.0323
Root mean squared error	0.1391
Relative absolute error	43.65%
Root relative squared error	72.33%
Total number of instances	768

algorithm (Table 7) followed by the Random Forest algorithm (Table 8) and the least performing one is the J48 algorithm (Table 9).

Table 7. Results for Naïve Bayes-algorithm.

Naïve Bayes-algorithm	Result
Correctly classified instances	96 (95.0%)
Incorrectly classified instances	5 (5.0%)
Kappa statistic	0.9352
Mean absolute error	0.0153
Root mean squared error	0.098
Relative absolute error	6.98%
Root relative squared error	29.7%
Total number of instances	243

Table 7 shows that the correctly classified instances are 96 or 95.0% for the Naïve Bayes Algorithm.

Table 8. Results for random forest-algorithm

Random forest -algorithm	Result
Correctly classified instances	94 (93.1%)
Incorrectly classified instances	7 (6.9%)
Kappa statistic	0.9074
Mean absolute error	0.1196
Root mean squared error	0.1924
Relative absolute error	54.6%
Root relative squared error	58.3%
Total number of instances	243

The Random Forest algorithm performance on correctly classified instances is 94 or 93.1%.

The J48 algorithm performance on correctly classified instances is 93 or 92.1%.

Table 9. Results for J48-algorithm

J48-algorithm	Result
Correctly classified instances	93 (92.1%)
Incorrectly classified instances	8 (7.9%)
Kappa statistic	0.8955
Mean absolute error	0.0225
Root mean squared error	0.14
Relative absolute error	10.2%
Root relative squared error	42.4%
Total number of instances	243

5 Conclusions

The main purpose of the research study was to investigate the performance of using three different machine learning algorithms on three different diabetes datasets. Taking this approach produced more comparable results and gave a better insight on the performance of the three different machine learning algorithms.

This research study focused on supervised learning algorithms specifically on these three classification algorithms:

- J48
- Naive Bayes
- Random Forest.

The evaluation was conducted by comparing the results and performances of each algorithm on a specific dataset described in the research methodology section. The main objective of this research study was to measure the performance in terms of the speed of execution and accuracy of the three chosen machine learning algorithms listed above on the three different datasets.

The datasets were chosen from two well-known public datasets and one dataset was collected from a research group. This private dataset represented the knowledge workflow that was built using the WEKA tool.

The results were compared for each dataset in terms of speed and accuracy. Test option cross-validation of ten folds was used for all the experiments. This is a technique that runs systematic repeated percentage splits. The dataset is divided into ten pieces where nine are used for testing and one for training. The results for all three chosen algorithms were presented for each dataset.

The differences in accuracy have been affected by the datasets that were selected for this study, thus proving the hypothesis. It can be concluded that the J48 and Random Forest classifiers are slightly slower in performance than the Naïve Bayes classifier for the datasets with large number of instances though more accurate and very powerful at finding very good results.

For future work, the recommendation is to combine the classifiers (algorithms) to compare how two or more classifiers would perform than using a single classifier.

References

1. Bansal, D., Chhikara, R., Khanna, K., Gupta, P.: Comparative analysis of various machine learning algorithms for detecting dementia. Procedia Comput. Sci. **132**, 1497–1502 (2018). https://doi.org/10.1016/j.procs.2018.05.102
2. Aher, S.B., Lobo, L.M.R.J.: Comparative study of classification algorithms. Int. J. Inf. Technol. Knowl. Manage. **5**(2), 239–243 (2012). http://csjournals.com/IJITKM/PDF%205-2/15_Sunita_B_Aher.pdf. Accessed 03 Aug 2021
3. Kevric, J., Jukic, S., Subasi, A.: An effective combining classifier approach using tree algorithms for network intrusion detection. Neural Comput. Appl. **28**, 1051–1058 (2017). https://doi.org/10.1007/s00521-016-2418-1. Accessed 03 Aug 2021
4. Kaur, G., Chhabra, A.: Improved J48 classification algorithm for the prediction of diabetes. Int. J. Comput. Appl. **98**(22), 13–17 (2014)
5. Bonaccorso, G.: Machine Learning Algorithms: Popular Algorithms for Data Science and Machine Learning. Packt Publishing, 2nd Edition (2018)
6. Samuel, A.L.: Some studies in machine learning using the game of checkers. IBM J. Res. Dev. **3**(3), 210–229 (1959). https://doi.org/10.1147/rd.33.0210
7. Rajkomar, A., Dean, J., Kohane, I.: Machine learning in medicine. New Engl. J. Med. **380**, 1347–1358, (2019). https://www.nejm.org/doi/full/10.1056/NEJMra1814259. Accessed 28 July 2021
8. Osisanwo, F.Y., Akinsola, J.E.T., Awodele, O., Hinmikaiye, J.O., Olakanmi, O., Akinjobi, J.: Supervised machine learning algorithms: classification and comparison. Int. J. Comput. Trends Technol. (IJCTT), **48**(3), 128–138 (2017). https://www.ijcttjournal.org/archives/ijctt-v48p126. Accessed 03 Aug 2021
9. Ayyadevara, V.K.: Pro machine learning algorithms. Andhra Pradesh: Apress Media, LLC (2018). https://doi.org/10.1007/978-1-4842-3564-5
10. Mohammed, M., Khan, M.B., Bashier, E.B.M.: Machine Learning Algorithms and Applications. 1st Edition. CRC Press, Boca Raton, 30 June 2020
11. https://data.world/uci/diabetes. Accessed 28 July 2021
12. https://data.world/data-society/pima-indians-diabetes-database. Accessed 28 July 2021
13. Tafa, Z., Pervetica, N., Karahoda, B.: An intelligent system for diabetes prediction. In: 4th Mediterranean Conference on Embedded Computing (MECO), pp. 378–382 (2015). https://doi.org/10.1109/MECO.2015.7181948

Author Index

Printed in the United States
by Baker & Taylor Publisher Services